T0348376

ADVANCES IN INTERNATIONAL ACCOUNTING

ADVANCES IN INTERNATIONAL ACCOUNTING

Series Editor: J. Timothy Sale

Volume 10:	Edited by T. S. Doupnik and S. B. Salter
Volume 11–15:	Edited by J. T. Sale
Volume 16:	Edited by J. Timothy Sale, S. B. Salter and D. J. Sharp
Volume 17:	Edited by J. Timothy Sale, S. B. Salter and D. J. Sharp

ADVANCES IN INTERNATIONAL ACCOUNTING

EDITED BY

J. TIMOTHY SALE

Department of Accounting, University of Cincinnati, USA

Associate Editors:

STEPHEN B. SALTER

Department of Accounting, University of Cincinnati, USA

DAVID J. SHARP

Accounting and Control Area, University of Western Ontario, Canada

2005

ELSEVIER
JAI

Amsterdam – Boston – Heidelberg – London – New York – Oxford
Paris – San Diego – San Francisco – Singapore – Sydney – Tokyo

ELSEVIER B.V.
Radarweg 29
P.O. Box 211
1000 AE Amsterdam,
The Netherlands

ELSEVIER Inc.
525 B Street, Suite 1900
San Diego
CA 92101-4495
USA

ELSEVIER Ltd
The Boulevard, Langford
Lane, Kidlington
Oxford OX5 1GB
UK

ELSEVIER Ltd
84 Theobalds Road
London
WC1X 8RR
UK

First edition 2005

British Library Cataloguing in Publication Data
A catalogue record is available from the British Library.

ISBN: 0-7623-1235-1
ISSN: 0897-3660 (Series)

♾ The paper used in this publication meets the requirements of ANSI/NISO Z39.48-1992 (Permanence of Paper).

Transferred to digital print on demand, 2006
Printed and bound by CPI Antony Rowe, Eastbourne

Working together to grow
libraries in developing countries

www.elsevier.com | www.bookaid.org | www.sabre.org

ELSEVIER   BOOK AID
             International   Sabre Foundation

CONTENTS

LIST OF CONTRIBUTORS

Wendy W. Achilles	East Carolina University, USA
C. Richard Baker	Adelphi University, USA
Yuk C. Q. Cheung	NTHYK Tai Po Secondary School, HK
Chee W. Chow	San Diego State University, USA
Frank L. Clarke	University of Newcastle, Australia
Yuan Ding	HEC School of Management, Paris, France
Simon S. Gao	Napier University, UK
Ahsan Habib	Lincoln University, New Zealand
Jerry Han	Hong Kong University Business School, Hong Kong
Alejandro Hazera	University of Rhode Island, USA
Saeed Heravi	Cardiff Business School, UK
Johanna Hyvönen	University of Oulu, Finland
Juha-Pekka Kallunki	University of Oulu, Finland
Pasi Karjalainen	University of Oulu, Finland
Dominica Suk-yee Lee	The Chinese University of Hong Kong, Hong Kong
Minna Martikainen	Laurea Polytechnic, Finland
Ken Ngangan	University of Papua New Guinea, Papua, New Guinea
Jussi Nikkinen	University of Vaasa, Finland
Jenice Prather-Kinsey	University of Missouri – Columbia, USA
Petri Sahlström	University of Vaasa, Finland

Shahrokh M. Saudagaran	Milgard School of Business, University of Washington – Tacoma, USA
Sandra Waller Shelton	Depaul University, USA
Hervé Stolowy	HEC School of Management, Paris, France
Rasoul H. Tondkar	Virginia Commonwealth University, USA
Joyce van der Laan Smith	Virginia State University, USA
Woody Wu	The Chinese University of Hong Kong, Hong Kong
Jason Zezheng Xiao	Cardiff Business School, UK
Joanna Yeoh	Institute of Chartered Accountants of New Zealand, New Zealand

EDITORIAL BOARD

REVIEWER ACKNOWLEDGMENT

The Editors of *Advances in International Accounting* wish to thank the following individuals who served as ad hoc reviewers for Volume 18.

Bikki Jaggi
Rutgers University, USA

CORPORATE GOVERNANCE AND INVESTOR REACTION TO REPORTED EARNINGS: AN EXPLORATORY STUDY OF LISTED CHINESE COMPANIES

Dominica Suk-yee Lee, Jerry Han, Woody Wu and Chee W. Chow

ABSTRACT

This study explores the determinants of listed Chinese companies' governance practices. It also examines how these companies' governance practices affect domestic investors' reaction to their earnings reports. Using publicly disclosed financial information and data directly collected from 148 domestically listed Chinese companies, the findings are consistent with investors in these companies basing their valuation decisions, at least in part, on these companies' earnings reports. This is indicated by the significant relationship between "unexpected" earnings and cumulative abnormal returns. However, the hypothesized effects of governance practice/choice are, on the whole, not supported. There also is no systematic relation between governance choice and ownership structure. We interpret these findings to imply that in the Chinese securities market, the

Advances in International Accounting
Advances in International Accounting, Volume 18, 1–25
ISSN: 0897-3660/doi:10.1016/S0897-3660(05)18001-5

institutional factors and infrastructure (e.g., legal liability, information intermediation, market for managers, and takeovers) are not yet sufficiently developed to permit individual domestic investors to exert significant influence via their actions in the capital markets.

INTRODUCTION

This study examines how listed Chinese companies' governance practices affect domestic investors' reaction to their earnings reports. It also explores the determinants of listed Chinese companies' governance practices. The objective is to both increase our understanding of the microstructure of the Chinese securities market, and to help Chinese authorities to better target and fine-tune their regulatory initiatives.

This topic is of interest because the total market capitalization of companies listed on China's two stock exchanges (Shanghai and Shenzhen) had reached 2,720.6 billion yuan by the beginning of the year 2000, or about one-fifth of the country's gross domestic product (*The Securities Daily*, January 1, 2000). This pooling of capital undoubtedly has fueled much of China's phenomenal economic growth of the past decade. As such, increased understanding of how investors evaluate listed Chinese firms can further enhance the effectiveness of this capital pooling process.

BACKGROUND ON THE CHINESE SECURITIES MARKET

A substantial body of empirical evidence (mostly from the developed economies) has shown that investors are not passive price takers in the market. Rather, they appraise the future prospects of different companies based on an evaluation of the available information on each company, often engaging the services of financial and information intermediaries. When a company's information is incomplete or not considered to be credible, investors will "price-protect" themselves via requiring a higher expected rate of return (i.e., lowering the price that they would pay for the company's shares). This finding suggests that both the total amount of ownership capital made available to listed companies (as compared to other uses of these resources, including consumption, direct investments in assets, and the granting of credit), and how this total amount is distributed among them, would depend on investors' evaluation of the available information. To the extent that these effects are also operational in the nascent Chinese securities market, they can significantly affect the speed and direction of that country's economic development.

Extensive studies have also shown that both the availability of information to investors, and the latter's use of this information are affected by a myriad of factors. These factors exist at many levels, from that of the economy (e.g., regulations regarding stock listing, legal liability, accounting methods, and disclosures), to that of institutions with a role in information production and dissemination (e.g., auditor certification requirements and competition for audit clients), to that of individual companies (e.g., ownership and asset structure, internal controls). Reviews of this literature are provided by Watts and Zimmerman (1986, 1990) among others. With the Chinese securities markets having a relatively short history, systematic studies of this type are only beginning to be performed in the Chinese setting. Some results consistent with those in the developed economies have been reported (e.g., DeFond, Wong, & Li, 1999). This suggests that at least some of the forces at work in the more developed economies also may be operational in the Chinese economy.

For its part, the Chinese government has taken actions aimed at increasing the integrity of financial transactions and their related disclosures. For example, a Securities Committee of the State Council and a China Securities Regulatory Commission were established in 1992 to oversee the operations of the securities markets and stock exchanges. Relating to accounting and disclosure, the first set of regulations was promulgated by the Ministry of Finance in 1992. Labeled "Accounting System for Selected Shareholding Companies," this regulation required listed Chinese companies to prepare balance sheets, income statements, and statements of changes in financial position in conformance with international accounting practices, and to make these available to the public in audited annual reports within 4 months of the fiscal year end (typically the same as calendar year end). Listed companies are also required to provide semi-annual reports by the end of August, although these do not have to be audited. In addition, the "Provisional Regulations Governing the Issuing and Trading of Shares," promulgated by the State Council in 1993, required the timely disclosure of significant events that may have material impacts on share prices.

Since issuance of these early regulations, ten other accounting and disclosure standards have been enacted amidst the issuance of over 30 exposure drafts of proposed standards (Li & He, 2000; Tang, 2000, also see Xiang, 1998; Pacter, 2001 for overviews of recent securities and accounting/

disclosure regulations in China). There are also recent initiatives to increase the legal liability of companies and auditors for fraudulent or deficient financial disclosure (DeFond et al., 1999). Many of these initiatives are patterned after those in the developed economies – especially the U.S. – and represent a big step forward from the relatively unregulated void of a decade ago. Nevertheless, collectively they still are quite limited in scope when compared to the range of standards and institutions of the more developed economies. China also has not yet developed a large corps of information intermediaries like financial analysts. As a result, the primary source of information on listed Chinese companies still tends to be the companies themselves (Poon, Firth, & Fung, 1998). As such, listed companies' earnings reports can have a proportionally much larger impact on securities prices (hence the amount and mix of capital made available to listed companies) in China than in the more developed economies.

Another salient feature of the Chinese securities market is that under Chinese securities law, listed companies are mandated to have three classes of ownership shares: state shares, institutional shares, and shares issued to individuals (Tang, Chow, & Cooper, 1994). State shares are held by the central government or government ministries, provincial, municipal, and city governments. These shares are prohibited from trading. Institutional shares (also called legal entity shares) are owned by separate legal entities, such as investment institutions, other enterprises, and the foreign partners of a corporatized joint venture. These shares also cannot be traded on the two exchanges, though they can be sold to other legal entities through a nationwide, computerized, Securities Trading Automated Quotation (STAQ) system. Finally, individual shares can be classified into ones restricted to trading domestically by Chinese citizens ("A shares"), and ones that can be sold to foreign individuals and entities ("B shares"). Some Chinese companies also are listed on the Hong Kong Stock Exchange ("H shares") and New York Stock Exchange ("Y shares"), but these are few in number. Another distinction between A and B shares is that the former are subject to domestic accounting and disclosure standards, whilst B shares are required to conform to International Accounting Standards. Thus, for a Chinese company with both A and B shares, two sets of financial reports have to be prepared, which typically are made available to the public on the same day. Comparisons of reported earnings under Chinese and international accounting standards have found them to have significant differences in many cases (Chen, Gul, & Su, 1999). However, the markets for A and B shares are effectively segmented, as these two types of shares have been found to trade at substantially different prices despite having the same rights to assets and dividends (Poon et al., 1998). Given this evidence on market segmentation, the current study focuses on the reactions of internal investors (owners of A shares) to domestically listed firms' annual earnings reports. Internal investors are, by far, the largest source of privately sourced capital to the listed companies. This domestic focus also helps to control for the effects of extraneous variables, such as the competition from companies from other countries and the variability of accounting and disclosure practices in the global capital markets.

CORPORATE GOVERNANCE AND INTEGRITY OF FINANCIAL REPORTING

The term "corporate governance" typically refers to the set of oversight activities undertaken by the board of directors to ensure that the firm appropriately discharges its fiduciary duties to stakeholders, including accurate information disclosures. Governance mechanisms are held to reduce the agency costs that arise when there is a separation of ownership and management, and attain this result via safeguarding assets and improving performance (Shleifer & Vishny, 1997; Agrawal & Knoeber, 1996; Brickley, Coles, & Terry, 1994), as well as guarding against fraudulent financial reporting (DeChow, Sloan, & Sweeney, 1996; Beasley, 1996; McMullen, 1996).

Aspects of corporate governance that have received attention include the size of, and mix between inside and outside members on the board of directors (Weisbach, 1988; Byrd & Hickman, 1992), whether the CEO also serves as the chairman of the board (Loebbecke, Eining, & Willingham, 1989; DeChow et al., 1996), and the existence of compensation, nomination, and audit committees (Beasley, 1996; DeChow et al., 1996; McMullen, 1996). Rosenstein and Wyatt (1990), for example, have found the appointment of outside directors to be associated with positive abnormal returns in the market. This finding is consistent with investors expecting outside directors to improve future performance. Focusing on management compensation, Core, Holthausen, & Larcker (1999) found that CEO compensation was higher at firms with ineffective governance structures, while the findings of Beatty and Zajac (1994) are consistent with the board of directors being less effective if the CEO also serves as its chairman. Relating to financial reporting, Beasley (1996) compared firms with financial reporting fraud to no-fraud firms, and found that the proportion of independent outside

directors on the board had a significant negative effect on the likelihood of
financial reporting fraud.

Focusing on committees of the board of directors, Braiotta (1994) identified audit committees as being "a significant element of corporate accountability and governance (that) help engender a high degree of integrity
in the financial reporting process." Indeed, McMullen and Raghunandan
(1996) have found that companies without financial reporting problems are
more likely to have audit committees consisting entirely of outside directors.
This finding suggests that the other committees of the board are also likely
to perform similar oversight functions relating to other major determinants
of manager actions.

Some governance mechanisms (e.g., a board of directors) have long been
part of company operations in the West and in the past decade, attention to
these mechanisms has significantly increased (e.g., COSO (U.S.), 1992;
CICA (Canada), 1995; CCG, Hampel Report (UK), 1998; OECD, 1999).
Chinese regulatory authorities are also paying increasing attention to the
governance practices of business enterprises. For example, several government agencies in Shanghai have jointly promulgated a set of guidelines on
the governance of state-owned-enterprises (*Jiefang Daily*, Dec 4, 1998).
More generally, Chinese government authorities have repeatedly expressed
the intent to introduce U.S.-type governance to establish a "modern enterprise system" (Tam, 1999, p. 40).

The increased attention to corporate governance implies acceptance that
governance practices can positively affect firm performance and/or the
soundness of financial reporting. There is indirect evidence supporting the
existence of linkages among companies' governance structures/processes
and financial disclosures. In the U.S. setting, DeAngelo (1988) has found
that earnings numbers are used by dissident stockholders who wage proxy
contests for seats on the board of directors, and also by incumbent managers who exercise their accounting discretion to defend themselves. A related study by Collins and DeAngelo (1990) found that market and analyst
reactions to reported earnings are more pronounced than in prior periods
during a proxy contest. From a different angle, Merchant's (1985a, b) finding from a field study, that net income targets are the most important form
of control imposed on managers, also suggests that companies are concerned with linking their controls to external financial reports.

In the case of China, a recent study by Xu and Wang (1999) has reported
a positive relationship between corporate governance and performance in
Chinese firms. However, performance was only narrowly defined as reported
earnings. More important, ownership structure was used to proxy for

governance, without attention to specific governance practices. As such, there is much room for further exploring the nature and impacts of governance practices in listed Chinese companies. To provide focus for an investigation pertaining to financial reporting, we specify the following (information) hypothesis based on the extant (Western) literature:

H1. (Information Hypothesis). Investor reactions to reported earnings by listed Chinese companies are higher for companies with stronger governance mechanisms.

Two points related to this information hypothesis are worthy of note. First, in focusing on companies' governance practices, it must be acknowledged that this is only one of the many factors that can affect firm valuation. Several studies have begun to examine other aspects of the Chinese securities market, such as the impacts of reporting using domestic versus International Accounting Standards (e.g., Bao & Chow, 1999), the pricing of initial public offerings (e.g., Mok & Hui, 1998), the effects of qualified audit opinions (e.g., Chen et al., 2000) and auditor switching behavior (e.g., DeFond et al., 1999). By extending attention to the role of governance practices, the current study complements these other efforts to develop a more holistic understanding of the Chinese securities market.

Second, an implicit assumption of the hypothesis is that there exist differences among listed Chinese companies' corporate governance mechanisms. This empirically testable expectation is premised on the well-established principal-agent theory and the large body of related empirical studies. The theory is that investors would price-protect themselves – thus reducing the value of the company – from potential actions that management may take to benefit at the expense of shareholders. The potential to reduce this dead-weight loss, in turn, creates incentives for company management to voluntarily adopt processes and mechanisms that reduce the potential for such opportunistic behavior. Tests of this theory in Western settings have consistently supported its predictions, and a comprehensive review of this literature is provided by Watts and Zimmerman (1986, 1990). Examples of mechanisms that managers have been found to voluntarily adopt include the terms of debt covenants (e.g., Leftwich, 1980), the use of external auditors (e.g., Chow, 1982), and voluntary disclosures (e.g., Leftwich, Watts, & Zimmerman, 1981; Chow & Wong-Boren, 1987; Meek & Gray, 1989). Since governance mechanisms are also expected to reduce management's potential for personal gain at the firm's expense, listed companies' governance structures should vary with the factors that affect the extent of the management versus investor conflict.

Applying the tenets of principal-agent theory to listed Chinese companies requires considering the unique features of the Chinese securities market. In particular, the mandated segmentation of ownership into several classes (discussed in the preceding subsection) suggests that there may be some divergence of interests among these classes of shareholders. Owners of state shares are unlikely to have earnings or asset integrity as primary concerns, in part because the government officials themselves are not the residual claimants, and in part because they often have other objectives for policy, such as full employment, social stability, and supporting the development of certain sectors. Owners of institutional shares likely will be more concerned with asset preservation and profitability, and given their block ownership, may be in a position to assert more influence, including direct interventions and gaining representation on the board of directors. Finally, individual share investors are most directly affected by firm profitability and reporting integrity. While dispersed ownership may dilute the influence of individual shareholders, concern for the reactions of such investors as a group still could create incentives for improved governance practices.

Much more research is needed to fully understand the incentives and avenues of influence of the three classes of shareholders. Nevertheless, there still seems to exist sufficient basis for expecting that a listed Chinese company's choice of governance practices would depend on the distribution of its share ownership among the three distinct groups. The following (governance choice) hypothesis reflects this general expectation of a systematic relationship:

H2. There is a systematic relationship between the ownership structures of listed Chinese companies and their governance practices.

METHODOLOGY

Testing the two hypotheses required data to be collected from different sources and using different methods. To facilitate explanation, the models used for hypothesis testing are first presented, and then used as the structure for explaining the nature of the variables and the data collection process.

Model and Variables for the Information Hypothesis (H1)

The model for testing H1 was of the following form, with company subscripts omitted:

$$UR(-2, +2) = \alpha_0 + \beta_0 UE + \beta_1 CEO + \beta_2 UE * CEO$$
$$+ \beta_3 OUTDIR\% + \beta_4 UE * OUTDIR\%$$
$$+ \beta_5 GOVERN + \beta_6 UE * GOVERN$$
$$+ \beta_7 INTAUD + \beta_8 UE * INTAUD$$
$$+ \beta_9 POLICY + \beta_{10} UE * POLICY$$
$$+ \beta_{11} UE * LTA + \beta_{12} UE * PUB\% \qquad (1)$$

where

UR $(-2, +2)$ = the cumulative market-adjusted "abnormal" return to company's A shares over the 5-day interval surrounding annual earnings announcement,

UE = unexpected earnings,

CEO = 0 if the chairman of BOD is the same person as the CEO, 1 otherwise,

OUTDIR% = percentage of directors who are outsiders,

GOVERN = average score for 5-item corporate governance scale,

INTAUD = equals 1 if there is an internal audit department, 0 otherwise,

POLICY = average score for 12 questions on the existence of formal work manuals or policies in making various operation decisions,

LTA = log of company's total assets, and

PUB% = percentage of ownership by individuals.

The general form of this regression is patterned after prior research on the informativeness of accounting disclosures (e.g., Alford, Jones, Leftwich, & Zmijewski, 1993; Amir, Harris, & Venuti, 1993; Barth & Clinch, 1996; Cho & Jung, 1991). As mentioned above, the dependent variable, UR $(-2, +2)$, was the cumulative market-adjusted "abnormal" return to the company's A shares over the 5-day interval surrounding annual earnings announcement. UE was unexpected earnings, and CEO, OUTDIR%, GOVERN, INTAUD, and POLICY measured various aspects of the company's governance practices. LTA and PUB% were included to control for the size of a company and its share ownership by individual (i.e., non-governmental and non-institutional) investors.

To calculate the cumulative abnormal returns, UR, daily returns were obtained from the *Taiwan Economic Journal* China Data Base. The equally weighted (with dividend) return of each exchange was used as the market return for deriving the market-adjusted abnormal returns. Annual earnings announcement dates were manually extracted from *China Securities Daily, Shanghai Financial Times, Shanghai Securities News, Shenzhen Journal of Commerce,* and the *Shenzhen Securities Times,* which are the primary venues for listed companies to publish their (required) annual financial reports. For deriving unexpected earnings (UE), an expectations model was required. Since the short histories of China's two stock exchanges (and the even shorter histories of most listings) precluded sufficient time series data for model estimation, we used the random walk to proxy for market expectations. The two control variables, LTA and PUB%, were derived from the listed companies' annual reports.

In contrast, the governance practice variables are not part of companies' annual reports, though most should be obtainable by an inquisitive outsider, and incentives exist for companies with stronger governance to make such data available to investors (the potential implications of these measures' public availability will be explored further in the results section). A survey approach was used to collect these data, where the surveys were personally delivered to a top manager of each sample company. Specifically, we sought the following information for each company:

CEO = whether the CEO also served as the chairman of the board (0 = yes, 1 = no).

OUTDIR% = the proportion of directors who were not employees.

INTAUD = whether the company had a distinct, internal audit department,

GOVERN = the company's average score on following five 0/1 questions:

1. Whether the Chairman of the BOD and the CEO are the same person?
2. Whether there were fixed terms on the board of directors?
3. Whether the board had an audit committee?
4. Whether the board had a nominations committee?
5. Whether the board had a compensation committee?

This set of four governance-related variables was broadly based on extant research on governance (e.g., Bacon, 1993; Beasley, 1996; Blair, 1995; Byrd & Hickman, 1992; Braiotta, 1994; DeChow et al., 1996; McMullen, 1996; Weisbach, 1988). The numerical value of GOVERN was the sum of the five answers divided by 5 (hence, the range of this variable was 0–1.0). With the assignment of the zero and one values to answers (reversed between the CEO measure and the other four), a higher score is consistent with the literature's concept of stronger governance.

Whereas CEO, OUTDIR%, GOVERN, and to some extent, INTAUD dealt with practices at the board of directors level, the POLICY variable focused more on the company's routine operations. Inclusion of these more internally focused variables is premised on the effectiveness of external mechanisms being dependent on internal governance structures that simultaneously operate in the firm (Demsetz & Lehn, 1985; Bathala & Rao, 1995; Daily, 1996). POLICY was the average score from questions asking, on 7-point scales, the degree to which the company had explicit written policies regarding operational 12 activities. This set of 12 activities was broadly based on extant research on management controls (e.g., Anthony, Dearden, & Govindarajan, 1992; Flamholtz, Das, & Tsui, 1985; Merchant, 1985a; Kren & Liao, 1988; Lincoln, Hanada, & McBride, 1986), with many specific items being from Khandwalla (1977) and Gordon and Narayanan (1984). The value of POLICY was the average of the numerical answers to questions regarding the existence of formal work manuals or policies in making the following 12 operation decisions, where the values assigned were $1 =$ none or unclear, and $7 =$ detailed and clear:

1. External financing;
2. Allocation of resources among internal units;
3. Development of new products and/or services;
4. Capital budgeting;
5. Sourcing of non-labor inputs;
6. Product or service pricing;
7. Product or service mix;
8. Hiring and firing of personnel;
9. Salary adjustments;
10. Personnel performance evaluation;
11. Bonus determination; and
12. Day to day operations.

To ensure that the wording and items on the questionnaire were relevant to the Chinese context, members of the research team conducted pilot interviews at several companies each in Shanghai and Shenzhen. Minor revisions were made based on the feedback from these pilot tests.

For each company, a packet was prepared that contained two copies each of the questionnaire and a cover letter that requested cooperation, explained the purpose of the questionnaire, and promised anonymity for both company and respondent. The use of two questionnaires was designed to allow for some validation across responses from each company.

Based on the research team's prior experience with similar endeavors in China, a personal approach to data collection was adopted where the top management of each company was contacted to secure its cooperation. Personal experience and prior research further suggested that the person(s) making the contact had to have the proper *guanxi* with the company's managers. In the Chinese business community, *guanxi* is cultivated mainly for the reciprocal exchange of favors (Luo, 1997). It denotes trust, facilitates action (Alston, 1989), and has long been valued as one of the most important factors in conducting business in China. For example, in an interview study of managers in Chinese state-owned, collectively hybrid, and private companies, Xin and Pearce (1996) found that *guanxi* is especially important for managers in private Chinese companies to secure resources and protection.

Given cost considerations and the importance of *guanxi*, it was decided to only target listed companies headquartered in the Shanghai and Shenzhen areas. For companies in the Shanghai area, two faculty members of the accounting and finance department of a leading university in Shanghai were engaged to personally visit each company. If the visit succeeded in gaining cooperation in the survey, then the packet of two questionnaires was left for distribution. Since the information being sought was more likely to be known to higher-level managers, the contact in each company was asked to target managers at higher ranks (including themselves). For the companies in Shenzhen, the research team was able to obtain the assistance of a top manager from one of the sample companies, who assisted in the distribution and collection of the questionnaires.

The personal contacts were initiated in 1998, such that data for 1997 were sought. This personal approach produced highly favorable response rates. Out of a target sample of 100 listed companies from Shanghai and 59 from Shenzhen, 184 completed questionnaires were received from 93 Shanghai companies, and 110 were received from 55 companies in Shenzhen (total = 148 companies). All but two of the companies (both were from Shanghai) returned two completed questionnaires.

Demographic data on the respondents suggest that they should be sufficiently informed and experienced to provide accurate answers to the questions. Out of the respondents from Shanghai, 77 reported that they were members of top management and 68 were from middle management, with only 35 being from other ranks. For Shenzhen, 21 respondents were from top management, 72 indicated that they were from the middle rank, and only 17 were from other ranks. In terms of years of employment with the current company, the means were 10.89 and 5.75 years for Shanghai and Shenzhen, respectively.

For statistical analysis, the two surveys from each company were arithmetically averaged to derive the values of variables. Owing to incomplete responses, the available sample size (in number of companies) for different governance measures ranged from 103 (for OUTDIR%) to 145 (GOVERN).

Model and Variables for the Governance Choice Hypothesis (H2)

The model for testing H2 was of the following form, with company subscripts omitted:

$$X_i = c + d_0 \text{ STATE\%} + d_1 \text{ LP\%} + d_2 \text{ PUB\%} + d_3 \text{ LMVE} + d_4 \text{ LISTYRS}$$

$$(2)$$

where

X_i stands alternately for each of the five governance measures, CEO, OUTDIR%, INTAUD, GOVERN, and POLICY,
STATE% = percentage of company's shares owned by the State,
LP% = percentage of shares owned by legal persons,
PUB% = percentage of company's shares owned by individual investors,
LMVE = the natural log of the market value of the company's equity,
LISTYRS is the number of years that the company had been listed.

LMVE was included as a control for size effects and LISTYRS was included to control for the potential effects of past history (current practice at the time of listing) and inertia in introducing change. Data on all of these variables were obtained from the companies' financial reports.

RESULTS

Descriptive Statistics

Table 1 presents descriptive statistics (mean, median, and standard deviation) for the company characteristics included in the models. Tables 2 and 3 present, respectively, details on the makeup of the composite measures for GOVERN and POLICY. Table 4 provides the Spearman and Pearson correlations among the variables. Since there were only minor differences

Table 1. Descriptive Statistics for Selected Company Characteristics.

Variable Name	N	Median	Mean	Std. Dev.
TA	148	10.38	19.70	33.46
STATE%	148	37.75	33.75	27.47
LP%	148	15.53	26.77	26.76
PUB%	148	21.79	25.63	19.60
MVE	148	4.47	9.36	19.64
CEO	144	1.00	0.87	0.34
TOTDIR	145	9.00	9.52	3.13
OUTDIR	112	3.00	3.58	2.65
OUTDIR%	103	0.33	0.37	0.24
INTAUD	137	1.00	0.66	0.47
GOVERN	145	0.40	0.41	0.17
POLICY	142	5.63	5.48	1.03

TA = total book value of assets, measured in RMB 100 million.
STATE% = percentage of shares owned by the State.
LP% = percentage of shares owned by legal persons.
PUB% = percentage of shares owned by the public.
MVE = market value of common equity, measured in RMB 100 million.
TOTDIR = total number of directors.
OUTDIR = number of outside directors.
OUTDIR% = percentage of directors who are outsiders.
GOVERN = average score for 5-item corporate governance scale.
CEO = 0 if the chairman of BOD is the same person as the CEO, 1 otherwise.
INTAUD = 1 if there is an internal audit department, 0 otherwise.
POLICY = average score for 12 questions on the existence of formal work manuals or policies in making various operation decisions.

between the Shanghai and Shenzhen companies, only aggregate data for the total sample are presented for parsimony.

Table 1 shows that on average, 33.75% of the sample companies' shares are owned by the state (STATE%). The percentages of ownership by legal persons (LP%) and individual domestic investors (PUB%) are similar (26.77 and 25.63%, respectively). Individually as well as collectively, these ownership percentages would seem adequate for exerting some influence on managerial behavior. It is also of interest to note that the three classes of ownership sum to less than 100%. The small shortfall represents ownership by foreign investors (B shares) as well as relatively small percentages of ownership by members of management and employees.

Table 2. Descriptive Statistics for Components of the
GOVERN Variable.

Component	Mean	Std. Dev.
1. Chairman and CEO are the same person? (1 = no, 0 = yes)	0.866	0.340
2. Fixed-term appointments for corporate directors? (1 = yes, 0 = no)	0.883	0.306
3. Existence of audit committee on the corporate board? (1 = yes, 0 = no)	0.159	0.357
4. Existence of nomination committee on the corporate board? (1 = yes, 0 = no)	0.055	0.229
5. Existence of compensation committee on the corporate board? (1 = yes, 0 = no)	0.066	0.245

Table 3. Descriptive Statistics for Components of the
POLICY Variable[a].

Component	Mean	Std. Dev.
1. Policy on raising financial resources.	5.755	1.217
2. Policy on allocating financial resources.	5.341	1.162
3. Policy on new product/service development.	5.323	1.291
4. Policy on major capital investment decisions.	5.844	1.212
5. Policy on finding non-labor resources.	5.168	1.392
6. Policy on product/service pricing.	5.529	1.358
7. Policy on product/service mix and marketing.	5.353	1.363
8. Policy on hiring and firing.	5.658	1.354
9. Policy on salary/wages adjustments.	5.560	1.292
10. Policy on performance evaluation.	5.346	1.331
11. Policy on bonus and compensation.	5.407	1.292
12. Policy on daily operations.	5.604	1.343

[a]Response scale: 1 = "None or unclear", 7 = "Detailed and clear".

Table 1 also shows that on an average, the sample companies' boards of directors have 9.52 members, with 37% (or 3.58 members) being outsiders. In most of the companies, the CEO does not simultaneously serve as the chairman of the board (CEO = 0.87), and the majority of the companies do have a distinct, internal audit department.

Regarding the aggregate GOVERN measure, the theoretical range was 0–1, and Table 1 shows that its mean value was 0.41. The details provided in Table 2 show that this relatively high number was primarily due to the CEO measure and most companies (88.3%) having fixed terms for board

Table 4. Correlations between Company Characteristics.

Variable	TA	STATE%	LP%	PUB%	MVE	OUTDIR%	GOVERN	CEO	INTAUD	POLICY
TA		0.095	−0.079	−0.145	0.231	−0.147	0.058	0.012	0.001	0.056
		(0.25)	(0.34)	(0.08)	(0.00)*	(0.12)	(0.49)	(0.89)	(1.00)	(0.51)
STATE%	0.187		−0.783	−0.329	−0.104	−0.231	0.037	0.015	0.188	−0.088
	(0.02)*		(0.00)*	(0.00)*	(0.21)	(0.01)*	(0.66)	(0.86)	(0.03)*	(0.30)
LP%	−0.099	−0.742		−0.117	−0.065	0.108	−0.083	0.096	−0.225	−0.034
	(0.23)	(0.00)*		(0.16)	(0.43)	(0.26)	(0.32)	(0.25)	(0.01)*	(0.68)
PUB%	−0.255	−0.277	−0.004		0.349	0.161	−0.014	−0.148	0.000	0.052
	(0.00)*	(0.00)*	(0.95)		(0.00)*	(0.09)	(0.87)	(0.08)	(1.00)	(0.54)
MVE	0.285	−0.143	−0.069	0.500		−0.053	0.244	−0.00	−0.155	0.104
	(0.00)*	(0.08)	(0.40)	(0.00)*		(0.58)	(0.00)*	(0.99)	(0.07)	(0.22)
OUTDIR%	−0.114	−0.169	0.002	0.130	−0.028		−0.062	0.103	0.109	0.187
	(0.23)	(0.07)	(0.98)	(0.17)	(0.77)		(0.52)	(0.28)	(0.27)	(0.05)*
GOVERN	−0.065	0.028	−0.045	−0.020	−0.010	−0.039		0.336	0.080	−0.010
	(0.44)	(0.74)	(0.59)	(0.81)	(0.91)	(0.68)		(0.00)*	(0.35)	(0.90)
CEO	0.023	0.001	0.118	−0.168	−0.082	0.079	0.389		−0.139	−0.096
	(0.79)	(0.99)	(0.16)	(0.04)*	(0.33)	(0.41)	(0.00)*		(0.10)	(0.26)
INTAUD	0.014	0.168	−0.204	−0.009	−0.073	0.097	0.094	−0.139		0.233
	(0.87)	(0.05)*	(0.02)*	(0.92)	(0.40)	(0.33)	(0.27)	(0.10)		(0.01)*
POLICY	0.049	−0.065	−0.065	0.028	0.105	0.202	−0.012	−0.096	0.288	
	(0.56)	(0.44)	(0.44)	(0.74)	(0.21)	(0.03)*	(0.89)	(0.26)	(0.00)*	

Notes: (1) Pearson correlations are reported on the upper-right part of the table.
(2) Spearman correlations are reported on the lower-left part of the table.
(3) Significance levels are shown in parentheses.
*Significant at $p = 0.05$.

members. All three measures related to the operations (as compared to setup) of the board of directors tended toward the low end, with only 15.9, 5.5, and 6.6%, respectively, of the sample companies reporting the existence of an audit committee, a nomination committee, and a compensation committee on the board.

Focusing on the POLICY variable (Table 3), most of the sample companies report that they have established rather extensive internal policies relating to the 12 aspects of operations. The mean values for all 12 components are above 5.5 (range: 5.168–5.844) on a response scale of 1 to 7.

Finally, consider the correlations among company characteristics (Table 4). Given the virtually identical patterns of significant correlations between the Pearson and Spearman results, only the former (upper-right part of the table) will be discussed.

Since a higher percentage ownership by one class of shareholders implies lower ownership percentages by other classes, it is not surprising to find negative and significant correlations between STATE% and LP%, and between STATE% and PUB%. But the correlation between LP% and PUB% is not significant, reflecting the fact that there are residual (and relatively minor) classes of other owners (e.g., employees). The positive and significant correlation between TA and MVE is similarly not surprising.

The positive and significant correlation between MVE and PUB% suggests that companies with larger total market values of equity tend to have higher percentages of ownership by individual investors. To the extent that listed companies with higher market values of equity also are more important to the Chinese economy (especially considering the significant and positive correlation between TA and MVE) this finding may give impetus to considering the role of individual investors in such companies.

Turning to the correlations with governance practices, STATE% has a negative and significant correlation with OUTDIR%. Thus, companies with higher percentages of their ownership in the hands of the state tend to have proportionally fewer outside directors, perhaps reflecting the relatively lower influence of non-state owners and state officials' preference for directly influencing company management. The positive and significant correlation between STATE% and INTAUD, in conjunction with the negative and significant correlation between LP% and INTAUD, suggest that state officials are more focused than the other classes of owners on internal controls. Finally, there is a positive and significant correlation between CEO and GOVERN, and ones between OUTDIR% and POLICY, and between INTAUD and POLICY. These correlations suggest that there may be some complementarities across governance practices. It is worthy of note, however, that except for the –0.783 correlation between ownership variables STATE% and LP%, all of the significant correlations are at very modest levels (0.349–0.187 in absolute values).

Test of the Governance Choice Hypothesis (H1)

Table 5 presents the results of a regression based on Eq. (1). The 1997 fiscal year was used to ensure that all variables were from the same time period. (Recall discussion of data collection for the governance variables.) Models using 3- and 11-day "windows" for cumulating abnormal returns, and various subsets of the independent variables yielded qualitatively similar results. Hence they are omitted.

Table 5 shows that the regression as a whole has an adjusted R^2 of 0.06. While this statistic is not remarkable, it is in the typical range for regressions of this type. Further, the equation as a whole has an F value of 2.59, which is significant at the 0.001 level.

Consistent with prior studies of the Chinese securities market (e.g., Abdel-khalik, Wong, & Wu, 1999; Haw, Qi, & Wu, 1999), there is a positive and significant correlation between UE and cumulative abnormal return. This suggests that domestic Chinese investors do make use of the listed companies' annual earnings reports. Focusing on the governance practice variables, H1 implies that there would be positive and significant coefficients for these variables' interaction terms with UE. This pattern is not uniformly observed, with the coefficients for UE $*$ CEO and UE $*$ GOVERN being negative, rather than positive as predicted (-0.451 and $–2.663$, respectively). The interactions that *are* positive are uniformly not statistically significant, while the negative coefficient for UE $*$ GOVERN is significant at the 0.05 level ($t = -2.12$). Overall, these results fail to support H1.

Since POLICY relates to companies' internal policies and process, one could attribute the lack of significance for this variable to outsiders' lack of access to such detailed information. However, such an explanation seems to be less tenable for the GOVERN variable, which pertains to the board of directors. In this case, the significant negative interaction term between GOVERN and UE implies that individual investors reacted less, rather than more, to the unexpected earnings reported by companies with stronger board of directors related governance structures. This is a decidedly counterintuitive result.

While the available data precluded an exhaustive investigation into the potential causes of this unexpected finding, some exploratory analysis still

Table 5. Cumulative 5-Day Abnormal Returns as a Function of Unexpected Earnings and Governance Practices.

Variable	Coeff.	*t*-statistic
Intercept	−0.011	−0.38
UE	2.172	2.35*
CEO	−0.007	−0.47
UE*CEO	−0.451	−0.73
OUTDIR%	−0.018	−0.97
UE*OUTDIR%	0.260	0.34
GOVERN	0.013	0.37
UE*GOVERN	−2.663	−2.12*
INTAUD	0.012	1.21
UE*INTAUD	0.006	0.03
POLICY	−0.001	−0.17
UE*POLICY	0.035	0.47
UE*LTA	−0.107	−1.01
UE*PUB%	−0.008	−1.60
Adjusted R^2 = 0.06		
F-value = 2.59		
Significance level = 0.00		

UE = unexpected earnings.
CEO = 0 if the chairman of BOD is the same person as the CEO, 1 otherwise.
OUTDIR% = percentage of directors who are outsiders.
GOVERN = average score for 5-item corporate governance scale.
INTAUD = 1 if there is an internal audit department, 0 otherwise.
POLICY = average score for 12 questions on the existence of formal work manuals or policies in making various operation decisions.
LTA = log of total assets.
PUB% = percentage of shares owned by individuals.
*Significant at 0.05 level.

was possible. We speculated that the governance practices of a company may have affected the timeliness of its annual reports, conditional on the favorable versus unfavorable nature of the earnings change. In turn, the timing of earnings announcement could have shifted investors' reactions to a period outside the days we had used to cumulate abnormal returns.

To evaluate the efficacy of the announcement date explanation, we collected data on the reporting delay for each sample company, defined as the number of days between fiscal year end and publication of the annual report. This measure was used as the dependent variable in a regression of the form in Eq. (1). Neither the main effect due to GOVERN, nor its interaction term with unexpected earnings was close to statistical significance.

As an added test, we cumulated each company's market-adjusted daily returns for the 12 months surrounding announcement of its 1997 earnings, and regressed this against the governance variables in a model of the form in Eq. (1). Again, both the main and interaction effects due to GOVERN were far from being statistically significant. Thus, our overall results fail to indicate a significant role for governance practices in domestic Chinese investors' use of reported earnings, and in addition leaves us with an unexpected result that calls for attention from future research.

Test of the Governance Choice Hypothesis (H2)

Recall that H1 was predicated on listed companies' governance choices being responsive to investor expectations. Hence, evidence on the relation between ownership structure and governance practices (the focus of H2) could shed light on the H1 results. Table 6 presents the results of regressions

Table 6. Regression Results on Governance Practices.

Dependent Variable	Intercept	STATE%	LP%	PUB%	LMVE	LISTYRS	Adj. R^2	F-value (sig. level)
CEO	0.886	0.003	0.004	−0.002	0.015	−0.004	0.05	2.59
	(4.92)	(1.40)	(1.78)	(−0.99)	(0.42)	(−2.82)*		(0.03)
OUTDIR%	0.570	−0.003	−0.001	0.001	−0.040	−0.001	0.05	2.19
	(4.02)	(−1.48)	(−0.61)	(0.68)	(−1.37)	(−0.77)		(0.06)
GOVERN	0.480	−0.001	−0.002	−0.001	0.010	0.001	0.0	0.67
	(5.22)	(−1.19)	(−1.55)	(−0.98)	(0.55)	(0.89)		(0.65)
INTAUD	0.824	−0.000	−0.004	0.002	−0.091	0.001	0.04	2.12
	(3.18)	(−0.03)	(−1.35)	(0.63)	(−1.79)	(0.62)		(0.07)
POLICY	6.307	−0.020	−0.019	−0.010	0.129	0.008	0.05	2.42
	(11.55)	(−2.85)*	(−2.74)*	(−1.53)	(1.19)	(1.77)		(0.04)

STATE% = percentage of shares owned by the State.
LP% = percentage of shares owned by legal persons.
PUB% = percentage of shares owned by the public.
LMVE = log of market value of common equity, measured in RMB 100 million.
LISTYRS = the number of years that the company had been listed.
CEO = 0 if the chairman of BOD is the same person as the CEO, 1 otherwise.
OUTDIR% = percentage of directors who are outsiders.
GOVERN = average score for 5-item corporate governance scale.
INTAUD = 1 if there is an internal audit department, 0 otherwise.
POLICY = average score for 12 questions on the existence of formal work manuals or policies in making various operation decisions.
Significance levels are shown in parentheses.
*Significant at 0.05 level.

using the model in Eq. (2). Each regression used a different governance measure as the dependent variable.

Table 6 shows that the regression for GOVERN is not significant. There is no relationship between this variable and the company characteristics that we had hypothesized would affect this choice. All four remaining regressions are at least moderately significant ($p = 0.07$–0.03). In the case of CEO, the only significant independent variable was the number of years that the company had been listed. The negative sign of its coefficient indicates that the separation between CEO and board chairmanship was proportionally less in companies with longer listing histories.

Table 6 also shows two other coefficients as being significant. Both are in the regression with POLICY as the dependent variable. They indicate that as the percentage of ownership by the state and legal persons increases, the company tends to have less developed sets of internal policies. Perhaps this reflects the power, and preference, of these two owner groups to exercise influence and/or oversight via other means, including direct interventions and directives. A caveat is that three significant regression coefficients out of a total of 25 does not strongly dispel the possibility that the results are due to chance. Perhaps future research can shed further light on this, and other possible explanations.

SUMMARY AND DISCUSSION

The key findings from this study are as follows. First, investors in the domestically listed Chinese companies do seem to base their valuation decisions, at least in part, on these companies' earnings reports. This was indicated by the significant relationship between "unexpected" earnings and cumulative abnormal returns. However, the hypothesized effects of governance practice/choice are, on the whole, not supported. Furthermore, one aspect of governance is found to have an effect opposite in direction to that expected.

Second, the Chinese companies' choices of governance practices are, on the whole, not systematically related to ownership structure. Though a couple of significant relations are found, the possibility that these are due to chance cannot be dismissed.

On the whole, we interpret these findings to imply that in the Chinese securities market, the institutional factors and infrastructure (e.g., legal liability, information intermediation, market for managers, and takeovers) are not yet sufficiently developed to permit individual investors to exert significant influence via their market reactions. The segmented nature of share ownership (e.g., state and legal person shares) also may be a contributory factor in at least two ways. One is that these two classes of owners tend to hold over half of the shares, so individual owners are in the minority and thus have proportionally limited influence. The other is that these two classes of owners may have objectives that differ from the (presumed) wealth maximization objective of individual owners. If China desires to attract more private capital to listed companies, and to increase these companies' attention to investor wealth maximization (in part via increased effectiveness and accountability), a potential implication is that the segmentation of company ownership needs to be loosened or eliminated, along with increasing the transparency of company operations.

In seeking policy implications of this type, it is important to recognize that, while this study has progressed over prior studies in getting more detailed measures of companies' governance practices, these measures are based on self-reporting in surveys. While the responses to board of director level governance practices may be more straightforward, those relating to internal operating processes and policies are more subject to judgmental error. Access to companies' internal data would improve the accuracy and reliability of these measures. Second, we have implicitly assumed that every component of governance practice plays an equally important or intensive role. Further investigation, such as focused surveys or interviews, could help to develop a more appropriate weighting scheme. Third, our measures may only capture the surface of phenomena. For example, we lack information on how outside board members are appointed. It may be that the appointment of outside board members is just "window dressing" (Menon & Williams, 1994; Wallace, 1995), and that companies are primarily concerned with the wishes of the state and legal person owners. Considerations like these suggest that there is much room for increasing both the scope and depth of the investigation, in particular relating to the potential conflict of interests among the three classes of owners, the avenues that each class has to exert influence, and how these affect the operations of listed Chinese companies.

ACKNOWLEDGEMENT

The authors are indebted to Shijun Cheng for his assistance in data collection, and to the Hong Kong Research Grants Council for its financial support (RGC grant number CUHK 160/96H).

REFERENCES

Abdel-khalik, A. R., Wong, K., & Wu, A. (1999). The association between disclosure of accounting information and security prices in China's emerging capital market. *International Journal of Accounting, 34*, 467–489.

Agrawal, A., & Knoeber, C. R. (1996). Firm performance and mechanisms to control agency problems between managers and shareholders. *Journal of Financial and Quantitative Analysis, 31*, 377–397.

Alford, A., Jones, J., Leftwich, R., & Zmijewski, M. (1993). The relative informativeness of accounting disclosures in different countries. *Journal of Accounting Research, 31*(Suppl.), 183–223.

Alston, J. P. (1989). Guanxi, and Inhwa: Managerial principles in Japan, China, and Korea. *Business Horizons, 32*, 26–31.

Amir, E., Harris, T. S., & Venuti, E. (1993). A comparison of the value relevance of U.S. versus Non-U.S. GAAP accounting measures using form 20-F reconciliations. *Journal of Accounting Research, 31*(Suppl.), 230–263.

Anthony, R. N., Dearden, J., & Govindarajan, V. (1992). *Management control systems.* Homewood, IL: Irwin.

Bacon, J. (1993). *Corporate boards and corporate governance.* New York: The Conference Board.

Bao, B., & Chow, L. (1999). The usefulness of earnings and book value for equity valuation in emerging capital markets: Evidence from listed Chinese companies in the People's Republic of China. *Journal of International Financial Management and Accounting, 10*, 85–104.

Barth, M. E., & Clinch, G. (1996). International accounting differences and their relation to share prices: Evidence from U.K., Australian, and Canadian firms. *Contemporary Accounting Research, 13*, 135–170.

Bathala, C., & Rao, R. P. (1995). The determinants of board composition: An agency theory perspective. *Managerial and Decision Economics, 16*, 59–69.

Beasley, M. (1996). An empirical analysis of the relation between the board of director composition and financial statement fraud. *The Accounting Review, 71*, 443–465.

Beatty, R. P., & Zajac, E. J. (1994). Managerial incentives, monitoring, and risk bearing: A study of executive compensation, ownership, and board structure in initial public offerings. *Administrative Science Quarterly, 39*, 313–335.

Blair, M. (1995). *Ownership and control: Rethinking corporate governance for the twenty-first century.* Washington, DC: Brookings Institute.

Braiotta, L. (1994). *The audit committee handbook.* New York: Wiley.

Brickley, J., Coles, J., & Terry, R. L. (1994). Outside directors and the adoption of poison pills. *Journal of Financial Economics, 35*, 371–390.

Byrd, J. W., & Hickman, K. A. (1992). Do outside directors monitor managers? Evidence from tender offer bids. *Journal of Financial Economics, 32*(Suppl.), 195–221.

Canadian Institute of Chartered Accountants (CICA). (1995). *Criteria of Control Board Guidance on Control (CoCo).* Toronto, Ontario, Canada: CICA.

Chen, C. J. P., Gul, F. A., & Su, X. (1999). A comparison of reported earnings under Chinese GAAP versus IAS: Evidence from the Shanghai Stock Exchange. *Accounting Horizons, 13*, 91–111.

Cho, J. Y., & Jung, K. (1991). Earnings response coefficients: A synthesis of theory and empirical evidence. *Journal of Accounting Literature, 10*, 85–116.

Chow, C. W. (1982). The demand for external auditing: Size, debt and ownership influences. *Accounting Review, 57,* 272–291.

Chow, C. W., & Wong-Boren, A. (1987). Voluntary financial disclosure by mexican corporations. *Accounting Review, 62,* 541–544.

Collins, D. W., & DeAngelo, L. E. (1990). Accounting information and corporate governance: Market and analyst reactions to earnings of firms engaged in proxy contests. *Journal of Accounting and Economics, 13,* 213–247.

Committee of Sponsoring Organizations of the Treadway Commission (COSO). (1992). *Internal control-integrated framework.* Jersey City, NJ: American Institute of Certified Public Accountants.

Committee on Corporate Governance (CCG). (1998). *Final report of committee (Hampel Report).* London, UK: Gee Publishing Company.

Core, J. E., Holthausen, R., & Larcker, D. F. (1999). Corporate governance, chief executive officer compensation, and firm performance. *Journal of Financial Economics, 51,* 371–406.

Daily, C. (1996). Governance patterns in bankruptcy reorganizations. *Strategic Management Journal, 17,* 355–375.

DeAngelo, L. E. (1988). Managerial competition, information costs, and corporate governance: The use of accounting performance measures in proxy contests. *Journal of Accounting and Economics, 10,* 3–36.

DeChow, P., Sloan, R., & Sweeney, A. (1996). Causes and consequences of earnings manipulation: An analysis of firms subject to enforcement actions by the SEC. *Contemporary Accounting Research, 13,* 1–36.

DeFond, M. L., Wong, T. J., & Li, S. H. (1999). The impact of improved auditor independence on audit market concentration in China. *Journal of Accounting and Economics, 28,* 269–305.

Demsetz, H., & Lehn, K. (1985). The structure of corporate ownership: Causes and consequences. *Journal of Political Economy, 98,* 1155–1177.

Flamholtz, E., Das, T., & Tsui, A. (1985). Toward an integrative framework of organizational control. *Accounting, Organizations and Society, 10,* 35–50.

Gordon, L. A., & Narayanan, V. K. (1984). Management accounting systems, perceived environmental uncertainty and organization structure: An empirical investigation. *Accounting, Organizations and Society, 9,* 33–48.

Haw, I. M., Qi, D., & Wu, Y. W. (1999). Value-relevance of earnings in an emerging capital market: The case of A-shares in China. *Pacific Economic Review, 4,* 337–347.

Khandwalla, P. N. (1977). *The design of organizations.* New York: Harcourt Brace Jovanovich.

Kren, L., & Liao, W. (1988). The role of accounting information in the control of organizations: A review of the evidence. *Journal of Accounting Literature, 7,* 280–309.

Leftwich, R. (1980). Market failure fallacies and accounting information. *Journal of Accounting and Economics, 2,* 193–211.

Leftwich, R., Watts, R., & Zimmerman, J. (1981). Voluntary corporate disclosure: The case of interim reporting. *Journal of Accounting Research,* (Suppl.), *19,* 50–77.

Li, R., & He, H. (2000). An analysis of the development and current situation of the civil legal liabilities of CPAs in China. *China Accounting and Finance Review 2, 1,* 104–120.

Lincoln, J., Hanada, M., & McBride, K. (1986). Organizational structures in Japanese and U.S. manufacturing. *Administrative Science Quarterly, 31,* 338–364.

Loebbecke, J., Eining, M., & Willingham, J. (1989). Auditors' experience with material irregularities: Frequency, nature, and detectability. *Auditing: A Journal of Practice and Theory, 9,* 1–28.

Luo, Y. (1997). Guanxi and performance of foreign-invested enterprises in China: An empirical inquiry. *Management International Review, 37*, 51–70.

McMullen, D. (1996). Audit committee performance: An investigation of the consequences associated with audit committees. *Auditing: A Journal of Practice and Theory, 15*, 87–103.

McMullen, D., & Raghunandan, K. (1996). Enhancing audit committee effectiveness. *Journal of Accountancy, 182*, 79–81.

Meek, G. K., & Gray, S. J. (1989). Globalization of stock markets and foreign listing requirements: Voluntary disclosures by continental European companies listed on the London Stock Exchange. *Journal of International Business Studies, 20*, 315–336.

Menon, K., & Williams, J. (1994). The use of audit committees for monitoring. *Journal of Accounting and Public Policy, 13*, 121–139.

Merchant, K. (1985a). *Control in business organizations.* Boston, MA: Pitman.

Merchant, K. (1985b). Organizational controls and discretionary program decision making: A field study. *Accounting, Organizations & Society, 10*, 67–85.

Mok, H. M. K., & Hui, Y. V. (1998). Underpricing and aftermarket performance of IPOs in Shanghai, China. *Pacific-Basin Finance Journal, 6*, 453–474.

Organization for Economic Cooperation and Development (OECD). (1999). Draft Principles of Corporate Governance, Washington, DC.

Pacter, P. (2001). Accounting standards in China: A progress report. *Accounting & Business, 4*(2), 22.

Poon, W. P. H., Firth, M., & Fung, H. G. (1998). Asset pricing in segmented capital markets: Preliminary evidence from China-domiciled companies. *Pacific-Basin Finance Journal, 6*, 307–319.

Rosenstein, S., & Wyatt, J. G. (1990). Outside directors, board independence and shareholder wealth. *Journal of Financial Economics, 26*, 175–191.

Shleifer, A., & Vishny, R. (1997). A survey of corporate governance. *Journal of Finance, 52*, 737–783.

Tam, O. K. (1999). *The development of corporate governance in China.* Cheltenham, UK and Northampton, MA: Edward Elgar.

Tang, Y. W. (2000). Bumpy road leading to internationalization: A review of accounting development in China. *Accounting Horizons, 14*(1), 93–102.

Tang, Y. W., Chow, L., & Cooper, B. (1994). *Accounting and finance in China – A review of current practice* (2nd ed.). Hong Kong: Longman.

Wallace, W. (1995). Are outside directors put on boards just for show? *Wall Street Journal*, B22.

Watts, R., & Zimmerman, J. (1986). *Positive accounting theory.* Englewood Cliffs, NJ: Prentice-Hall.

Watts, R., & Zimmerman, J. (1990). Positive accounting theory: A ten-year perspective. *Accounting Review, 65*, 131–156.

Weisbach, M. (1988). Outside directors and CEO turnover. *Journal of Financial Economics, 20*, 431–460.

Xiang, B. (1998). Institutional factors influencing China's accounting reforms and standards. *Accounting Horizons, 12*, 105–119.

Xin, K. R., & Pearce, J. L. (1996). Guanxi: Connections as substitutes for formal institutional support. *Academy of Management Journal, 39*, 1641–1658.

Xu, X., & Wang, Y. (1999). Ownership structure and corporate governance in Chinese stock companies. *China Economic Review, 10*, 75–98.

CULTURAL INFLUENCES ON INDIGENOUS USERS' PERCEPTIONS OF THE IMPORTANCE OF DISCLOSURE ITEMS: EMPIRICAL EVIDENCE FROM PAPUA NEW GUINEA

Ken Ngangan, Shahrokh M. Saudagaran and Frank L. Clarke

ABSTRACT

This study investigates the cultural determinism hypothesis that financial statement users from different cultural groups will have different perceptions regarding the importance of accounting information disclosure. Examination of the perceptual differences of three cultural groups from: (1) Papua New Guinea, (2) other developing countries, and (3) developed western countries, shows that while significant differences exist in accounting information perception between financial statement users from the developed western countries and developing countries (including Papua New Guinea), there appears to be no significant difference in the perceptions of users in the developing countries. In general, the results support the cultural determinism thesis in accounting. This has implications for the

Advances in International Accounting
Advances in International Accounting, Volume 18, 27–51
Copyright © 2005 by Elsevier Ltd.
ISSN: 0897-3660/doi:10.1016/S0897-3660(05)18002-7

designing of appropriate accounting and reporting systems for use in the developing countries. It also raises questions about some of the country classifications traditionally reported in the international accounting literature. An important implication is the warning it sends to the International Accounting Standards Board and any other aspiring global standard setters about their penchant for selling Anglo-American standards, packaged as 'international' or 'global' standards, to the developing countries.

INTRODUCTION

Over the past decade, the effort to harmonize financial reporting globally has gathered momentum under the auspices of the International Accounting Standards Committee (IASC) and its successor – The International Accounting Standards Board (IASB). Underlying the push for the international harmonization of accounting standards is the implicit assumption that the accounting information needs of users are similar notwithstanding their different socio-economic and political backgrounds. However, a growing body of literature argues that significant and influential differences exist between the cultural environments of the developed and developing countries which may engender differences in the information needs of financial statement users in each (Briston, 1978; Wallace, 1988; Perera, 1989a; Baydoun & Willett, 1995; Chow, Shields, & Wu, 1999; Patel, 2003). Accounting practices in developed countries are a product of the economic, regulatory, social, and political conditions that prevail in those countries (Mueller, 1967; Meek & Saudagaran, 1990).[1] Transporting those practices, either overtly or in the guise of 'international accounting standards (IASs)', to developing countries with underlying environments that differ markedly from the developed countries, should not be expected to have optimum results for constituents in the developing countries.

Studies have been conducted mainly in the developed countries to examine the information needs of financial statement users both within a country (e.g., Firth, 1978; McNally, Eng, & Hasseldine, 1982; Wallace, 1988; Abu-Nassar & Rutherford, 2000) and users across different countries (e.g., Baker, Chenhall, Haslem, & Juchau, 1977; Chang & Most, 1981; Choi & Levich, 1990; Salter, Roberts, & Kantor, 1995). Whereas different methods have been used in the analyses and somewhat different conclusions reached, there is a consensus that the information needs of users differ between various user groups within a single country and between users of the same class across different countries. However, much of this work has focused primarily on user groups in developed countries. Little empirical research has investigated the information needs of users in developing countries.

This chapter reports the examination of differences and similarities in user preferences for different aspects of accounting information disclosure, with a view to explain the difference in preferences in terms of cultural grouping affiliations. It develops and tests the general hypothesis that no significant difference exists in the perceptions of financial statement users of different nationalities, specifically from developed and developing countries, regarding the disclosure of accounting information in financial statements.

We investigate the cultural determinism hypothesis that financial statement users from different cultural groups will have different perceptions regarding the importance of accounting information disclosure. We do this by investigating the perceptions of financial statement users of different nationalities based in Papua New Guinea (PNG). We include financial statement users of other nationalities to facilitate comparison and determine whether (1) the information needs of users from a developing country are different from those of users from a developed country (Perera, 1985), and (2) the information needs of users from a developing country are similar to those of users from other developing countries (Wallace, 1988). Examination of the perceptual differences of three cultural groups from: (1) PNG, (2) other developing countries (ODC), and (3) developed western countries (DWC), shows that while significant differences exist in accounting information perception between financial statement users from the DWC and developing countries (including PNG), there appears to be no significant difference in the perceptions of users in the developing countries. In general, the results support the cultural determinism thesis in accounting. This has implications for the designing of appropriate accounting and reporting systems for use in the developing countries. It also raises questions about some of the multicountry classifications (i.e., British Commonwealth group) traditionally reported in the international accounting literature. Finally, an important implication is the warning it sends to the IASB and any other aspiring global standard setters about their penchant for selling Anglo-American standards, packaged as 'international' or 'global' standards, to the developing countries.

CULTURAL GROUPING AFFILIATION AND HYPOTHESES FORMULATION

Culture has been subject to numerous interpretations in the social science literature. An early view was that culture could be explained only by reference to specific cultures (e.g., White, 1949). After reviewing the literature on culture, Kroeber and Kluckhohn (1952, p. 181) concluded that no consensus existed. Jahoda (1984, p. 140) noted that 'culture is arguably the most elusive term in the vocabulary of the social sciences' and Segall (1984, p. 153) emphasized the point by asserting that 'no single definition [of culture] is embraced even by all anthropologists, in whose discipline the concept is central.' Consequently, Segall noted that there was no need to push for a definition of culture:

> We of course cannot (and don't) do without culture but it matters not at all that we cannot pin down the concept. We don't need to. When we try to, we may end up with a definition that leads us erroneously to a conclusion that we are studying the wrong things. (1984, pp. 161–162)

Certainly most definitions of culture have emphasized on values, ideas, beliefs, and meaning systems. An early definition proposed by Kroeber and Kluckhohn (1952) also included ideas and values. After reviewing uses of the concept over 150 years, Kroeber and Kluckhohn proposed the following definition:

> Culture consists of patterns, explicit and implicit, of and for behavior acquired and transmitted by symbols, constituting the distinctive achievements of human groups, including their embodiments in artifacts; the essential core of culture consists of traditional (i.e., historically derived and selected) ideas and especially their cultural systems may on the one hand be considered as products of action, on the other hand as conditioning elements of further action. (1952, p. 181)

Other early definitions of culture included that by Fayerweather (1959, p. 7) who defined culture as 'the attitudes, beliefs and values of a society.' Whitely and England (1977) reviewed the 164 definitions analyzed by Kroeber and Kluckhohn (1952) and redefined culture as 'the knowledge, beliefs, art, laws, morals, customs and other capabilities of one group distinguishing it from other groups.' More recently, Rohner (1984, pp. 119–120) defined culture as 'the totality of equivalent and complementary learned meanings maintained by a human population, or by identifiable segments of a population, and transmitted from one generation to the next.' Similarly, Takatera and Yamamoto (1987) noted that culture is often regarded as an expression of norms, values, and customs. Perera (1989b) noted that culture is used to refer to the fact that members of a given group tend to share common frameworks of meanings, social understandings, values, beliefs, and symbols, a notion similar to Hofstede's (1980, p. 25) definition of culture as 'the collective programming of the mind which distinguishes the members of one human group from another'. More informally, Hofstede (1984, p. 113) referred to culture as 'a system of meanings in the heads of multiple individuals within a population.' He described the content of mental programs as values and identified four sets of norm values, which he termed dimensions of culture (Hofstede, 1980).[2] His explication of the concept pervades most of the accounting studies relating to the influence of culture on national accounting practices.

Given the frequent reference to Hofstede (1980) in the literature, it appeared reasonable for this study to likewise adopt Hofstede's definition, for it emphasizes values and meaning systems that are consistent with a majority of definitions of culture over the years (Rohner, 1984). Its use here allows this inquiry to mesh with those preceding it (e.g., Gray, 1988; Perera, 1989b; Belkaoui & Picur, 1991). In the Hofstede tradition, culture is characterized as a system of shared cognition of a group of individuals, a system entailing their knowledge-in-common and their holding of beliefs-in-common. This follows Goodenough's (1971) view of culture where he proposed that culture can be viewed as a system of shared cognition in which the mind generates a culture by means of finite number of rules or by means of unconscious logic. As a system of shared cognition it may be seen as 'a unique system for perceiving and organizing materials, phenomena, events, behaviors, and emotions' (Rossi & O'Higgins, 1980, p. 63). Such a focus usefully captures the idiosyncratic national settings in which accounting is employed and the information it produces is used. Culture in this sense is the coordinating force that facilitates the orderly functioning of the society embracing it.

Our focus is on the idiosyncratic and indigenous perceptions of accounting information. Accordingly, a cognitive functioning view of culture is adopted to investigate the influence of culture on accounting. Using the cognitive emphasis, different categories of nationalities act as networks of subjective meanings or shared frames of reference, which in general, members of each category enjoy. To that end Belkaoui and Picur (1991, p. 119) noted that the different cultural groups in accounting create different cognition or systems of knowledge for communication within and between cultures. That is the focus of this study.

This chapter pursues those differences with respect to three nationality groupings regarding the disclosure of accounting information: (1) Papua New Guineans, (2) nationals from selected DWC, and (3) nationals from selected ODC.[3] Each of the three groupings of nationalities is identified as a *cultural category* in which the members share substantial common cognitive characteristics distinguishing them from the members of the other categories. This fits Hofstede's survey results (1983, pp. 335–355) that demonstrated significant cultural differences between Anglo-American countries and many developing countries.

Justification for this study of national cultures within the developed and developing country categories arises from the argument in the extant international accounting literature to the effect that significant differences exist in the cultural environments of developed and developing countries (Jaggi, 1975; Perera, 1989b; Wallace, 1990; Saudagaran & Diga, 1997). Jaggi (1975) examined the cultural environment and value orientations on the reliability of disclosures in annual reports of developed and developing countries. He noted that culture has an impact on the value orientation of managers in the two categories of countries. Perera (1989b) examined Hofstede's four societal value dimensions and found significant cultural differences between the DWC and many developing countries. Differences are most easily identifiable in the areas associated with Hofstede's individualism versus collectivism and large versus small power distance cultural dimensions.

A pervading issue in the normative literature on accounting in developing countries, questions the appropriateness of the transfer of accounting technology from the developed countries to the developing countries, mainly through colonialism. Those transfers have emerged mainly through colonization:

> The real issue to resolve in respect of transfer of accounting technology is the *tension* between national cultures of developing countries and cultures of exporting countries. (Emphasis added; Wallace, 1990, p. 5)

By virtue of the different economic, social, and legal systems under which (so often) importers and exporters of accounting and other commercial practices operate, that tension is not surprising.

It is further argued in the international accounting literature that notwithstanding considerable diversity, similarities in the cultural environments may also be observed between countries. Wallace (1990) for example, noted that although the developing countries are not a homogeneous group they have similar cultural characteristics. They are often viewed as being at the 'threshold of economic growth.' Most developing countries have imported accounting technology from those developed countries that were once their colonizers (Briston, 1978; Hove, 1989; Saudagaran & Diga, 2003). It has traditionally been postulated that as a result of the colonization period cultural characteristics inherited from the colonizers within the developing country category may lead to similar cognition or systems of knowledge regarding the perception of accounting information disclosure. This can be widely observed in the international accounting classification studies that typically lump a group of countries in the category generally labeled 'British influence'. The common link between these countries is that they were all British colonies at some point in their history (Mueller, 1968; American Accounting Association, 1977; Nair & Frank, 1980; Doupnik & Salter, 1993). However, based on a study of postcolonial accountancy regimes in five Southeast Asian countries, Saudagaran and Diga (2003) question the significance of the colonial link relative to other variables shaping accounting regimes in developing countries and conclude that 'conventional explanations in terms of each country's colonial history were found to be wanting because they provided few insights to the prevalent dynamics in these countries' (p. 76). This is of relevance this study since, as described in the next section, the subjects in the study are all from countries that are former British colonies.

Whereas several previous attempts have been made to examine the influence of national culture on accounting (e.g., Soeters & Schreuder, 1988; Belkaoui & Picur, 1991; Zarzeski, 1996; Patel, 2003), unlike them, this study examines the influence of nationality on perceptions of accounting information. Hofstede's (1987) definition of national culture as the shared mental programming of most members of a nation is extended here to encompass a group of nations wherein, the literature argues, the populace share similar cultural characteristics. Hence, the extended definition of national culture for this study is *the shared idiosyncratic mental programming peculiar to most members of each category of nationalities.*

Other studies (e.g., Soeters & Schreuder, 1988; Belkaoui & Picur, 1991) have established that culture influences the cognitive structure and knowledge systems of individuals within the various cultural groups in accounting. Previous studies have identified also significant differences in the cultural environments of developed and developing countries (Wallace & Briston, 1993). As a result of those differences, the cognitive structures and knowledge systems regarding the importance of accounting information disclosure are likely to differ between the nationality groupings of users of financial statements. To test this relationship, the following hypotheses are stated in their null form.

The overall null hypothesis tested is:

There is no significant difference between the perceptions of financial statement users of different nationalities regarding the importance of accounting information disclosure.

The null hypotheses associated with the pairs of the three cultural groups are:

H1. There is no significant difference between the perceptions of users from PNG and those in the DWC regarding the importance of accounting information disclosure.

H2. There is no significant difference between the perceptions of users from PNG and those in the ODC regarding the importance of accounting information disclosure.

H3. There is no significant difference between the perceptions of users from the DWC and those in the ODC regarding the importance of accounting information disclosure.

SAMPLE, DATA, AND RESEARCH DESIGN

Selection of Information Items

A questionnaire was developed and administered among subjects in PNG. Construction of a list of items of financial and nonfinancial information that a reporting company might be expected to disclose in its financial statements in PNG, was the initial step in the development of the questionnaire. Selection of items for inclusion in the survey instrument was based on four general criteria, that:

1. the item, relevant to developing countries, had been included in one or more of the previous studies;
2. the item is required to be disclosed by the Papua New Guinea Association of Accountants' (PNGAA) standards, the adopted IASs and is required disclosure under the PNG Companies Act and other legal rules which specify the disclosure of such items in the financial statements;
3. the item relates to a controversial issue in the country such as the claim for compensation by land owners in areas where major resource projects are undertaken or to control the importation of raw materials into the country by companies;
4. the item is generally regarded in the literature as being of relevance and significance to users of financial statements in developing countries.

An item was selected if it met one or more of the above criteria. On the basis of the above criteria 40 information items were selected for inclusion in the questionnaire survey (see the appendix).

Research Instrument

Respondents were asked to examine each of the 40 items and indicate the degree of importance they attached to each in the context of financial information disclosure. In judging each item of information they were asked to use as a frame of reference, the anticipated approach of a person using the annual reports as a major input in reaching a financial decision about a company. This was consistent with the decision-usefulness theme coursing through the conceptual framework exercises in the developed countries that might be regarded as exemplars by those in the developing countries.

As the focus of the study was on general purpose financial reporting, no particular decision was specified. Thus, the decisions may be to buy, hold, or sell shares of a company; to bargain on behalf of employees for more wages or better working conditions; to lend money to the company; to refuse/grant a company supplier's credit, or government import license or tax holiday; or to ascertain the contributions of the company to society.

The expected responses were structured according to the following five-point Likert scale:

1. the item is unimportant
2. the item is slightly important
3. the item is moderately important
4. the item is important
5. the item is very important

Sample Selection

The population from which the sample was selected was located in Port Moresby (the capital city of PNG). A total of 726 questionnaires were mailed to subjects selected from the PNG population of users of financial statement, employing the stratified sampling technique used in similar studies (e.g., Firth, 1978; Wallace, 1988). In this study, it facilitated the acquisition of data with a known level of precision regarding the necessary subdivisions of the population (e.g., Cochran, 1977). The total sample of 726 subjects consisted of 400 Papua New Guineans, 156 subjects from the DWC, and 170 from ODC. The sample from the DWC included subjects from Australia, New Zealand, and the United Kingdom. The sample from ODC included subjects from Uganda, Tanzania, India, and Sri Lanka.

Survey Responses

Postage prepaid envelopes were provided with the questionnaires and the responses were reviewed upon receipt. Each useable response was numbered in the order in which it was received. Responses, which were

Table 1.   Summary of Survey Response Rates.

Nationality Group	Total Sampled	Useable Responses	Response Rates (%)
Papua New Guinea	400	209	52.25
Developed country	156	68	43.59
Developing country	170	41	24.12
Overall	726	318	43.80

either incomplete or improperly completed, were eliminated from the analysis. As respondents did not disclose their addresses, such questionnaires could not be returned for rectification. Information on the sample and response rates by each of the three nationality groups is presented in Table 1.

Response rates refer to the number of useable completed questionnaires. A total of 12 responses were eliminated from the analysis because they were either incomplete or were not properly completed. Of the 400 questionnaires distributed to PNG nationals, 209 responses were received for a response rate of 52.25%; 68 of 156 questionnaires distributed to nationals of DWC were completed for a response rate of 43.59%; and of the 170 questionnaires distributed to nationals of ODC 41 were completed for a response rate of 24.12%. Thus, of the total 726 questionnaires mailed to the user groups, 318 completed questionnaires were received for an overall response rate of 43.8% from respondents (financial statement users) in PNG.

The response rate of 43.8% is reasonable when compared with other similar previous studies (e.g., Wallace, 39.2%; Firth, 40.27%; Chenhall & Juchau, 46.44%). However, the presence of nonresponse bias (with respect to the other 56.2%) could entail a viewpoint significantly different from that of the respondents and affect the validity of the results of the research. In an attempt to establish whether the response rate resulted in any bias, the data obtained were examined using the Oppenheim test (1966) to determine whether the responses of the first 50 returns were significantly different from the last 50 returns. The t-test was then applied to examine whether there was any statistically significant difference between the mean scores of the two groups. Table 2 presents the results of the test of nonresponse bias indicating no significant difference at the 0.05 level between the two groups of responses. Accordingly, the results of the returned samples can comfortably be generalized to represent the entire population of users of corporate annual reports sampled for the study.

In this study, the 40 disclosure items were halved and the correlation between the two scores is calculated to test for reliability (Carmines &

Table 2. Test of Nonresponse Bias.

Group	Cases	Mean	Std. Dev.	F	Prob.	t	df	Prob.
1	50	3.6915	0.637	1.18	0.562	1.36	98	0.177
2	50	3.5250	0.586					

Notes: Prob. = 2-tail probability; df = degrees of freedom. Not significant at the 0.05 level.

Table 3. Reliability Coefficients for the 40 Disclosure Items.

Correlation between forms	0.7396
Guttman split-half	0.8488
Spearman–Brown	0.8503
Alpha for part 1	0.8966
Alpha for part 2	0.8909

Notes: The Spearman–Brown coefficient for both equal and unequal lengths = 0.8503; No. of items = 40; 20 items in part 1 and 20 items in part 2; No. of cases = 318.

Zellar, 1981). Table 3 presents the results of the test of reliability of the 40 disclosure items. It reveals that both the Guttman split-half and the Spearman–Brown correlation coefficients are high. The alpha coefficients for the separate sections used for the split-half computations and for the whole test, are also reported in Table 3.

Data Analysis

The number of items included in the survey presents problems for analysis. One accommodating mechanism is to reduce the 40 information items into relatively homogeneous groups. Factor analysis was used to effect the reduction to identify patterns of relationships amongst the variables (Kim, 1978) and to generate an understanding of underlying structure so as to combine the variables into new variables (factors) smaller than the original set they encompass. In this study, the factor analysis performed on the 40 information items extracted 10 factors that satisfied Kaiser's (eigenvalue greater than one) criterion and accounted for 65.4% of the variance.

The research hypotheses were tested using one-way analysis of variance (ANOVA) to compare the means of the 10 factors extracted by the factor analysis. One-way ANOVA was employed because of its common use in the previous studies investigating user preferences for disclosure items. Upon testing the significance of the difference among the means of the three groups simultaneously, the next step in the analysis was to determine which group means were significantly different from one another. Again, ANOVA was used to test for differences between the three pairs of nationality groupings.[4]

RESULTS

The overall null hypothesis of no group differences was examined by testing for a between-subjects effect of the three nationality groupings. The results presented in Table 4 show that the hypothesis of no group difference is rejected at the 0.05 level. Except for factors 8 and 9 significant differences were found. Significant differences were found to exist across all three nationality groupings. Basically, the different cultural groups in accounting represented different cognition or systems of knowledge regarding the perception of accounting information disclosure. Cultural affiliations could be inferred to lead to different cognition or systems of knowledge, which in turn, has the potential for inducing different perceptions of the relative importance of particular disclosure items.

Hypotheses 1–3 were tested by examining differences between the three pairs. The results presented in Table 5 show that the hypothesis of no difference between PNG and the DWC is rejected at the 0.05 level. Except for factors 6, 8, and 9 significant differences in perception were found with respect to all the other factors. Thus, significant differences were found to exist between Papua New Guineans and nationals of the DWC. Membership in the two cultural groups in accounting, entailed different cognition or systems of knowledge in respect to perceptions of accounting information disclosure.

The results presented in Table 6 show that the hypothesis of no difference between PNG and ODC is accepted at the 0.05 level. Except for factors 6 and 7, no significant differences were found. Papua New Guineans were thereby found to entertain generally similar perceptions as those of the nationals of ODC. This suggests that the cognitive structures of the two groups of respondents from developing nations were the same, or substantially similar, in respect of the named disclosure items. Affiliations in the two cultural groups appear therefore to lead to similar cognition or systems of knowledge, leading in turn to similar perceptions of disclosure items.

Table 4. Test of Hypothesis for Differences between Papua New Guinea, Developed Western Countries, and Other Developing Countries.

Factors		Mean of Responses			Test of Significance	
		PNG	DWC	ODC	*F*-ratio	*F*-prob.
F1	Employment and training	3.439	2.746	3.429	24.484	0.000*
F2	Comparative figures	3.626	3.276	3.793	4.948	0.008*
F3	Share ownership	3.832	3.382	4.012	12.227	0.000*
F4	Company background details	3.754	3.279	3.764	10.868	0.000*
F5	Future events	4.040	3.673	4.031	6.607	0.002*
F6	Related companies/businesses	3.951	4.029	4.358	4.887	0.008*
F7	Forecasted statements	3.895	3.142	3.594	18.217	0.000*
F8	Details of company directors and managers	3.414	3.463	3.402	0.067	0.935
F9	Investment financing	3.887	3.726	4.049	2.974	0.053
F10	Transactions in foreign currency	3.435	2.860	3.524	9.652	0.000*
	Sample size	209	68	41		

Notes: PNG = Papua New Guinea, DWC = Developed Western Countries, ODC = Other Developing Countries.
*Significant at the 0.05 level.

Table 5. Test of Hypothesis for Difference between Papua New Guinea and Developed Western Countries.

Factors		Mean of Responses		Test of Significances	
		PNG	DWC	*F*-ratio	*F*-prob.
F1	Employment and training	3.439	2.746	48.658	0.000*
F2	Comparative figures	3.626	3.276	7.210	0.008*
F3	Share ownership	3.832	3.382	18.670	0.000*
F4	Company background details	3.754	3.279	21.288	0.000*
F5	Future events	4.039	3.673	11.958	0.001*
F6	Related companies/businesses	3.951	4.029	0.531	0.467
F7	Forecasted statements	3.895	3.142	38.342	0.000*
F8	Details of company directors and managers	3.414	3.463	0.122	0.727
F9	Investment financing	3.887	3.725	3.022	0.083
F10	Transactions in foreign currency	3.435	2.860	17.792	0.000*
	Sample size	209	68		

Notes: PNG = Papua New Guinea, DWC = Developed Western Countries.
*Significant at the 0.05 level.

Table 6.   Test of Hypothesis for Difference between Papua New Guinea
and Other Developing Countries.

	Factors	Mean of Responses		Test of Significances	
		PNG	ODC	*F*-ratio	*F*-prob.
F1	Employment and training	3.439	3.429	0.006	0.939
F2	Comparative figures	3.626	3.793	1.241	0.266
F3	Share ownership	3.832	4.012	2.163	0.143
F4	Company background details	3.754	3.764	0.006	0.938
F5	Future events	4.041	4.031	0.006	0.939
F6	Related companies/businesses	3.951	4.358	9.499	0.002*
F7	Forecasted statements	3.895	3.594	4.088	0.044*
F8	Details of company directors and managers	3.414	3.412	0.004	0.950
F9	Investment financing	3.887	4.049	1.935	0.165
F10	Transactions in foreign currency	3.435	3.524	0.278	0.598
	Sample size	209	41		

Notes: PNG = Papua New Guinea, ODC = Other Developing Countries.
*Significant at the 0.05 level.

The results presented in Table 7 show that the hypothesis of no difference
between the DWC and ODC is rejected at the 0.05 level. Except for factor 8,
significant differences were found with respect to the others. Thus, significant differences were found to exist between the nationals of the DWC and
the developing countries, suggesting that the cognitive structure of the two
cultural groups differed, potentially creating different cognition or systems
of knowledge for the perception of disclosure items.

Discussion

The overall hypothesis relating to the three nationality groups (PNG, DWC,
and ODC) was rejected at the 0.05 level suggesting that significant differences exist in the perceptions of financial statement users across different
nationalities. That result is consistent with the findings of other cross-cultural studies investigating user preference for accounting information disclosure (e.g., Baker et al., 1977; Chang & Most, 1981) and has direct
implications for the adoption of IASs. Success, failure, and future directions
of international convergence efforts depend on an understanding of the

Table 7. Test of Hypothesis for Difference between Developed Western Countries and Other Developing Countries.

Factors		Mean of Responses		Test of Significances	
		DWC	ODC	*F*-ratio	*F*-prob.
F1	Employment and training	2.746	3.429	21.983	0.000*
F2	Comparative figures	3.276	3.793	6.387	0.013*
F3	Share ownership	3.382	4.012	16.928	0.000*
F4	Company background details	3.279	3.764	9.987	0.002*
F5	Future events	3.673	4.031	5.531	0.021*
F6	Related companies/businesses	4.029	4.358	5.528	0.021*
F7	Forecasted statements	3.142	3.594	4.902	0.029*
F8	Details of company directors and managers	3.463	3.402	0.085	0.772
F9	Investment financing	3.726	4.049	4.904	0.029*
F10	Transactions in foreign currency	2.860	3.524	10.835	0.001*
	Sample size	68	41		

Notes: DWC = Developed Western Countries, ODC = Other Developing Countries.
*Significant at the 0.05 level.

extent to which proposed accounting mechanisms are universal or culturally dependent. A similar view is shared by Cooke and Wallace (1990, p. 83):

> If accounting is determined by its environment, present efforts at international accounting harmonization will have to rely on the ability of national accounting bodies or governments to impose international accounting standards on their environments regardless of their desirability.

It is to be noted that the nationalities of subjects surveyed here were all traditionally grouped under the British sphere of influence. Thus, the development of accounting and reporting practices in these countries have accordingly been influenced by the British accounting model (Walton, 1986). The survey results demonstrate that different cultural groups in accounting create different cognition or systems of knowledge for communication between cultures. Thus, differences in perceptions regarding the use of accounting information exist across countries even within the British sphere of influence. As such, the effectiveness of the British accounting model as a proviso of relevant accounting information for the sort of decisions on hand in each country is very much debatable.

The test of difference between pairs of nationality groups yielded some interesting results. The hypothesis of no difference between PNG and nationals of other developing nations was accepted at the 0.05 level indicating that no significant difference exists in perception between users from PNG and the ODC (with a British colonial background) regarding the type of accounting information that may be needed for decision making within the developing country contexts. The results support the development of regional accounting associations between the developing nations and the sharing of accounting techniques and principles among developing countries.

The hypotheses of no difference between PNG and DWC and between the DWC and the developing countries were rejected at the 0.05 level. The results indicate a significant linkage between cultural groupings and differences in perceptions regarding accounting information disclosure. The results also suggest significant differences between information disclosure perceptions in DWC and developing countries (with the same [British] cultural backgrounds). These results further cast doubt on the wisdom of the proliferation of IASs and their acquiescent adoption by developing countries. IASs are often characterized to be an internationalization of western accounting standards, especially those of Britain and the U.S.A. (Hove, 1989; Perera, 1985). If, as it appears, the information needs differ between the developing countries and the developed countries, advocacy of the IASC and the IASB's standards is most likely misplaced. Those engaging in that advocacy might be better employed redirecting their efforts to assist the accountancy bodies of the developing nations to design the indigenous accounting standards and reporting systems appropriate to their needs.

CONCLUDING REMARKS

Just as the United States' accounting practices are not entirely appropriate in the United Kingdom or France, neither are U.S., U.K., or French accounting practices entirely appropriate in developing countries such as PNG. While the general need for information exists in all these countries, the specific nature, structure, focus, and quantity of information needed in developed and developing countries respectively, may vary considerably. Thus, unless the business environments and user needs in developed and developing countries correspond, it is unlikely that the export of developed country accounting systems to and the import of them into a developing country such as PNG will be harmonious. As evidenced in this study, this also applies to countries in the same accounting cluster (i.e., British Commonwealth countries).

This study provides further evidence questioning the continued adoption of IASs and the promotion of that practice by the developing countries in general and by PNG in particular. In light of the evidence adduced through this study, developing countries would appear to be well advised to reassess their strategies and accordingly design accounting and reporting systems geared toward meeting the information needs of users within the specific developing country contexts. The development of an appropriate accounting model for a developing country seems a far cry from the mere adoption of IASs.

Some have argued that, like most other technologies, accounting has to be transferred to the developing countries initially. This means that a pattern of growth of accounting technology, such as that in the U.S., U.K. and other developed countries, has not yet occurred in developing countries. Part of the reason is that developing countries are trying to catch up very rapidly, resulting in many social and economic imbalances in the process. As Mirghani (1982, p. 68) stated:

> Developing countries cannot afford to wait for accounting to evolve as it has in developed countries because the influences that shaped accounting in developed countries are unlikely to occur in developing countries to the same degree. Instead, a carefully designed strategy for the development of accounting as an effective tool for the economic development process must be adopted by each developing country in view of its own specific environment.

Accordingly, we argue that although a developing country is dependent initially upon the transfer of accounting technology from more developed countries, it is not in its long-run interest to depend entirely, or uniquely, on such a transfer. Thus, the indigenous accounting professions in each developing country should appraise the adopted accounting technology and adjust it to make it compatible with their local economic, political, social, and cultural environments. As Needles (1976, p. 50) observed:

> Far from being substitutes for each other, the obtaining of accounting technology from advanced countries and the building up of an indigenous accounting technological and professional capacity are complementary.

Further research is needed to investigate the information needs of users in the developing country context, especially in terms of the investigation of the varying effects of culture as cognition on the one hand and the impact of indigenous nation specific cultures on the other. Nation-specific cultures include, organizational culture, occupational culture, level and country of education, and membership in professional associations. Observations in this study, point to the need for further conceptual and empirical research on the nature and consequences of cultural determinism in accounting, especially in the developing country context.

NOTES

1. The term 'accounting practices' is used here in the sense defined by the American Institute of Certified Public Accountants that stated, "No attempt is made here to distinguish between principles, practices and methods. The term 'practices' is generally used to include all of these. It is also used with regard to presentation, classification and disclosure of items in financial statements" (AICPA, 1964, p. 22).

2. The norm values (cultural dimensions) enunciated by Hofstede (1980) are: (1) *power distance* – the extent to which hierarchy and an unequal distribution of power in institutions and organizations are accepted, (2) *uncertainty avoidance* – the degree to which society feels uncomfortable with ambiguity and an uncertain future, (3) *individualism (versus collectivism)* – a preference for a loosely knit social fabric or an independent, tightly knit social fabric, and (4) *masculinity (versus femininity)* – the extent to which gender roles are differentiated and performance and visible achievement (traditional masculine values) are emphasized over relationships and caring (traditional feminine values).

3. A common approach taken to group countries in the developed and developing category is to use Hofstede's four value dimensions (e.g., Harrison, 1993). However, since the nationalities of subjects in this study, especially for the developing country category, were not included in Hofstede's survey, no attempt was made to group nationalities according to the four dimensions of culture proposed by Hofstede (1980). Instead, the international accounting literature was surveyed to see how researchers classified the countries concerned. A similar approach was taken by Wallace (1990) to classify countries based on their level of development in his literature review on accounting in developing countries.

4. The test for differences between pairs of nationality groupings can also be conducted using the Scheffe test, a multiple comparison technique for all possible pairs. The results of the Scheffe test for all three pairs of nationality groupings were similar to the results of the one-way ANOVA test reported in this study.

ACKNOWLEDGMENT

The authors wish to thank workshop participants at the University of Papua New Guinea, the University of Newcastle (Australia), the Congress of the European Accounting Association in Copenhagen, the Asian Academic Accounting Association conference in Penang, and the Asia-Pacific Conference on International Accounting Issues in Rio De Janeiro for their helpful comments. Ken Ngangan thanks AuSAid and the University of Papua New Guinea for the financial support provided during his Ph.D. candidature.

REFERENCES

Abu-Nassar, M., & Rutherford, B. A. (2000). External reporting in less developed countries with moderately sophisticated capital markets: A study of user needs and information provision in Jordan. *Research in Accounting in Emerging Economies, 4*, 227–246.

American Accounting Association. (1977). Report of committee on international accounting operations and education 1975–76. *Accounting Review*(Suppl.), 65–132.

American Institute of Certified Public Accountants. (1964). *Professional accounting in twenty five countries*. New York: AICPA.

Baker, H. K., Chenhall, R. H., Haslem, J. A., & Juchau, R. H. (1977). Disclosure of material information – A cross national comparison. *International Journal of Accounting, 13*(1), 1–18.

Baydoun, N., & Willett, R. J. (1995). Cultural relevance of Western accounting systems to developing countries. *Abacus, 31*(1), 67–92.

Belkaoui, A., & Picur, R. D. (1991). Cultural determinism and the perception of accounting concepts. *International Journal of Accounting, 26*, 118–131.

Briston, R. J. (1978). The evolution of accounting in developing countries. *International Journal of Accounting, 14*(1), 105–120.

Carmines, E. G., & Zellar, R. A. (1981). *Reliability and validity assessment*. Beverly Hills, CA: Sage Publications.

Chang, L. S., & Most, K. S. (1981). An international comparison of investor uses of financial statements. *International Journal of Accounting, 17*(1), 43–60.

Choi, F. D. S., & Levich, R. M. (1990). *The capital market effects of international accounting diversity*. Homewood, IL: Dow Jones-Irwin.

Chow, W. C., Shields, M. D., & Wu, A. (1999). The importance of national culture in the design and preference for management controls for multinational operations. *Accounting Organizations and Society, 24*, 441–461.

Cochran, W. G. (1977). *Sampling techniques*. New York: Wiley.

Cooke, T. E., & Wallace, R. S. O. (1990). Financial disclosure regulation and its environment: A review and further analysis. *Journal of Accounting and Public Policy, 9*(2), 79–110.

Doupnik, T. S., & Salter, S. B. (1993). An empirical test of a judgmental international classification of financial reporting practices. *Journal of International Business Studies, 24*(1), 41–60.

Fayerweather, J. (1959). *The executive overseas*. Syracuse: Syracuse University Press.

Firth, M. (1978). A study of the consensus of the perceived importance of disclosure of individual items in corporate annual reports. *International Journal of Accounting, 14*(1), 57–70.

Goodenough, W. H. (1971). *Culture, language and society*. MA: Addison-Wesley.

Gray, S. J. (1988). Towards a theory of cultural influence on the development of accounting systems internationally. *Abacus, 24*(1), 1–15.

Harrison, G. (1993). Reliance on accounting performance measures in superior evaluative style – The influence of national culture and personality. *Accounting, Organizations and Society, 18*(4), 319–339.

Hofstede, G. (1980). *Culture's consequences*. Beverly Hills, CA: Sage Publications.

Hofstede, G. (1983). Dimensions of national cultures in fifty countries and three regions. In: J. B. Deregowski, S. Dziurawiec & R. C. Annis (Eds), *Explanations in cross-cultural psychology*. London: Sweet and Zeitlinger.

Hofstede, G. (1984). The cultural relativity of the quality of life concept. *Academy of Management Review, 3,* 389–398.

Hofstede, G. (1987). The cultural context of accounting. In: B. E. Cushing (Ed.), *Accounting and culture.* Sarasota, FL: AAA.

Hove, M. R. (1989). The inappropriateness of international accounting standards in LDC: The case of IAS No. 24 – Related party disclosures – Concerning transfer pricing. *International Journal of Accounting, 24*(2), 165–179.

Jaggi, B. L. (1975). The impact of the cultural environment on financial disclosures. *International Journal of Accounting, 10*(2), 75–84.

Jahoda, G. (1984). Do we need a concept of culture? *Journal of Cross-Cultural Psychology, 15*(2), 139–151.

Kim, J. (1978). *Factor analysis: Statistical methods and practical issues.* Beverly Hills, CA: Sage Publications.

Kroeber, A. L., & Kluckhohn, C. (1952). *Culture: A critical review of concepts and definitions.* Cambridge, MA: Peabody Museum.

McNally, G. M., Eng, L. H., & Hasseldine, C. R. (1982). Corporate financial reporting in New Zealand: An analysis of user preferences, corporate characteristics and disclosure practices. *Accounting and Business Research, 13*(Winter), 11–20.

Meek, G. K., & Saudagaran, S. M. (1990). A survey of research of financial reporting in a transnational context. *Journal of Accounting Literature, 9,* 145–182.

Mirghani, A. M. (1982). A framework for a linkage between microaccounting and macroaccounting for purposes of development planning in developing countries. *International Journal of Accounting, 18*(1), 57–68.

Mueller, G. G. (1967). *International accounting.* New York: Macmillan.

Mueller, G. G. (1968). Accounting principles generally accepted in the United States versus those generally accepted elsewhere. *International Journal of Accounting, 3*(2), 91–104.

Nair, R. D., & Frank, W. G. (1980). The impact of disclosure and measurement practices on international accounting classifications. *Accounting Review*(July), 426–450.

Needles, B. E. (1976). Implementing a framework for the international transfer of accounting technology. *International Journal of Accounting, 12*(1), 45–62.

Oppenheim, A. N. (1966). *Questionnaire design and attitude measurement.* London: Heinemann.

Patel, C. (2003). Some cross-cultural evidence on whistle-blowing as an internal control mechanism. *Journal of International Accounting Research, 2,* 69–96.

Perera, M. H. B. (1985). *The relevance of international accounting standards to developing countries.* Working Paper 85-8. School of Financial Studies. University of Glasgow, Scotland, UK

Perera, M. H. B. (1989a). Accounting in developing countries: A case for localised uniformity. *British Accounting Review, 21*(2), 141–158.

Perera, M. H. B. (1989b). Towards a framework to analyze the impact of culture on accounting. *International Journal of Accounting, 25*(1), 42–57.

Rohner, R. P. (1984). Toward a conception of culture for cross-cultural psychology. *Journal of Cross-Cultural Psychology, 15*(2), 111–138.

Rossi, I., & O'Higgins, E. (1980). The development of theories of culture. In: I. Rossi (Ed.), *People in culture.* New York: Praeger.

Salter, S. B., Roberts, C. B., & Kantor, J. (1995). Financial reporting practices in the Caribbean: A comparison and analysis in light of the import model of financial reporting. *Research in Accounting in Emerging Economies, 3,* 99–122.

Saudagaran, S. M., & Diga, J. (1997). Accounting regulation in ASEAN: A choice between the global and regional paradigms of harmonization. *Journal of International Financial Management and Accounting, 8*(1), 1–32.

Saudagaran, S. M., & Diga, J. (2003). *Post-colonial accountancy regulation in ASEAN: Accounting ideology in a transnational context.* Working Paper. Oklahoma State University, Stillwater, Oklahoma.

Segall, M. H. (1984). More than we need to know about culture, but are afraid not to ask. *Journal of Cross-Cultural Psychology, 15*(2), 153–163.

Soeters, J., & Schreuder, U. (1988). The interaction between national and organizational cultures in accounting firms. *Accounting Organizations and Society, 13*(1), 75–85.

Takatera, S., & Yamamoto, M. (1987). The cultural significance of accounting in Japan. Paper presented at workshop on accounting and culture. European Institute for Advanced Studies in Management (EIASM), Brussels.

Wallace, R. S. O. (1988). Intranational and international consensus on the importance of disclosure items in financial reports: A Nigerian case study. *British Accounting Review, 20*(December), 223–265.

Wallace, R. S. O. (1990). Accounting in developing countries: A review of the literature. In: R. S. O. Wallace, J. M. Samuels & R. J. Briston (Eds), *Research in third world accounting.* London: JAI Press.

Wallace, R. S. O., & Briston, R. (1993). Improving the accounting infrastructure in developing countries. *Research in Accounting in Emerging Economies, 2*, 201–224.

Walton, P. (1986). The export of British accounting legislation to Commonwealth countries. *Accounting and Business Research, 16*(3), 353–357.

White, L. (1949). *The science of culture.* New York: Grove Press.

Whitely, W., & England, G. W. (1977). Managerial values as a reflection of culture and the process of industrialization. *Academy of Management, 20*(3), 439–453.

Zarzeski, M. T. (1996). Spontaneous harmonization effects of culture and market forces on accounting disclosure practices. *Accounting Horizons, 10*(1), 18–37.

APPENDIX. RESEARCH INSTRUMENT

No.	Question	Very Important	Important	Moderately Important	Slightly Important	Unimportant
1	Discussion of major factors likely to influence next year's financial results	5	4	3	2	1
2	Details of company directors (e.g., names, salaries, outside affiliations)	5	4	3	2	1
3	Details of senior management (e.g., names, ages, salaries, functional responsibilities)	5	4	3	2	1
4	Statement of company objectives	5	4	3	2	1
5	Historical summary of important operating and financial data	5	4	3	2	1
6	Breakdown of borrowings (e.g., long-term/short-term, date of maturity, security)	5	4	3	2	1
7	Forecast of next year's profits	5	4	3	2	1
8	Information relating to investments (e.g., names, % ownership)	5	4	3	2	1
9	A statement of value added	5	4	3	2	1
10	Information on dividend per share (e.g., % growth, dividend policies)	5	4	3	2	1
11	Source and use of funds statement	5	4	3	2	1
12	Earnings per share details (e.g., amount, growth rate)	5	4	3	2	1

		5	4	3	2	1
13	Information relating to research and development (e.g., progress with new product development, planned expenditures)	5	4	3	2	1
14	Information on transactions with Government (e.g., money exchanged with government such as government guaranteed loans)	5	4	3	2	1
15	Inflation adjusted annual accounts as supplementary statements	5	4	3	2	1
16	Brief narrative history of the company	5	4	3	2	1
17	Information relating to capital expenditures (e.g., expenditure in past year, planned expenditures)	5	4	3	2	1
18	Information on major industry trends in which the company operates	5	4	3	2	1
19	Forecasted cash flow for the next 2–5 years	5	4	3	2	1
20	Structure of share ownership	5	4	3	2	1
21	Information on tax payment status of company (e.g., deferred tax, tax expense)	5	4	3	2	1
22	Statement of the rate of return required by the company on its projects	5	4	3	2	1
23	Number of employees	5	4	3	2	1
24	Indications of employee morale (e.g., labor turnover, strikes, absenteeism)	5	4	3	2	1
25	Details of foreign representatives (e.g., managers, directors, financiers)	5	4	3	2	1

APPENDIX. (*Continued*)

No.	Question	Very Important	Important	Moderately Important	Slightly Important	Unimportant
26	Amount expended on human resources (e.g., training, welfare facilities)	5	4	3	2	1
27	Information relating to the company's employee pension plan	5	4	3	2	1
28	Information on corporate social responsibility (e.g., attitude of company, expenditures)	5	4	3	2	1
29	Advertising and publicity information (e.g., expenditure in past year, planned expenditure)	5	4	3	2	1
30	Competitive position of the company in the industry in which it operates	5	4	3	2	1
31	Company's contribution to PNG's economic development (e.g., amount of exports)	5	4	3	2	1
32	Factors affecting company's future	5	4	3	2	1
33	Detailed related multinational enterprises (e.g., names, % ownership, other subsidiaries)	5	4	3	2	1
34	A statement of transactions in foreign currency	5	4	3	2	1
35	Comparative income statement figures for the last 2 years	5	4	3	2	1

		5	4	3	2	1
36	Comparative income statement figures for the last 5 years	5	4	3	2	1
37	Comparative balance sheet figures for the last 2 years	5	4	3	2	1
38	Comparative balance sheet figures for the last 5 years	5	4	3	2	1
39	Directors' declaration on the veracity (correctness) of annual reports	5	4	3	2	1
40	Information relating to the company's subsidiaries (e.g., names, % ownership)	5	4	3	2	1

FIRM-SPECIFIC DETERMINANTS OF INCOME SMOOTHING IN BANGLADESH: AN EMPIRICAL EVALUATION

Ahsan Habib

ABSTRACT

The purpose of this chapter is to empirically examine the existence of income smoothing and determinants of smoothing behavior in Bangladesh. Using Eckel's (1981), Abacus (June), 28–40, "comparison of the variance of sales and profit" method, this study finds that a fair number of Bangladeshi firms engage in income smoothing. Particularly, 46 firms out of a sample of 107 firms with available data, engage in at least one type of income-smoothing behavior. Further, a logistic regression result indicates that firms characterized by sponsors having the largest ownership stake among all the equity holders and smaller firms engage more in income smoothing. Also, firms that have high debt to equity ratio engage more in smoothing behavior.

INTRODUCTION

The purpose of this chapter is to empirically examine the existence of income smoothing and the determinants of managerial income-smoothing

Advances in International Accounting
Advances in International Accounting, Volume 18, 53–71
ISSN: 0897-3660/doi:10.1016/S0897-3660(05)18003-9

behavior in Bangladesh. Simply put, income smoothing refers to minimizing fluctuations in earnings over time. Givoly and Ronen (1981, p. 175) define smoothing, "as a form of signaling whereby managers use their discretion over the choice among accounting alternatives within generally accepted accounting principles so as to minimize fluctuations of earnings over time around the trend they believe best reflects their views of investors' expectations of the company's future performance."

The topic of income smoothing is an extensively researched one with Hepworth (1953) being credited with first generating the idea of income smoothing.[1] Numerous researchers over the last four decades or so have enriched the income-smoothing literature by focusing on: the concept of income smoothing, the existence of income smoothing, the techniques used to smooth income, and the motivations for smoothing.[2]

There are two different types of smooth income streams: those that are naturally smooth and those that are intentionally smoothed by management. A naturally smooth income stream results from an income generating process that produces a smooth income stream. An intentionally smoothed income stream can be the result of real smoothing or artificial smoothing. As the name implies, real smoothing occurs when management takes action to structure the revenue-generating events of the organization to produce a smooth income stream. Artificial smoothing, on the other hand, occurs when management manipulates the timing of accounting entries to produce a smooth income stream (Albrecht & Richardson, 1990, p. 713).

Initial studies on income smoothing were concerned with the issue of how to appropriately measure income smoothing. While the results of early studies were inconclusive, recent evidence (Moses, 1987; Belkaoui & Picur, 1984) generally has supported the hypothesis of existence of income smoothing. This finding has prompted a second era in the literature investigating what firm characteristics are associated with income smoothing.

This chapter is the first of its kind in Bangladesh, and hence looks at both the existence of smoothing and firm characteristics associated with such smoothing. Using Eckel's (1981) 'comparison of the variance of sales and profit' method, this study finds that a fair number of Bangladeshi firms engage in income smoothing. Particularly, 46 firms out of a sample of 107 firms with available data, engage in at least one type of income-smoothing behavior. Further, a logistics regression result indicates that firms characterized by sponsors having the largest ownership stake among all the equity holders and smaller firms engage more in income smoothing. Also, firms that have high debt to equity ratio engage more in smoothing behavior.

This chapter will be of interest to regulators, i.e., the Securities & Exchange Commission of Bangladesh (BSEC) in deciding whether to police income-smoothing behavior of firms in Bangladesh. If BSEC perceives income smoothing to be a form of earnings management that needs to be constrained for efficient operation of the capital market, then this argument sounds quite logical. However, for that to happen, BSEC needs to know what firm characteristics are associated with income smoothing.

Also domestic and foreign institutional investors as well as individual investors will find the results useful in allocating their portfolios. If they perceive income smoothing as a desirable property of firm earnings on the ground that it smoothes out the year-to-year variability of earnings, then they will include firms in their portfolio that engage in income-smoothing behavior. However, the opposite will occur if they believe that smoothing is a form of earnings management and management expropriates their resources by engaging in such behavior.

APPROACHES TO THE STUDY OF INCOME SMOOTHING

Albrecht and Richardson (1990) identify three approaches to the study of income smoothing based on the extant literature:

1. *The classical approach*: The classical approach to studying income smoothing involves an examination of the relation between the choice of a smoothing variable (operating expenses, ordinary expenses, or extraordinary items) and its effect on reported income. However, these studies suffer from at least three shortcomings. First, the studies typically utilize an expectancy model (linear, first-difference model, etc.) of 'normalized' income that may not be representative of the underlying earnings process. Second, these studies concentrate on one smoothing variable and this may well bias the results. Some companies could use that variable alone or in combination with other, while some companies may not use that variable at all. Third, some studies consider the effects of the smoothing variable in one period only, ignoring the intertemporal effects.

2. *The income variability approach*: Imhoff (1977) was the first researcher to attempt to separate management's artificial-smoothing behavior from real smoothing actions or naturally smooth income stream. He asserts that, sales revenue of a company represents the real economic actions of the firm, and would therefore incorporate real smoothing activities if they

exist. Then artificial smoothing behavior can be discerned by comparing
the variance of ordinary income to the variance of sales. Imhoff, however,
implicitly assumed that artificial and real smoothings were mutually exclusive, and hence, studied the effects of smoothing on only those companies that exhibited high sales variability. Eckel (1981) corrected for this
by including firms that exhibited low variability of sales from his sample.

3. *The sector approach*: Another popular approach for studying income
   smoothing is based on the idea of dual economy sector derived from
   models of sectorial economic differentiation. This model divides the industrial structure of the economy into two distinct sectors consisting of
   the core and periphery sectors. As the name implies, the firms in the core
   economy sector are noted for high productivity, high profits, intensive
   utilization of capital, high incidence of monopoly elements, and a high
   degree of unionization. On the one hand, peripheral industries are characterized by their small firm size, labor intensity, low profits, low productivity, intensive product–market competition, lack of unionization,
   and low wages. It is hypothesized that firms in the core industry face less
   uncertainty and hence less need for income smoothing. On the other,
   firms in the periphery industry have more opportunity and predisposition
   to smooth both their operating flows and reported income measures.
   Using this classification scheme, Belkaoui and Picur (1984) separate 171
   companies from 42 industries into 114 core and sector firms and 57 periphery sector firms. They compare the change in operating income and
   change in ordinary income to the change in expenses. Their findings
   indeed show that firms in the periphery sector show a greater depth of
   smoothing behavior than do firms in the core sector. Using a sample of
   512 companies over 1974–1985, Albrecht and Richardson (1990), however, fail to find support for the differential-smoothing behavior in the
   core and periphery sectors.

The early literature focused mainly on identifying whether income
smoothing exists or not. This literature was criticized for its failure to incorporate the motivations for smoothing. Lambert (1984) suggests that the
proper test for smoothing is to determine whether smoothing is more in
evidence when there is relatively greater incentive for it to exist. The following discussion identifies the following incentives for smoothing:

1. Firm size,
2. Debt financing,
3. Firm profitability, and
4. Ownership structure.

Firm Size

Arguments for larger firms to engage in more smoothing activities are hypothesized because:

1. Larger firms get more public as well as regulatory and governmental actions. Regulators may consider large upward earnings fluctuations to be a sign of monopolistic practice, while large downward fluctuations may signal crisis and cause panic (Moses, 1987, p. 362).
2. Larger firms have a wide array of smoothing instruments (e.g., research and development expenditure, non-recurring items, etc.,) available compared to smaller firms.
3. Large, mature firms should have synchronized revenue and expense cycle because of fewer uncertainties in the environment. Thus, the earning streams of large firms are probably naturally smoothed.

Debt Financing

When firms raise money through debt financing (be it long-term bank loans or public debt), capital providers rely on lending agreements or debt covenants. This agreement restricts (many of these restrictions are expressed in terms of accounting numbers) certain managerial actions that could be detrimental to the interests of the lenders (like issuing more debt, paying out dividend in excess of a certain percentage of earnings, etc.). If the cost of violating this agreement is fairly high for the lender, then the party will in extreme cases engage in earnings management to avoid violating debt covenant or will engage in smoothing to give the impression that the company maintains a steady flow of income, which will assure the payment due to the lenders.

Firm Profitability

A manager's ability to smooth income is largely limited by the firm's profit potential even though the conventional income smoothing studies have typically presupposed that a manager has unlimited ability to smooth income. Firm with successive years of poor performance will have fewer instruments available to smooth income. Hence, firms with higher profitability will have greater potential for smoothing income.

Ownership Structure

If a corporation has a diffuse ownership structure and a manager has little equity stake in the company (typical of U.S. and U.K. companies), then the manager of this management-controlled firm might try to present the operating result of the firm in the most favorable manner possible in order to avoid stockholder unrest, or to lessen the probability of takeover attempts. Contrary to this, if the ownership is concentrated with few blockholders (usually family members), then the manager (in most cases nominated by the family) does not need earnings manipulation as a job-preserving strategy, because the owners possess control of the firm. The arguments suggest that in Bangladesh (characterized by concentrated ownership structure) (Habib, 2003; Chowdhury, 1999), ownership concentration and income smoothing should be negatively associated.

Extant literature identifies the existence of management compensation schemes to be one determinant of income smoothing. If executives are awarded stock options and the market price of stock can be increased through a smoothed stream of income, then a positive relationship is expected between compensation schemes and income smoothing. However, in Bangladesh, no listed company grants stock options to its executives. Even though an annual bonus is paid (annual reports just note the gross amount paid), no detailed information is available as to the content of the plans. Hence, whether managers in Bangladesh smooth income to make sure that they are entitled to a steady flow of bonus, cannot be empirically examined.

REVIEW OF RELATED LITERATURE

As mentioned previously, the early literature on income smoothing typically utilized an expectancy model (linear, first-difference model, etc.) of 'normalized' income. Imhoff (1977) is the first one to suggest that normalized earnings could be a function of an independent variable-like sales assuming that sales revenue is not subject to smoothing. He first regresses income and sales on time. He then defines variability as the size of the R^2 for each regression. For example, if the sales $(R^2) >$ income (R^2), then the sales time series is defined as less variable than the income time series. Additionally, Imhoff regresses income on sales $(I = f(S))$ to determine the extent to which income is related to sales. Imhoff applies the following two criteria to classify smoothers:

1. Smooth income stream and a weak association between sales and income, or
2. A smooth (variable) income (sales) stream.

Using 94 industrial companies, he fails to find any evidence of smoothing.

Eckel (1981, p. 33) provides an alternative conceptual framework that addresses the shortcomings of Imhoff's methodology. Particularly, he notes that:

> . . . it is not the degree of variability in the income time series that the income smoothing hypothesis is addressing, but rather whether or not the reported income variability is a function of any overt actions undertaken on the part of management to explicitly reduce the variability of reported income and distort the representation of the economic reality of the firm.

Eckel proposes that the coefficient of variation (CV) of change in gross sales should be greater than the CV of change in income for a firm to be smoother. Using 62 firms from 1951–1970, he identifies only two firms (3%) to be income smoother compared to eight firms (13%) according to Imhoff's definition. He interprets his results as documenting the lack of smoothing behavior in contrast to most other studies that provide evidence of earnings smoothing.

Michelson, Jordan-Wagner, and Wootton (1995) evaluate three major propositions: (a) the tendency of firms to become income smoothers; (b) the difference in the returns of smoothing and non-smoothing firms' common stocks; and (c) the relationship between perceived market risk and income smoothing. Employing four different smoothing variables (operating income after depreciation, pre-tax income, income before extraordinary items, and net income), the authors show that investors do not give preference to smoother income streams and smoothing does not increase the market value of the firm as smoothers consistently under-perform non-smoothers. On the issue of market perception of risk, their results indicate that smoothing firms have consistently lower betas than non-smoothers. The difference, however, is not statistically significant.

Moses (1987) tests for a relationship between income smoothing and various firm-specific factors that have been used in the economic consequence literature. Moses takes accounting change to be the smoothing device because of its purely discretionary nature. To operationalize expected earnings, Moses uses a simple random walk model (as a robustness check he uses prior year's earnings plus average earnings growth over 5 preceding years, 5 years' average of return on assets, etc.). Over the period 1975–1980, Moses analyzes

212 discretionary accounting changes and finds that size, bonus compensation, and pre-change earnings deviation were significantly positively associated with income smoothing. Ownership control (defined as the percentage of the largest single party stock ownership) is not associated with smoothing.

Carlson and Bathala (1997), on the other hand, find evidence that as the proportion of inside ownership increases, there is a corresponding increase in the probability of the firm being an income smoother. This result implies that managers with more ownership have more discretion to alter reported income in such a manner as to enhance their own personal well being (Gordon, 1964). They also find that the share of institutional investors, debt financing, dispersion of stock ownership, profitability, and compensation variables are positively related to smoothing, but size is negatively related. They had a sample of 265 firms with 172 (93) being classified as smoothers (non-smoothers), respectively.

RESEARCH DESIGN

As noted earlier, the purpose of this chapter is to find out the existence of smoothing among the listed firms of Bangladesh and to empirically examine the firm-specific characteristics associated with smoothing. To do that, sample companies are categorized into smoothers and non-smoothers based on the "comparison of the variance of sales and profit" method proposed by Eckel (1981).

Because managers could choose a combination of smoothing instruments, the following four measures of income are chosen as the instruments of smoothing:

1. Gross profit (GP) = Sales−cost of goods sold (COGS),
2. Earnings before interest and taxes (EBIT) = Sales−COGS−operating expenses,
3. Pre-tax profit (PRETAXPRO) = Sales−COGS−operating expenses−interest cost,
4. Net income (NI) = Sales−COGS−operating expenses−interest cost−tax provision.

Using the Eckel's approach, the relative coefficient of variation is computed in the following manner

$$CV_I(\text{coefficient of variation of income}) = (\sigma\,\Delta\text{income})/(\mu\,\Delta\text{income}) \quad (1)$$

where σ Δincome is the standard deviation of change in income over the sample period for each firm, μ Δincome the mean change in income over the sample period for each firm, Δincome = ΔGP, ΔEBIT, ΔPRETAXPRO, and ΔNI over the sample period for each firm, and Δsales the mean of change in sales over the sample period for each firm.

$$CV_s(\text{coefficient of variation of sales}) = (\sigma\,\Delta\text{sales})/(\mu\,\Delta\text{sales}) \qquad (2)$$

where σ Δsales is the standard deviation of change in sales over the sample period for each firm, and μ Δsales is the mean of change in sales over the sample period for each firm.

$$CV_{IS}(\text{relative coefficient of variation in income}) = CV_I/CV_S \qquad (3)$$

If the CV_{IS} ratio is less than one, then the firm will be classified as an income smoother. Since the standard deviation and mean of the changed income and sales series are to be calculated, a restriction is imposed in selecting the sample. To have a sufficient number of observations to get meaningful coefficient of variation measure, sample firms need to have at least 5 years of changed income and sales series. For example, a firm with income and sales data available from 1997–2002 will be included as there will be changed data series available from 1998 to 2002 (because of first differencing, the observation pertaining to 1997 will be lost).

Four measures are used to determine if a firm is a smoother or non-smoother based on the four smoothing variables (GP, EBIT, PRETAX-PRO, and NI). First, the absolute value of CV_{IS} ($|CV_{IS}|$) is calculated for each firm for each of the four income measures. Then firms are classified into four categories as follows:

- SMOOTH_1: Firms are classified as smoothers if any of the $|CV_{IS}|$ for the four income measures (GP, EBIT, PRETAXPRO, and NI) are between 0 and 1.00.
- SMOOTH_2: A little more restrictive criterion is imposed for firms belonging to this model. Firms are classified as smoothers if the $|CV_{IS}|$ for at least two of the four income measures are between 0 and 1.00.
- SMOOTH_3: A somewhat more restrictive criterion applies in this model. Firms are classified as smoothers if the $|CV_{IS}|$ for at least three of the four income measures are between 0 and 1.00
- SMOOTH_4: This is the most restrictive of all models. Firms are classified as smoothers if the $|CV_{IS}|$ for all the four income measures are between 0 and 1.00.

Discussion so far has focused on research design issues dealing with the existence of smoothing. To identify the firm-specific determinants of smoothing, the following logistic regression model is used:

$$\text{SMOOTH}_{it} = \beta_0 + \beta_1 \text{ SIZE}_{it} + \beta_2 \text{ DEBT}_{it} + \beta_3 \text{ PROFIT}_{it} + \beta_4 \text{ OWN}_{it} + \varepsilon_{it} \quad (4)$$

where SMOOTH, the dependent variable, takes a value of one if the firm is classified as an income smoother, and zero otherwise; SIZE is the natural logarithm of total assets; DEBT is total liabilities divided by total assets; PROFIT is proxied by return on sales (ROS) defined as the ratio of net income to sales; and OWN is a dummy variable representing ownership of share capital taking a value of one when ownership by sponsors is the largest ownership category among all the equity holders, and zero otherwise (equity holders besides sponsors are foreign owners, government shareholders, individual shareholders, institutional shareholders, shareholding by employees and others.).

Four separate regressions are run to account for the different smoothing categories (SMOOTH_1, SMOOTH_2, SMOOTH_3, and SMOOTH_4).

Based on the discussion above, SIZE, DEBT, and PROFIT are expected to have positive coefficients while the sign for OWN is expected to be negative. The independent variables for each firm are averaged over the available sample years (minimum of 6 and maximum of 11 years).

SAMPLE SELECTION

Firms listed with the Dhaka Stock Exchange (DSE) and having at least 5 years of changed sales and four measures of smoothing instruments (GP, EBIT, PRETAXPRO, and NI) are selected over the sample period of 1991–2001. Financial firms are excluded (with DSE code 100, 150, and 700). The nature of the operation of firms belonging to these categories renders their managerial decision-making non-comparable to other firms. Because of the longer time series required to perform relative coefficient of variation measure and the fact that many firms do not report details about their ownership structure, a final sample of 107 firms with a sufficient longer time series of Sales, GP, EBIT, PRETAXPRO, and NI and complete ownership data are selected for conducting the empirical analysis (financial data are from Bangladesh Bank 2002, 2001, and 1998). Table 1 gives the time series available for calculating the coefficient of variation measure and their industry composition.

Table 1. Sample Periods and Industry Composition.

Panel A: Sample Periods

Period Covered	Firms	Percentage	Cumulative (%)
1992–2001	50	46.7	46.7
1992–2000	7	6.5	53.3
1992–1999	3	2.8	56.1
1992–1998	1	0.9	57.0
1992–1997	1	0.9	57.9
1993–2001	3	2.8	60.7
1993–2000	3	2.8	63.6
1994–2001	4	3.7	67.3
1995–2001	7	6.5	73.8
1995–2000	3	2.8	76.6
1995–1999	1	0.9	77.6
1996–2001	9	8.4	86.0
1996–2000	6	5.6	91.6
1997–2001	9	8.4	100.0
Total	107	100.0	

Panel B: Industry Composition

Industry	Number	Percentage
Engineering	15	14.0
Food & allied products	21	19.6
Fuel and Power	3	2.8
Jute	4	3.7
Textiles	26	24.2
Pharmaceuticals & chemicals	19	17.8
Paper & printing	3	2.8
Services and real estate	3	2.8
Miscellaneous	13	12.1
Total	107	100.0

Out of 107 sample firms with sufficient data, 47% (fifty firms) have 10 years of changed data while the remaining 53% are scattered over various fiscal years. Looking at the industry composition in Panel B it is evident that the maximum number of firms belong to textile industry (26 or 24%) followed by firms in the food & allied products sector (21 or 19%). Pharmaceuticals and chemicals, and engineering sectors, too, are heavily represented in the sample.

EMPIRICAL RESULTS

Table 2, Panel A shows the CV measure of sales and four smoothing instruments. Median values show that CV_Δsales has the least relative variability (1.37) followed by CV_ΔGP (1.79). Although mean change in sales are negative in 22% of the cases, this figure rises to 37% when it comes to the net income measure.

Panel B shows the descriptive statistics for the absolute value of the smoothing measure. This is arrived at by dividing the coefficient of various income measures (CV_ΔGP, CV_ΔEBIT, CV_ΔPRETAXPRO, and CV_ΔNI) by the coefficient of sales. Firms are classified as smoothers if

Table 2. Descriptive Statistics for Sales and Income Smoothing Instruments.

Panel A: Coefficient of variation

Variable	Mean	Median	% Negative
CV_Δsales	0.41	1.37	22
CV_ΔGP	3.89	1.79	24
CV_ΔEBIT	17.61	2.55	29
CV_ΔPRETAXPRO	0.21	2.21	36
CV_ΔNI	0.36	2.08	37

Panel B: Absolute values of CV_{IS} for smoothing measures

Smoothing measure	Mean	Median	1st Quartile	3rd Quartile
CV_ΔGP/CV_Δsales	2.67	1.26	0.81	2.32
CV_ΔEBIT/CV_Δsales	6.57	2.03	1.11	3.99
CV_ΔPRETAXPRO/CV_Δsales	4.75	1.98	1.14	3.57
CV_Δ NI/CV_Δsales	5.42	2.06	1.07	3.38

Panel C: Classification of firms by smoothing measure

Smoothing measure	Number of Firms		Percentage (%)
	Sample	Smoothing	
GP	107	46	43
EBIT	107	29	27
PRETAXPRO	107	20	19
NI	107	14	13

Note: Maximum number of sample years represented is 11 spanning from 1991 to 2001 while the minimum is six, spanning from 1996 to 2001.

the absolute score lies in the range of 0–1.00. The mean and median value of absolute smoothing scores of 107 firms lie well above the upper bound of 1.00. Only the 1st quartile value of CV_ΔGP/CV_Δsales is below 1.00 meaning that 25% of 107 firms have an absolute smoothing score of 0.81 or below based on the CV_ΔGP/CV_Δsales measure.

Panel C makes a finer partition of the result in Panel B by classifying firms as smoothers based on the four categories that increasingly become more restrictive. Forty-six firms or 43% of the sample firms engage in some form of smoothing, i.e., for these firms any of the $|CV_{IS}|$ of the four income measures (GP, EBIT, PRETAXPRO, and NI) are between 0 and 1.00. This percentage is monotonically decreasing with only 14 firms or 13% of the sample firms engaging in smoothing by employing all four income measures.

Table 3 presents descriptive statistics of the variables that are expected to influence managerial income-smoothing decisions. Overall, firms are highly leveraged with a mean (median) of 0.78 (0.66), respectively and

Table 3. Descriptive Statistics and Differences in Means for Independent Variables.

Panel A: Descriptive Statistics

Variable	Mean	Median	1st Quartile	3rd Quartile
DEBT	0.78	0.66	0.53	0.85
PROFIT (ROS)	−0.03	0.02	−0.06	0.08
SIZE	3.39	3.45	3.06	3.72
OWN	0.62			

Panel B: Differences in Means of Independent Variables

Variable	Mean		Difference	*t* statistic	*p* (two-tailed)
	Smoother	Non-Smoother			
DEBT	0.91	0.68	−0.23	−2.19	0.03
PROFIT (ROS)	−0.06	−0.005	0.055	0.93	0.32
SIZE	3.25	3.50	0.25	2.32	0.02
OWN	0.54	0.67	0.13	1.35	0.18

Notes: Number of firms is 107. Maximum number of sample years represented is 11 spanning from 1991 to 2001 while the minimum is 6, spanning from 1996 to 2001. All independent variables are averaged over the sample period pertaining to the respective firms. To eliminate the influence of extreme values, ROS values exceeding 1.00 and −1.00 are winsorized at 1.00 and −1.00, respectively.

characterized by low profitability with a median return on sales of just 2%. In 66 firms out of a sample pool of 107 firms, ownership by the sponsors is the largest among all the equity holders.

Panel B compares the difference in means of the independent variables among the smoother and non-smoother firms. The result is based on Model 1 where 46 (61) firms are classified as smoother (non-smoother), respectively. Smoothing firms are more leveraged, less profitable, lower in size, and have a comparatively small number of cases where ownership by sponsors is the largest among the equity holders. However, only the difference in leverage and size are statistically significant. Thus, the univariate statistics support the debt covenant hypothesis as well as the ownership hypothesis. However, the results on size and profitability variable is contrary to what is hypothesized.

CORRELATION ANALYSIS

Table 4 presents Pearson correlation coefficients among the smoothing measures and variables hypothesized to influence smoothing decision. As expected all the smoothing variables (SMOOTH_1–SMOOTH_4) are significantly positively related at the 1% level. However, as one moves down vertically from SMOOTH_1 to SMOOTH_4, the correlation coefficients on smoothing variables decrease monotonically (from 0.70 to 0.45). On the other hand, as one goes horizontally, say from, SMOOTH_4, coefficients increase monotonically from 0.45 to 0.81.

For the sake of brevity, the discussion on the relationship between smoothing measures and other independent variables focuses on SMOOTH_1 alone. SMOOTH_1 is significantly positively related to DEBT ($r = 0.21, p = 0.03$), and significantly negatively related to SIZE ($r = -0.22$, $p = 0.02$). Although, SMOOTH_1 is negatively related to OWN, the relationship is not statistically significant ($r = -0.13, p = 0.18$). Such is the case with PROFIT.

Regarding the correlation among the independent variables, PROFIT and DEBT are significantly negatively correlated ($r = -0.24, p = 0.01$). So are SIZE and DEBT ($r = -0.22, p = 0.02$). OWN has no significant relationship with any of the other three independent variables.

REGRESSION ANALYSIS

Table 5 presents the main regression results. Four models (SMOOTH_1, SMOOTH_2, SMOOTH_3, and SMOOTH_4) are treated as the dependent

Table 4. Pearson Correlation Coefficients for Smoothing Categories and Variables Hypothesized to Influence Smoothing Decisions.

	SMOOTH_1	SMOOTH_2	SMOOTH_3	SMOOTH_4	DEBT	PROFIT	SIZE	OWN
SMOOTH_1	1.000							
SMOOTH_2	0.702**	1.000						
	(0.000)							
SMOOTH_3	0.552**	0.786**	1.000					
	(0.000)	(0.000)						
SMOOTH_4	0.447**	0.636**	0.809**	1.000				
	(0.000)	(0.000)	(0.000)					
DEBT	0.209*	0.136	0.163*	0.197*	1.000			
	(0.031)	(0.162)	(0.093)	(0.042)				
PROFIT (ROS)	-0.091	-0.015	0.063	0.078	-0.239*	1.000		
	(0.353)	(0.882)	(0.521)	(0.425)	(0.013)			
SIZE	-0.221*	-0.183	-0.196*	-0.133	-0.224*	0.078	1.000	
	(0.022)	(0.059)	(0.044)	(0.174)	(0.020)	(0.0423)		
OWN	-0.131	-0.082	0.033	0.021	-0.029	-0.136	-0.053	1.000
	(0.179)	(0.403)	(0.738)	(0.832)	(0.765)	(0.162)	(0.518)	

Notes: Number of firms is 107. Maximum number of sample years represented is 11 spanning from 1991 to 2001 while the minimum is 6, spanning from 1996 to 2001. All independent variables are averaged over the sample period pertaining to the respective firms. Two-tailed significance level in parentheses. To eliminate the influence of extreme values, ROS values exceeding 1.00 and −1.00 are winsorized at 1.00 and −1.00, respectively.
*Significant at the 0.05 level (two-tailed).
**Significant at the 0.01 level (two-tailed).

Table 5. Logistic Regression Results.

Variable	SMOOTH_1	SMOOTH_2	SMOOTH_3	SMOOTH_4
Constant	2.02	1.37	0.74	−0.72
z-statistic	1.34	0.88	0.43	−0.37
p	0.18	0.38	0.67	0.71
DEBT	0.72	0.34	0.47	0.65
z-statistic	1.45	0.88	1.18	1.57
p	0.15	0.38	0.24	0.12
PROFIT (ROS)	−0.53	−0.20	0.21	0.23
z-statistic	−1.00	−0.37	0.42	0.46
p	0.32	0.71	0.68	0.65
SIZE	−0.72	−0.70	−0.82	−0.56
z-statistic	−1.83	−1.67	−1.71	−1.04
p	0.07	0.10	0.09	0.30
OWN	−0.71	−0.47	0.16	0.18
z-statistic	−1.65	−1.02	0.30	0.28
p	0.10	0.31	0.76	0.78
Log likelihood	−67.13664	−59.69459	−48.71872	−39.32016
Restricted log likelihood	−73.11188	−62.51782	−51.54403	−41.51413
LR statistic (4 df)	11.95048	5.646465	5.650621	4.387948
Probability (LR stat)	0.017723	0.227152	0.226804	0.356041
McFadden R^2	0.081727	0.045159	0.054814	0.052849

Notes: Number of firms is 107. Maximum number of sample years represented is 11 spanning from 1991 to 2001, while the minimum is 6, spanning from 1996 to 2001. All independent variables are averaged over the sample period pertaining to the respective firms. Two-tailed significance level in parentheses. To eliminate the influence of extreme values, ROS values exceeding 1.00 and −1.00 are winsorized at 1.00 and −1.00, respectively. The LR statistic tests the joint null hypothesis that all slope coefficients except the constant are zero. This is the analog of the F-statistic in linear regression models and tests the overall significance of the model. Restricted log likelihood is the maximized log likelihood, when all slope coefficients (except for the constant term) are restricted to zero.

variable one at a time while DEBT, PROFIT, SIZE and OWN act as the independent variables.

In the regression that uses SMOOTH_1 as the dependent variable, SIZE enters the regression with a significantly negative coefficient (−0.72 and a $p = 0.07$). This result is contrary to what was hypothesized, i.e., larger firms are expected to engage in more smoothing. One interpretation of this finding is that in Bangladesh executive stock option schemes do not exist (Chowdhury, 1999, p. 66) and hence managers do not have the incentive to produce a smoothed income stream that will boost the stock price up. Usually it is the larger firms that are potential candidates for awarding executive stock options. If management believes that accounting fundamentals do not play any role in share valuation, then they will not bother with borrowing from the future to make current performance look better (if they find current performance to be poor) or deferring current period income for the future to make future performance look better (if the future performance is expected to be poor).

Smaller firms, on the other hand, suffer from leverage problems. Correlation analysis shows that firm size and leverage is significantly negatively correlated. If the cost of violating debt agreements is fairly high, then the borrower could engage in smoothing income to give the impression that the company maintains a steady flow of income that will assure the payment due to the lenders.

OWN enters the regression with a negative sign and the coefficient is marginally significant (-0.71 and a $p = 0.10$). This implies that firms characterized by sponsors having the largest stake among all the equity holders engage in less smoothing. If the ownership is concentrated with few blockholders (usually family members), then the manager (in most cases nominated by the family) does not need earnings manipulation as a job preserving strategy because the owners possess control of the firm. The coefficient on DEBT is positive as expected but not statistically significant (0.72 and a $p = 0.15$). Firm with higher debt engage in more smoothing to create the impression that these firms do have a smoothed income stream that will make them unlikely to default on their principal and interest payment obligations. The coefficient on PROFIT is neither statistically significant, nor does it have the expected sign. The SMOOTH_1 has an R^2 of about 8% and the model fit is significant at the 2% level with an LR statistic of 11.95.

SUPPLEMENTAL ANALYSIS

To see whether observations belonging to 1992–2001 time frames had a different impact on the regression coefficients, the regression in Table 5 was rerun with the 1992–2001 sample data ($n = 50$) and all other observations excluding the 1992–2001 time frame ($n = 57$). Unreported results with the 1992–2001 data show that SIZE is significantly negative as in the full sample. However, OWN loses its significance. All other variables are statistically insignificant. The result from regression excluding the 1992–2001 observations fared worse with no coefficient having statistical significance.

INDUSTRY INFLUENCE

As noted in the sample selection section, the textile, food & allied product and pharmaceutical industries are heavily represented in the sample with 24, 19 and 18% of the total sample, respectively. To assess the possible industry influence, a dummy variable was added to represent one of these three industries. Untabulated results indicate that the textile industry dummy was significantly negatively related to the dependent variable SMOOTH_1 (-1.41 with $p = 0.01$). The coefficient on SIZE and OWN, however, remained significantly (marginally significantly) negatively related to SMOOTH_1. Similarly, when a dummy was included to account for the food & allied industry, the coefficient was negative but not significant (-0.85 with $p = 0.14$). The significance level of SIZE and OWN became stronger when the food dummy was added. Finally, the dummy variable for pharmaceutical industry was positive but not statistically significant (0.70 with $p = 0.21$). SIZE and OWN, however, remained negatively related to SMOOTH_1.

CONCLUDING REMARKS

This study has empirically examined whether income smoothing exists in the context of Bangladesh and if so, what firm-specific characteristics are associated with managerial smoothing behavior. Using a sample of 107 firms listed with the Dhaka Stock Exchange, the study finds that about 46 firms (43% of the sample observations) engage in at least one type of income smoothing behavior. Firms that are smaller in size, ownership concentrated with sponsors, and having higher leverage engage more in income smoothing.

This study has just looked at what motivates managers to smooth income. An important extension of this research would be to see how the market reacts to smoothing. Usually, smoothing connotes a negative tone but as mentioned in the introductory section, smoothing could well act as a signaling device in an environment where alternate corporate disclosure practices are not well developed.

NOTES

1. However, Buckmaster (1992) documents a frequent and continuing recognition of income smoothing properties and management preferences for smooth accounting income time-series in the accounting and business literature from the beginning of the twentieth century up to the publication of Hepworth's 1953 article.

2. For a comprehensive overview of the income smoothing literature around these issues, see Stolowy and Breton (2000).

ACKNOWLEDGMENTS

I thank anonymous reviewers for their constructive comments. Professor Santi Narayan Ghosh provided insightful comments on an earlier version of this paper. All remaining errors are mine.

REFERENCES

Albrecht, W. D., & Richardson, F. M. (1990). Income smoothing by economy sector. *Journal of Business Finance & Accounting, 17*(5), 713–730.

Bangladesh Bank, Statistics Department. (2002), (2001) and (1998). Balance sheet analysis of Joint Stock Companies listed on the Dhaka and Chittagong Stock Exchange. Dhaka, Bangladesh.

Belkaoui, A., & Picur, R. D. (1984). The smoothing of income numbers: Some empirical evidence on systematic differences between core and periphery industrial sectors. *Journal of Business Finance & Accounting, 11*(4), 527–545.

Buckmaster, D. (1992). Income smoothing in accounting and business literature prior to 1954. *The Accounting Historians Journal, 19*(2), 147–171.

Carlson, S. J., & Bathala, C. T. (1997). Ownership differences and firms' income smoothing behavior. *Journal of Business Finance & Accounting, 24*(2), 179–196.

Chowdhury, D. (1999). *Performance-related pay: An assessment of profit-sharing and employee share ownership schemes* Bureau of Business Research, Dhaka: University of Dhaka.

Eckel, N. (1981). The income smoothing hypothesis revisited. *Abacus, 17*(1), 28–40.

Givoly, D., & Ronen, J. (1981). "Smoothing" manifestations in fourth quarter results of operations: Some empirical evidence. *Abacus, 17*(2), 174–193.

Gordon, M. (1964). Postulates, principles and research in accounting. *The Accounting Review, 39*, 251–263.

Habib, A. (2003). *Governance through ownership: A synthesis of research on causes and consequences of corporate ownership structure and preliminary empirical evidence from Bangladesh.* Working Paper, University of Dhaka.

Hepworth, S. R. (1953). Smoothing periodic income. *The Accounting Review, 28*(1), 32–39.

Imhoff, E. A., Jr (1977). Income smoothing – A case for doubt. *Accounting Journal* (Spring), 85–100.

Lambert, R. (1984). Income smoothing as rational equilibrium behavior. *The Accounting Review, 59*(4), 604–618.

Michelson, S. E., Jordan-Wagner, J., & Wootton, C. W. (1995). A market based analysis of income smoothing. *Journal of Business Finance & Accounting, 22*(8), 1179–1193.

Moses, O. D. (1987). Income smoothing and incentives: Empirical tests using accounting changes. *The Accounting Review, 62*(2), 358–377.

Stolowy, H., & Breton, G. (2000). *A framework for the classification of accounts manipulations.* Working Paper, HEC School of Management, France.

BANK EARNINGS MANAGEMENT IN EMERGING MARKET ECONOMIES: THE CASE OF MEXICO

Alejandro Hazera

ABSTRACT

In the mid-late 1990s, developing countries in several parts of the world experienced severe currency devaluations that were accompanied by deep economic downturns. For some regions, international financial organizations have documented that deficient financial reporting standards and practices contributed to the onset and magnitude of the crises by understating banks' problem loans and capital adequacy problems. However, little research has been conducted concerning the role of financial reporting in the post-devaluation reconstruction of financial systems. As such, this paper examines the role of financial reporting in the post-1994 devaluation restructuring of the Mexican banking system. Emphasis is placed on examining whether the country's three largest banks delayed the recognition of loan losses in the late 1990s. The results provide evidence that banks took advantage of weaknesses in financial reporting standards to delay the recognition of loan losses.

Advances in International Accounting
Advances in International Accounting, Volume 18, 73–95
ISSN: 0897-3660/doi:10.1016/S0897-3660(05)18004-0

INTRODUCTION

In recent years the financial reporting standards published by the International Accounting Standards Board (IASB) and the Financial Accounting Standards Board (FASB) have been promoted as alternative bodies of accounting standards available for the adoption of uniform sets of standards by all countries. To a large extent, several developing countries have adopted or declared their intention to adopt IASB Standards (IASs). Even with this progress, standard setters have raised concerns that the adoption of IASs by developing countries is not occurring sufficiently rapidly and that some countries may be adopting IASs in a "piecemeal" fashion that allows companies to affect the reliability and transparency of financial reports.

To some extent, the adoption of IASs by developing countries is most urgently needed for the countries' financial sectors. Since the mid-1990s, developing countries in several regions of the world have experienced severe currency devaluations that have been accompanied by financial sector collapse. These crises have included such nations as Mexico (1994), Thailand (1997), Korea (1998), and Russia (1998). In some instances, international financial authorities have argued that inadequate financial reporting standards for banks' loan loss provisions and reserves enabled financial institutions to conceal the extent of their loan and capital adequacy problems.[1] Accordingly, in a recent report, the International Monetary Fund (IMF) (2000, p. 126), states that authorities should ensure that:

> new private and privatized banks are subject to effective corporate governance, as well as proper regulation and supervision to avoid abuses, including insider lending. In addition, accompanying reforms of the legal and regulatory environment – including the accounting framework...will also be required.

To a large extent, the Mexican financial crisis of the 1990s provides the most comprehensive illustration of the relationship between emerging market financial crises and financial reporting reforms. In December 1994, the country experienced a severe currency devaluation that initiated a credit and capital crisis in the country's banks that lasted during the latter half of the 1990s. In response, the country undertook several steps to support its flagging banking system. The government sought international financial assistance to recapitalize the country's financial institutions. New financial reporting standards for banks were promulgated. The country's financial system was reorganized by merging smaller domestic banks with larger ones and permitting foreign institutions to purchase domestic banks.

In undertaking the final step, it was widely recognized in the country's financial press that the government had "bought time" in the post-devaluation period for small banks to merge with larger institutions by promulgating new financial reporting standards, which permitted banks to report artificially low loan loss provisions and reserves. A larger issue, however, may have concerned the country's larger banks. After the initial consolidation of the country's smaller banks (1995–1998), large banks stated in their 1998 annual reports that they had returned to profitability and that they possessed adequate capital. During 1999, however, two of these banks reported sharp increases in their loan loss provisions. Also, the banks continued to transfer large amounts of (current) commercial loans to government agencies. By 2001, the write-offs had become so large that all the three banks had been acquired by foreign financial institutions. As a result, for the first time in the country's history, virtually the entire financial system was owned by foreign financial institutions.

Given these events, this paper examines whether the country's largest banks engaged in earnings and capital management from the final quarter of 1997 to the final quarter of 2000. Emphasis is placed on assessing whether the banks used new, "post-crisis" financial reporting standards to delay the recognition of loan losses. An examination is also made of whether banks may have transferred loans to government agencies instead of reserving those loans.

THE RECENT EVOLUTION OF THE MEXICAN BANKING SYSTEM

The Mexican banking system traditionally possessed two dominant characteristics.[2] First, in a reflection of the country's traditional nationalism, only Mexican nationals were allowed to own Mexican banks. Second, in a pattern common throughout much of Latin America, three banks, Banco Nacional de Mexico (BANAMEX) Banco de Comercio (Bancomer), and Banco Serfin (Serfin), continually possessed a disproportionate share of the financial system's loans and deposits. In the early 1980s, the system was permanently altered as the collapse of the international petroleum market, chronic corruption in the financial system, and the increasing dominance of the "big three" banks, compelled the outgoing administration of Lopez Portillo (1976–1982) to nationalize the nation's financial institutions in September of 1982.[3]

In the latter part of that decade, as the economy recovered, the presidential administration of Carlos Salinas de Gortari (1988–1994) attempted to relieve the country of its persistent crises by modernizing and restructuring the Mexican economy.[4] As part of this effort, the government proposed to reprivatize the country's banks. The legal basis for the privatization was the 1990 *Ley para Regular Las Agrupaciones Financieras* (Law to Regulate Financial Groups) (Comisión Nacional Bancaria y de Valores, 1990). The statute's purpose was to encourage the formation of large, Mexican-controlled financial services holding companies. However, in contrast to the past exclusion of foreign investors from participation in the financial system, the law allowed for minority foreign ownership in the financial groups' holding companies.

From 1991 through 1994, the law accomplished its objectives. The number of official financial groups listed in the Mexican Stock Exchange's *Anuario Financiero* (Financial Annual) (Bolsa Mexicana de Valores, 1991–1994) increased from 6 in 1991 to 22 in 1994. Also, in keeping with the law's opening to foreign investors, the capital structures of 15 groups incorporated minority foreign ownership. Even with this reorganization, however, the three groups associated with the traditionally three largest banks, Banco Nacional de Mexico Accival (BANACCI), Grupo Financiero Bancomer (GFB), and Grupo Financiero Serfin (GFSERFIN), accounted for approximately 53.71% of the total assets of the 16 groups for which data are provided in the Stock Exchange's 1994 *Anuario Financiero* (Financial Annual).

In December 1994, the country entered another prolonged economic crises as a major currency devaluation initiated a period of recession, high inflation, and high interest rates. Correspondingly, a credit and capital crisis in the country's financial system commenced. By the beginning of 1995, the severity of the crisis compelled the Mexican government to appeal to the United States and international financial organizations for a "bailout" package to recapitalize the nation's financial system. The final plan totaled 47.5 billion U.S. dollars. Twenty billion dollars of the loan package were loaned by the United States and $10 billion were provided by the Bank for International Settlement. As a precondition for the aid, the Mexican government was required to gradually adopt international capital adequacy standards and Generally Accepted Accounting Principles (GAAP).

Internationalization of Capital Requirements

As a precondition for international financial assistance, Mexico was compelled to gradually adopt the requirements of the 1988 Basel Accord and its

1996 amendment. The 1988 Basel Accord, adopted by the G-10, formally links credit risk to minimum capital requirements. The accord requires that "eligible capital" be a minimum (currently) 8% of risk-weighted assets. The 1996 amendment, which was to be implemented by member banks by 1998, allows banks to use internal models to manage market risk and provides guidance on implementation of models. However, banks are also required to maintain a prudential level of capital to address specific risk.

In order to begin complying with these accords, the country's National Banking and Securities Commission (NBSC), the primary government agency responsible for overseeing banks and issuing financial reporting standards for banks, issued circular 1423 (1999) (Comisión Nacional Bancaria y de Valores, 1999). The circular requires banks to establish risk committees and audit committees, prepare formal risk control manuals, and form independent internal audit departments. In addition, the NBSC issued circulars 1480 (2000) (Comisión Nacional Bancaria y de Valores, 2000) and 1506 (2001) (Comisión Nacional Bancaria y de Valores, 2001). Circular 1480 provides more stringent standards for assessing commercial credit and provides guidance on the corresponding reserves that should be established for each level of credit risk. Circular 1506 addresses banks' operating risk and provides guidance on the formation and operation of audit committees.[5]

In general, the circulars encouraged a rapid movement toward compliance with the Basel accords. Most notably, the International Monetary Fund, in the 2001 (p. 63) assessment of Mexico's financial system stability, concluded that almost all Mexican banks "...comply with international capital adequacy standards." In support of this assertion, the report states that the "...adjusted net worth for the eight largest privately-owned banks was... estimated to have risen from 2.7 percent of risk weighted assets at end-1999 to 8.6 percent at end 2000...".

Internationalization of Financial Reporting Standards

In conjunction with the gradual movement toward adopting international capital requirements, the NBSC began forming a new set of financial reporting standards for banks. The initial standards were published in Circular 1343 (1997) (Comisión Nacional Bancaria y de Valores, 1997). The most urgent need involved standards regarding the classification of loans as past-due and the size of loan loss reserves.

Prior to the 1994 devaluation, in accordance with NBSC standards, Mexican banks' financial statements usually utilized only the term "past-due." In general, loans were considered "past-due" when a payment had not been received within 15–30 days of its due date. However, only the missed payment was considered "past-due" while the remainder was considered "current." Also, in a possible indication of a lack of recognition given to the concept of "non-performance," banks were allowed to continue accruing interest for 60 days on the (partial) amounts classified as past-due. The amounts recognized as "current" (i.e., the remainder of the loan) continued to accrue interest indefinitely. By contrast, U.S. standards require the recognition of a loan as "non-performing" after an installment on the loan has not been received 90 days after its due date. Once a payment has not been received (within 90 days) the entire amount of the loan is classified as non-performing. Also, interest accrual on the loan ceases.

Regarding the size of loan reserves, prior to the 1994 devaluation, official Mexican methods for estimating the underlying risk in loan portfolios were similar to the methodology of many countries. For example, as in many countries, NBSC standards required banks to estimate debtors' credit quality on the basis of several qualitative factors. On the basis of this assessment, loan portfolios were classified into five "risk" levels labeled as "A," "B," "C," "D," and "E." Loans labeled as "A" were considered current and collectible; thus, no reserves were established against this category. The other categories represented increasing degrees of risk that required banks to reserve the following minimum percentages against each category: B – 1%, C – 20%, D – 60%, and E – 100%. The total reserve, however, was required to equal a minimum of 60% of the banks' "past-due" loan portfolios (as defined above).

In Circular 1343, the NBSC modified the standards regarding loan loss provisions and reserves in several respects. With regard to loans, the standards required that Mexican banks classify the entire amount of a loan as past-due after a payment is 90 days overdue. However, in an indication of a recognition given to the concept of non-performance, banks were required to cease accruing interest on "past-due" loans. Thus, banks' financial statements should now provide a more accurate picture of past-due loans. Nevertheless, the new Mexican standards only require that banks reserve 45% of past-due loans; thus, loan reserves should be considerably less than 100% of past-due loans.

To a large extent, the new standards seemingly improved the financial reporting practices of Mexican banks. Most notably, for the 1998 reporting year, nine of the ten banks, which filed financial statements with the Mexican stock exchange indicated in their financial statement footnotes that they had followed the provisions of circular 1343 in accounting for their loan loss provisions and reserves. Thus, in accordance with international

GAAP, these banks followed the practice of classifying the entire amount of a loan as past-due when payment had not been received within 90 days of the due date. Also, the banks did not accrue interest on loans classified as past-due. However, in following a provision that may be weaker than international GAAP (i.e., the "45% rule"), the banks may have established loan reserves that were less than 100% of their past-due loan portfolios.

RESTRUCTURING OF THE FINANCIAL SYSTEM

On the basis of the financial aid and regulatory reforms discussed above, the Mexican government undertook an unprecedented restructuring and opening of the financial system. The focal point of the program was the Fondo Bancario de Proteccion al Ahorro (FOBAPROA) (Fund for the Protection of Savings). The agency was similar to the Resolution Trust Corporation (RTC) formed by the United States during the Savings and Loans crisis of the late 1980s. As such, FOBAPROA's main activities were to provide assistance to depositors, intervene in insolvent banks, and purchase the non-performing loan portfolios of banks. In 1999, as the financial system stabilized, FOBAPROA's non-performing loan portfolio was consolidated with the debt of the Mexican government. Also, FOBAPROA was replaced with Instituto para la Proteccion de Ahorro Bancario (IPAB, Institute for the Protection of Savings). IPAB was generally charged with the same mission as FOBAPROA.

As individual banks came under greater financial stress in the late 1990s, large amounts of non-performing loans were transferred to FOBAPROA. Under the typical loan transfer arrangement, the banks would transfer non-performing loans to FOBAPROA. The banks would then receive Mexican government grade bonds for the amount of the loans. Quite frequently, however, the agreement would include a "loss sharing" provision, which would obligate the bank to reimburse FOBAPROA for 25% of uncollectible loans.

As the pace of transfers increased, a two-stage reorganization of the banking system commenced. During the first stage (1995–1997) smaller banks that had been rendered insolvent by the financial crisis were either merged with other (domestic and foreign) financial institutions or liquidated and taken over by the government. By the end of this phase of consolidation (approximately the end of 1998), only 10 banks listed on the Mexican stock exchange. As shown in Table 1, however, the same "big three" banks, dominated the money markets. BANACCI possessed 19.92% of total loans and 25.23% of demand deposits; BANCOMER possessed 21.56% of total

Table 1. Relative Size of Big Three Institutions – 12/31/98.

Bank	Current Loans		Demand Deposits		Time Deposits	
	Pesos	%	Pesos	%	Pesos	%
Banacci	155,582.48	19.92	63,267.88	25.23	98,312.03	17.37
Bancomer	168,366.92	21.56	56,678.62	22.61	119,409.22	21.10
GFSerfin	106,002.57	13.57	26,849.51	10.71	75,535.84	13.35
Other	351,102.23	44.95	103,921.28	41.45	272,591.44	48.17
Total	781,054.20	100.00	250,717.29	100.00	565,848.53	100.00

Note: Monetary amounts are in thousands of pesos.
Source: Mexican National Banking and Securities Commission, 2000 Annual Report on Financial Institutions.

loans and 22.61% of demand deposits; and GFSERFIN possessed 13.57% of total loans and 10.71% of demand deposits.

At the end of 1998, these banks expressed optimism about their capital adequacy. For example, BANCOMER, in its 1998 annual report (Grupo Financiero Bancomer, 1998, p. 56) stated that its ratio of net capital to assets at risk had reached 16.4% at the end of 1998. In a similar manner, in its 1998 annual report (Grupo Financiero Banacci, 1998, p. 54) BANACCI stated that its ratio of net capital to assets at risk was 18.8% as of the end of 1998. Both the banks also emphasized that these levels of reserves were substantially above regulatory requirements.

However, in a contrary signal, the institutions continued to transfer large amounts of commercial loans to government agencies, especially FOBAPROA. These negative signals were confirmed when the banks began the second wave of consolidation. In March of 2000, Bancomer agreed to be acquired by Banco Bilbao Vizcaya of Spain. In May 2000, Banco Santander Mexicano, the affiliate of the Spanish bank, acquired a controlling interest in Serfin from IPAB. Finally, on May 17, 2001, the foreign takeover of the "big three" was completed as Citibank announced that it would acquire a controlling interest in BANACCI.

THE "BIG THREE" FINANCIAL INSTITUTIONS AND FINANCIAL MANAGEMENT

As discussed above, the financial crisis of the late 1990s forced the Mexican government to restructure the country's financial system. Concurrently, the

government attempted to adopt international capital adequacy requirements and rewrote the financial reporting standards for Mexican financial
institutions. As a result of these efforts, by 1998, the system incorporated a
smaller number of banks. However, the same "big three" banks continued
to dominate the loan and deposit markets. Initially, these institutions reported a return to profitability and expressed optimism about their capital
adequacy. However, in a signal contrary to the institutions' optimism, during 1999, the institutions transferred large amounts of commercial loans to
government agencies. Shortly thereafter in 2000 and 2001, the institutions
were acquired by foreign institutions. Given these contrary signals concerning the banks' financial position, concerns were expressed that, as the
possibility of foreign acquisition of the three largest banks became more
imminent, the banks had delayed the establishment of loan reserves for non-
performing loans. Such a pattern for troubled banks in developing countries
was discerned in a study by Beattie et al. (1995, pp. 123, 124), who state that:

> Supervisory concerns arise in particular where banks, for whatever reason, have been
> consistently under provisioning against likely loan losses. In such cases the need for
> large-scale catch up provisions or loan-write-offs may arise, typically in periods of re-
> cession and generalised financial distress. .... Supervisory authorities may then be faced
> with a choice between (belatedly) enforcing stringent provisioning standards, thereby
> depleting banks' stated regulatory capital and aggravating financial instability, and
> adopting a policy of forebearance under which banks are permitted to mask their pro-
> spective loan losses in the hope that the passage of time will enable them to repair their
> balance sheets.

In the Mexican context, this pattern would have been manifested by super-
visory authorities' allowing banks to underreport loan losses and subsequently providing the banks with capital infusions that allowed banks
to record large "catch-up" provisions. Thereafter, in the period leading up
to acquisition by foreign institutions, the banks would have been required to
follow more stringent standards regarding loans.

In order to investigate the possibility of this scenario, the big
three's financial statements for the period starting the final quarter of
1997 and ending the final quarter of 2000 were examined. The financial
statements were those published in the NBSC's annual report Comisión
Nacional Bancaria y de Valores, 1997–2000 on the country's banking
system. This period provides the most comparable data since the new financial reporting standards for banks were initially implemented in 1997
and took effect at the beginning of 1998. Also, this period incorporates the
transition of the big three banks from domestic to foreign owned financial
institutions.

Two aspects of the cases are examined. First, the banks' financial margins are examined in order to obtain evidence on whether banks under-reserved non-performing loans and subsequently recorded a "catch-up" adjustment. This examination encompasses three steps. First, interest income and expense are examined to ascertain movements in the banks' pre-provision financial margin. Second, movements in the financial margin after considering the loan loss provision are examined to determine if the banks may have recorded any unusually large changes in the provision, which may have represented a "catch-up" adjustment. Finally, trends in loan loss reserves on the banks' balance sheets are examined to determine whether the banks recorded any large increases in their loan reserves in conjunction with the large increase in the provision.

After examining the banks' financial margins, trends in the banks' capital adequacy are examined in order to obtain evidence on whether the banks may have transferred loans to the government in lieu of establishing loan reserves. This examination is based on two assumptions. First, it is assumed that past-due loans are deemed uncollectible and written off before loans categorized as "current." Second, it is assumed that any increase in FOBAPROA loans during the period offsets any corresponding decrease in consumer/commercial loans.

On the basis of these parameters, a three step process is used to examine the banks' capital adequacy. First, in order to ascertain a preliminary perspective of the banks' capital adequacy under the level of reserves as reported in their balance sheets, the reported shareholders equity to current loans ratio (hereafter referred to as the "capital ratio") is compared to the ratio that would have been reported had the bank provisioned 100% of its non-performing loans. Second, in order to ascertain the amount of loan transfers to FOBAPROA and other government agencies, any increase in loans to the government is compared with the decrease in consumer/commercial loans. The amount of possible capital contribution by FOBAPROA is then calculated by deducting the amount of reserves available to absorb non-performing current loans from the amount of loans effectively transferred to the government. Finally, the possible impact on capital adequacy of the FOBAPROA capital contribution is obtained by comparing the capital ratio, as reported by the bank, with the capital ratio that would have been reported if the amount of loans transferred by the bank to FOBAPROA had been reserved. GFSERFIN, the country's most troubled bank is examined first. BANCOMER and BANACCI, the second largest and the largest banks, are subsequently considered.

GFSERFIN

As stated above, GFSERFIN was traditionally the country's third largest bank. During the early 1990s, in order to overcome its perennial "third place" status, the bank undertook an aggressive loan program. However, the low credit quality of some of its new clients exacerbated the bank's credit and capital problems after the 1994 peso devaluation. In the second quarter of 1999, the bank's shareholders informed the Mexican government that they would no longer provide needed capital. Thus, the government was compelled to takeover the bank and provide it with an additional 1.3 billion dollars in capital.

The bank's perennial difficulties are reflected in its income statement. As shown in Table 2, interest income remained at approximately the same level for 1998 (42.18 million pesos) and 1999 (41.16 million pesos). Interest expense constituted 85 and 93% of interest income for 1998 and 1999, respectively, while the pre-provision financial margin declined from 22 to 11% of interest income during the same period.

Examination of the post-provision financial margin shows that the bank may have recorded a "catch-up" provision in the second quarter of 1999. For 1998, the provision for loan losses ranged from less than 1% of interest income for the first quarter to 15% for the third quarter. Subsequently, in the second quarter of 1999, the bank recognized a provision equaling 73% of the interest income. As a result, the bank's (post-provision) financial margin, which had varied from 8 to 26% of interest income during 1998, dropped abruptly to 65% for the second quarter of 1999. Net income, which had remained at low/stable levels during 1998 (and the first quarter of 1999), correspondingly dropped to a loss of 54% for the second quarter of 1999.

This sharp variation in the bank's loan loss provision was made possible by the aforementioned 45% rule. As shown in Table 3, from the fourth quarter of 1997 through the third quarter of 1998 the loan reserve varied between 61 and 67% of past-due loans. This percentage was above the 45% Mexican GAAP minimum but below a 100% provisioning requirement. However, for the fourth quarter of 1998 the reserve rose to 74% of past-due loans and abruptly jumped to 126% for the second quarter of 1999. Thereafter, the reserve exceeded past due loans.

Comparison of the bank's reported capital ratio with the ratio that would have been reported under a "100%" reserve indicates that the bank was experiencing a severe lack of capital in the periods before the adjustment. As shown in Table 3, based on a loan reserve/past-due loan ratio of 60–75%, the bank was able to maintain an equity/loan ratio between 7 and 9% from

Table 2. Percentage Income Statements for the "Big Three" Banks.

Income Statement Percentages

	Total	Total	1999				Total	1998			
	2000	1999	IV	III	II	I	1998	IV	III	II	I
GFSerfin											
Interest income[a]	27.09	41.16	10.67	9.55	8.94	11.99	42.18	13.41	11.21	9.29	8.26
Interest income (%)	100	100	100	100	100	100	100	100	100	100	100
Interest expense	(82)	(93)	(90)	(88)	(98)	(95)	(85)	(88)	(84)	(85)	(84)
Adjustment for inflation	(0)	4	1	3	5	6	8	9	6	6	10
Pre-financial margin (%)	18	11	11	15	7	11	22	21	23	21	26
Loan loss provision	(0)	(20)	(12)	(4)	(73)	2	8	9	15	7	0
Post-financial margin (%)	18	(9)	(1)	11	11	9	14	12	8	14	26
Other	(14)	(2)	2	(9)	(65)	(9)	(13)	(11)	(8)	(12)	(25)
Net income (%)	3	(11)	1	2	(54)	1	1	1	0	2	1
Bancomer											
Interest income[a]	57.32	61.75	14.33	14.47	14.16	18.78	64.06	20.42	15.92	13.94	13.79
Interest income (%)	100	100	100	100	100	100	100	100	100	100	100
Interest expense	(74)	(74)	(71)	(74)	(75)	(75)	(77)	(76)	(79)	(77)	(75)
Adjustment for inflation	3	3	3	2	3	5	4	6	4	3	2
Pre-financial margin (%)	29	29	32	28	27	30	27	30	25	26	27
Loan loss provision	(6)	13	28	9	6	10	7	10	7	4	5
Post-financial margin (%)	23	16	5	20	21	20	20	19	18	22	22
Other	(21)	(12)	(3)	(16)	(17)	(12)	(18)	(13)	(20)	(26)	(18)
Net income (%)	3	5	1	3	4	8	2	6	2	4	4

Banacci

	62.52	70.89	16.12	16.59	16.67	21.51	70.51	23.78	17.58	14.64	14.50
Interest income[a]	62.52	70.89	16.12	16.59	16.67	21.51	70.51	23.78	17.58	14.64	14.50
Interest income (%)	100	100	100	100	100	100	100	100	100	100	100
Interest expense	(65)	(66)	(65)	(65)	(67)	(67)	(71)	(66)	(76)	(73)	(73)
Adjustment for inflation	2	2	2	0	1	3	3	2	2	2	5
Pre-financial margin (%)	37	36	37	36	34	36	31	36	27	29	31
Loan loss provision	5	18	7	21	30	15	9	11	8	7	8
Post-financial margin (%)	32	18	30	14	4	21	22	25	18	22	23
Other	(19)	(6)	(16)	(4)	8	(11)	(14)	(8)	(24)	(12)	(13)
Net income (%)	14	12	14	11	12	10	9	17	6	11	10

Source: Mexican National Banking and Securities Commission, 2000 Annual Report on Financial Institutions.
[a]Interest Income in millions of pesos.

Table 3. Selected Balance Sheet Ratios – Big Three Banks.

Item	2000				1999				1998				1997
	IV	III	II	I	IV	III	II	I	IV	III	II	I	IV
GFSerfin													
Loan reserves/past due loans (%)	766	243	238	215	157	126	126	70	74	67	66	61	61
Equity/loans (as reported) (%)	11	9	8	6	7	7	7	9	9	9	9	9	9
Equity/loans (adjusted for 100% reserve) (%)	16	14	13	9	11	9	9	6	6	5	5	4	4
Bancomer													
Loan reserves/past due loans (%)	118	135	84	80	80	67	58	58	58	58	58	58	58
Equity/loans (as reported) (%)	11	13	14	14	14	15	14	13	12	10	11	12	12
Equity/loans (adjusted for 100% reserve) (%)	13	15	12	12	12	10	7	7	6	5	5	6	6
Banacci													
Loan reserves/past due loans (%)	106	100	100	100	106	100	75	63	61	61	61	61	55
Equity/loans (as reported) (%)	21	19	19	24	23	22	20	18	16	15	16	17	16
Equity/loans (adjusted for 100% reserve) (%)	21	19	19	24	24	22	16	11	9	8	9	9	7

1998 through the first quarter of 1999. However, a 100% LLR/NPL ratio would have reduced this ratio to 4–6%. Thus, the bank would have needed a capital infusion to maintain its capital adequacy.

Movements in the bank's loan reserves and loan portfolio suggest that it received a capital infusion from the government. Regarding the loan portfolio, as shown in Table 4, current loans increased from 137.17 million pesos at the end of 1997 to 148.16 million pesos at June 30, 1999. This rise was largely attributable to a rise in FOBAPROA loans of 25.3 million pesos. The new FOBAPROA loans, however, were partially offset by a decline in Commercial/Consumer loans of 10.31 million pesos. Thus, FOBAPROA loans may have effectively replaced non-performing commercial loans.[6]

Movements in the bank's loan reserves suggest that the bank would have been unable to maintain a positive capital ratio without this FOBAPROA support. As shown in Table 5, the bank's loan loss reserves increased from 9.41 million pesos on December 31, 1997 to 14.07 million pesos on June 30, 1999. During this same period, the bank added a provision of 14.74 million pesos. Thus, a total of 10.08 million pesos in loans were written off during this period. In this same period, past-due loans decreased by 4.26 million pesos. Thus, an amount of 5.82 million pesos that constitutes approximately one-half of the decrease of 10.31 million pesos (43.53 million pesos to 33.22

Table 4. Changes in Composition of Loan Portfolios of Big Three Banks 1998-Catch Up Adjustment.

	GFSerfin			Bancomer			Banacci		
	12/31/97	6/30/99	Change	12/31/97	9/30/99	Change	12/31/97	9/30/99	Change
Total current loans	137.17	148.16	10.99	221.69	177.57	−44.12	180.54	175.73	−4.81
FOBAPROA	76.13	101.43	25.30	49.27	50.34	1.07	43.3	43.97	0.67
Other governmental	17.51	13.51	−4.00	18.5	35.58	17.08	5.11	21.44	16.33
Commercial/consumer	43.53	33.22	−10.31	153.92	91.65	−62.27	132.13	110.32	−21.81
Other	1.09	2.25	1.16	0.30	0.01	−0.29	0.00	0.00	0.00

Note: Monetary amounts are in thousands of pesos.
Source: Mexican National Banking and Securities Commission, 2000 Annual Report on Financial Institutions.

Table 5. Movements in "Big Three" Banks' Loan Reserves 12/31/97 Through Date of Catch Up Adjustment.

	GFSerfin	Bancomer	Banacci
Balance 12/31/97	9.41	18.48	22.62
Add: Additional provision 12/31/97 to 9/30/98	14.74	8.58	17.94
Less: Balance date of catch up adj.	−14.07	−14.49	−25.31
Loans written off 1/1/98-"catch-up adjustment"	10.08	12.57	15.25
Decrease in past-due loans	−4.26	−10.66	−15.57
Amount of reserve available for current loans	5.82	1.91	−0.32
Change in loans to FOBAPROA	25.30	17.08	0.67
Change in loans to other governmental	−4.00	1.07	16.33
Total change in government loans	21.03	18.15	17.00
Less: Amount of reserve available for current loans	−5.82	−1.91	0.32
Implied capital contribution	15.48	16.24	17.32
Current equity (as reported)	10.05	25.94	38.09
Current loans (as reported)	148.15	177.57	175.73
Current loans/current equity (as reported) (%)	6.78	14.61	21.68
Equity, assuming transfers to government constitute capital contribution	−5.43	9.70	20.77
Current loans, assuming transfers to government constitute capital contribution	132.67	161.33	158.41
Current loans/current equity, assuming transfers to government constitute capital contribution (%)	−4.09	6.01	13.11

Note: Monetary amounts are in millions of pesos. GfSerfin's "catchup" date is June 30, 1999. The "catchup" date for Bancomer and Banacci is September 30, 1999.
Source: Mexican National Banking and Securities Commission, 2000 Annual Report on Financial Institutions.

million pesos) in Commercial/Consumer loans during the period was available to absorb non-performing current loans. If this amount is deducted from the total increase in FOBAPROA and government loans, the bank may have received an effective capital contribution of 15.48 million pesos.

As shown in Table 5, if this portion of loans had been written off, the bank's reserve ratio would have decreased from 6.78 to −4.09%. Thus, without the FOBAPROA loans, the bank may have been unable to maintain a positive capital ratio.

In the post-catch up period, the bank's loan reserve policy improved markedly. As stated above, from the second quarter of 1999 through the fourth quarter of 2000, the bank maintained reserves, which were considerably greater than the past due loans. Also, as shown in Table 6, from the second quarter of 1999 to the first quarter of 2000, the bank's past-due loans decreased by 10.55 million pesos, an amount only slightly greater than the decline of 9.53 million pesos in its loan loss reserves. Thus, after the catch-up adjustment, the bank continually maintained sufficient reserves to absorb possible credit risk in its current loan portfolio.

BANCOMER

As indicated above, BANCOMER was traditionally the country's second largest bank. During the early 1990s, the bank pursued more conservative lending policies than GFSERFIN. Thus, BANCOMER entered the sample period in a stronger financial position than its smaller competitor. This relative financial strength is shown in the bank's financial statements.

As shown in Table 2, interest income rose from 13.79 million pesos in the first quarter of 1998 to 20.42 million pesos in the last quarter of that year; however, by the last quarter of 1999, interest income had declined to 14.33 million pesos. The "pre-provision" financial margin remained in a relatively stable range of 25–32% of interest income during 1998 and 1999.

Movements in the "post-provision" margin, however, suggest the possibility of a "catch-up" adjustment. As shown in Table 2, the provision for loan losses constituted 5% of interest income for the first quarter of 1998 and fluctuated between 4 and 10% of interest income through the third quarter of 1999. In the fourth quarter of 1999, however, the provision leapt to 28%. Correspondingly, the "post-provision" financial margin, which had fluctuated between 18 and 22% of interest income from the first quarter of 1998 through the third quarter of 1999, dropped to 5% for the fourth quarter of 1999.

The bank seemingly used the 45% rule to delay the recognition of losses that might have been recognized under a "100% rule." As derived from the bank's balance sheet (Table 3), loan loss reserves constituted 58% of past-due loans from the final quarter of 1997 through the second quarter of 1999.

Table 6.   Comparison of Change in Past-Due Loans and Loan Loss
Reserves Date of Catch-Up Adjustment to 12/31/00.

	Date of Catch-Up Adjustment	December 31, 2001	Net Change
GFSerfin[a]			
Past-due loans	11.14	0.59	−10.55
Loan-loss reserve	14.07	4.54	−9.53
Net change			−1.02
Bancomer[b]			
Past-due loans	21.47	20.68	−0.79
Loan-loss reserve	14.49	23.12	8.63
Net change			7.84
Banacci[b]			
Past-due loans	25.23	7.61	−17.62
Loan-loss reserve	25.31	8.18	−17.13
Net change			−0.49

Note: Monetary amounts are in millions of pesos.
Source: Mexican National Banking and Securities Commission, 2000 Annual Report on Financial Institutions.
[a]6/30/99.

However, in a sign that the bank moved rapidly to recognize non-performing loans, the ratio leapt to 67 and 80% at the end of the third and fourth quarters of 1999, respectively. In an admission of its use of the 45% rule, the bank states in its 1999 annual report (p. 66) that the increment in the loan loss provision in 1999 resulted from a decision to increase reserves "... to 80% (from 58% in 1998)..." of past-due loans. Even with this increase, however, the bank's loan reserves did not exceed past-due loans until the third quarter of 2000.

In an indication of a capital adequacy problem, adherence to a reserve equal to 100% of past-due loans in the periods prior to the "catch-up" adjustment would have severely lowered the bank's equity/loan ratio. As shown in Table 3, based on a reserve ratio of 58%, the bank was able to maintain an equity/loan ratio between 10 and 15% from 1998 through the second quarter of 1999. However, with a reserve ratio of 100%, the equity/loan ratio for 1998 and the first half of 1999 would have decreased to approximately 5–7%.

As a result, the bank would have required a probable infusion of capital from the government to maintain its capital ratio. As shown in Table 4, current loans decreased from 221.69 million pesos at the end of 1997 to 177.57

million pesos by September 30, 1999. Most of this decline was attributable to commercial/consumer loans, which decreased by 62.27 million pesos. However, while loans from FOBAPROA remained at approximately the same level during this period (49.27 million pesos by December 31, 1997 and 50.34 million pesos by September 30, 1999), loans to other governmental agencies increased by 17.08 million pesos. Thus, non-performing commercial loans may have been transferred to the government in lieu of being reserved.

Movements in the bank's loans provisions and reserves suggest that the bank's capital ratio would have been significantly reduced without FOBAPROA support. As shown in Table 5, BANCOMER's loan loss reserves decreased from 18.48 million pesos by December 31, 1997 to 14.49 million pesos by September 30, 1999. During this same period, the bank added a provision of 8.58 million pesos. Thus, a total of 12.57 million pesos in loans were written off from the end of 1997 through the third-quarter of 1999. Correspondingly, as shown in Table 5, past-due loans decreased by 10.66 million pesos. Thus, if the assumption is made that the decrease in past-due loans was attributable to the write-off of loans, only 1.91 million pesos of reserves were available to absorb non-performing current loans during this period. Given the large decrease in commercial loans (62.27 million pesos), it is unlikely that the bank could have maintained its capital ratio without a capital contribution by the government. In this context, as shown in Table 5, if the 1.91 million pesos of remaining reserves are considered, 16.24 million pesos of non-performing current loans may have been effectively transferred to the government. As shown in Table 5, without this implied re-capitalization, the bank's equity/loan ratio would have decreased from approximately 14.61 to 6.01%.

As in the case of GFSERFIN, in the post catch-up period, the bank seems to have established a more conservative reserve policy. As stated above, from the third quarter of 1999 to the third quarter of 2000 the bank increased its loan reserve to past-due loan ratio from 57.52 to 135.1%. Also, as shown in Table 6, after the catch-up adjustment, past-due loans decreased by only 0.79 million pesos while 8.63 million pesos was added to loan loss reserves. Thus, after the "catch-up," the bank continuously established sufficient reserves to compensate for both its past due loans and any credit risk in its current loan portfolio.

BANACCI

As described above, Banco Nacional de Mexico (BANACCI) was traditionally Mexico's largest bank. In the years before the financial crisis, the bank maintained relatively high credit standards. As a result, BANACCI, which was cited by analysts as the institution most capable of surviving the financial crisis, entered the sample period in the strongest financial position of any of the "big three" institutions.

The relative financial stability is reflected in the bank's income statements. As shown in Table 2, interest income for the first quarter of 1998 was 14.50 million pesos and then fluctuated between 14.64 million pesos and 23.78 million pesos for the remaining quarters of 1998 and 1999. Interest expense ranged between 65 and 76% of interest income during the same period. The margin before deducting loan reserves fluctuated between 27 and 37%.

As in the case of GFSerfin and Bancomer, movements in the loan loss provision suggest the possibility of a "catch-up" adjustment. As shown in Table 2, the provision rose from 8% of interest income for the first quarter of 1998 to 30% of interest income for the second quarter of 1999. Correspondingly, the post-provision margin declined from 23 to 4% of interest income from the first quarter of 1998 to the second quarter of 1999.

As in the case of its sister institutions, BANACCI may have used the 45% rule to delay the recognition of non-performing loans. As shown in Table 3, the loan loss reserve approximated 61% of past-due loans during 1998 and rose to 75% of past-due loans for the second quarter of 1999. Thereafter, loan loss reserves approximated past-due loans.

Adherence to a 100% ratio would have lowered the bank's equity/loan ratio. As shown in Table 3, based on a loan reserve to past-due loan ratio of approximately 61%, the bank was able to maintain an equity/loan ratio of 16 to 17% from the fourth quarter of 1997 through 1998. However, with a reserve ratio of 100%, the equity/loan ratio for this period would have been 7 to 9%.

As in the case of its sister institutions, BANACCI seems to have replaced some of its consumer/commercial loans with FOBAPROA loans. As shown in Table 4, the bank's current loan portfolio declined by 4.81 million pesos from the final quarter of 1997 to the third quarter of 1999. A decline in commercial/consumer loans of 21.81 million pesos was partially offset by increases in loans to FOBAPROA of 0.67 million pesos and loans to other governmental agencies of 16.33 million pesos. Thus, loans to governmental agencies seem to have replaced 17 million pesos in commercial loans.

As shown in Table 5, BANACCI's loan loss reserves increased from 22.62 million pesos by December 31, 1997 to 25.31 million pesos by September 30, 1999. During this same period, the bank added a provision of 17.94 million pesos. Thus, 15.25 million pesos in loans were written off from the end of 1997 through the third quarter of 1999. As shown in Table 5, non-performing loans decreased by 15.57 million pesos. Accordingly, if the assumption is made that the decrease in past-due loans was attributable to the write-off of past-due loans, 0.32 million pesos of the reserves were available to absorb non-performing current loans. Accordingly, the bank may have received a capital contribution of 17.32 million pesos from the government. As shown in Table 5, without this capital contribution, the bank's current equity/loan ratio would have decreased from 21.68 to 13.11%. As a result, while the bank's capital ratio would have declined without the government contribution, the bank still would have adhered to approximate regulatory standards (i.e., 8%).

As in the case of its sister institutions, BANACCI seems to have adopted a more stringent reserve policy in the post catch-up period. As stated above, in the post catch-up period the bank established reserves that were virtually equal to its past-due loans. Also, as shown in Table 6, in the post catch-up period the bank's past-due loans decreased by 17.62 million pesos while its loan reserves decreased by a (virtually equal) 17.13 million pesos. Thus, either the bank did not cover the credit risk in its current loan portfolio or it felt that all of its credit risk had been transferred and was reflected in its past-due loan portfolio. Given the general optimism regarding BANACCI, the latter seems more likely.

CONCLUSION

In the late 1990s, Mexico suffered a severe economic downturn that resulted from the 1994 peso devaluation. As a result, its banks experienced severe credit and capital crises. In response, the Mexican government received foreign assistance, established a bank bailout agency, rewrote the financial reporting principles for its banks, and engaged in a two stage restructuring of the banking system.

During the first stage, some smaller banks were consolidated with larger financial domestic institutions and others were sold to foreign financial institutions. The Mexican press asserted that, in order to expedite this process, the government had promulgated accounting principles that would allow the banks to understate the loan loss provision and reserves. In the second phase of the consolidation, the country's larger banks were eventually sold to foreign entities.

This paper has examined the three largest banks' financial data for the period 1998–2000 to ascertain whether larger institutions, like their smaller counterparts, may have managed their earnings and/or capital. In general, the case of the three largest banks suggests that the new accounting standards allowed banks to establish reserves that were far less than their past-due loan portfolios. As a result, banks were allowed to delay or avoid recognition of loan losses. Also, in the pre-catch-up period, banks were seemingly able to transfer large amounts of loans to either FOBAPROA or "other government agencies" without first recognizing either the non-performance of the loans or the corresponding loan losses. In the post-catch-up period, however, banks established reserves equal to their past-due loan portfolios and seemingly transferred loans to past-due status on a more expedient basis.

In general, these patterns suggest that the economic pressures presented by the imminent acquisition of the banks by foreign institutions rather than the earlier promulgation of new standards was the impetus that caused the banks to follow more stringent practices. Given this tendency, financial reporting authorities should encourage developing countries to adopt stringent standards that comply with internationally accepted norms. Additionally, mechanisms should be adopted for ascertaining whether countries are adhering to international standards. Finally, banks and governments should be encouraged to disclose the rationale and balance sheet effects of capital contributions. Some may argue that such standards will place a great deal of stress on banks attempting to survive. However, only early recognition of loan losses will reduce the ultimate cost of restructuring developing countries' financial systems.

NOTES

1. See for example, Petersen (1998).
2. For a description of the traditional Mexican financial system, see Brothers and Solis (1966), Thompson (1979), and Maxfield (1990).
3. For an explanation of the nationalization, see Tello (1984).
4. As part of this effort, the government eased restrictions on foreign investment, balanced the federal budget, liberalized trade, and privatized several government-owned industries.
5. The circular requires that the audit committee be involved in designing the bank's internal control system, designating the external auditor, designing the institution's code of ethics, and reviewing the institution's financial statements. Also, regarding the internal audit function, the circular states that internal auditors should consistently review and test the internal control system, review the bank's financial statements, and provide information to the bank's external auditors.
6. In a manner that suggests the possible improper classification of non-performing loans, examination of the bank's balance sheet shows that the increase in FOBAPROA loans effectively replaced a virtually equal decrease in "other assets."

REFERENCES

Beattie, V. A., Casson, P. D., Dale, R. S., McKenzie, G. W., Sutcleffe, C. M. S., & Turner, M. J. (1995). *Banks and bad debts*. Chichester: Wiley.

Bolsa Mexicana de Valores. (1991–1994). *Anuario financiero (financial annual)*. México, DF: Bolsa Mexicana de Valores.

Brothers, D. S., & Solis, M. (1966). *Mexican financial development*. Austin, TX: University of Texas Press.

Comisión Nacional Bancaria y de Valores. (1990). *Ley Para Regular las Agrupaciones Finacieras*. México, DF: Comisión Nacional Bancaria y de Valores.

Comisión Nacional Bancaria y de Valores. (1997–2000). *Informacion estadistica (Statistical information)*. Mexico, DF: Comisión Nacional Bancaria y de Valores (www.cnbv.gob.mx).

Comisión Nacional Bancaria y de Valores. (1997). *Circular no. 1343*. México, DF: Comisión Nacional Bancaria y de Valores.

Comisión Nacional Bancaria y de Valores. (1999). *Circular no. 1423*. México, DF: Comisión Nacional Bancaria y de Valores.

Comisión Nacional Bancaria y de Valores. (2000). *Circular no. 1480*. México, DF: Comisión Nacional Bancaria y de Valores.

Comisión Nacional Bancaria y de Valores. (2001). *Circular no. 1506*. México, DF: Comisión Nacional Bancaria y de Valores.

Grupo Financiero Banacci. (1998). *Informe annual 1998*. Mexico, DF: Grupo Financiero Banacci.

Grupo Financiero Bancomer. (1998). *Informe annual 1998*. Mexico, DF: Grupo Financiero Bancomer.

International Monetary Fund. (2000). *World economic outlook – focus on transitional economies*. Washington, DC: International Monetary Fund (October).

International Monetary Fund (Monetary and Exchange Affairs and Western Hemisphere Departments). (2001). *Mexico – financial system stability assessment*. Washington, DC: International Monetary Fund (October).

Maxfield, S. (1990). *Governing capital, international finance and Mexican politics*. Ithaca, NY: Cornell University Press.

Petersen, M. (1998). UN Report Faults Big Accountants in Asia Crisis. *New York Times*. October 24, C1.

Tello, C. (1984). *La nacionalización de la banca en México (The nationalization of banks in Mexico)*. México, DF: Veintiuno Editores.

Thompson, J. K. (1979). *Inflation, financial markets, and economic development – the experience of Mexico*. Greenwich, CT: JAI Press.

ADOPTION AND BENEFITS OF MANAGEMENT ACCOUNTING SYSTEMS: EVIDENCE FROM FINLAND AND AUSTRALIA

Johanna Hyvönen

ABSTRACT

This study provides empirical evidence on management accounting practices in Finnish manufacturing companies. It identifies the adoption of the management accounting practices, received benefits from the adoption and intentions to emphasize the practices in the future. The results indicate that financial measures like product profitability analysis and budgeting for controlling costs is likely to be important in the future, but it is also clear that greater emphasis will be placed on newer practices like customer satisfaction surveys and employee attitudes. The results of the management accounting practices are compared to the findings of a similar study based on Australian data.

INTRODUCTION

The importance of the relative benefits that firms obtain by using financial or non-financial performance measures has been of particular interest in the

Advances in International Accounting
Advances in International Accounting, Volume 18, 97–120
ISSN: 0897-3660/doi:10.1016/S0897-3660(05)18005-2

accounting literature (see, for instance, Chenhall & Langfield-Smith, 1998; Lynch & Cross, 1992). The increasing importance of non-financial measures is reported in many surveys (Bhimani, 1994; Banerjee & Kane, 1996; Roberts, 1995; Lebas, 1996; Groot, 1996). As Ittner and Larcker (1998) point out, one of the main reasons for growing interest in non-financial measures is the fact that they can provide information about future profits or firm value that is not present in current profits. Kaplan and Norton (1996) state that non-financial indicators or investments in intangible assets may be better predictors of future financial performance than historical accounting figures. It has also been noticed that traditional management accounting techniques are not optimal for firms operating in the environment of global competition, rapid technological change and the development of new management approaches like total quality management (TQM) or just-in-time (Bromwich & Bhimani, 1994; Bunce, Fraser, & Woodcock, 1995; Chenhall & Langfield-Smith, 1998). Recently developed techniques, like activity-based costing (ABC), value chain analysis, target costing, product life-cycle analysis, shareholder value analysis, customer satisfaction surveys, employee-based methods, balanced performance measures, and benchmarking are proposed as ways of linking operations to the company's strategies and objectives.

This chapter investigates the management accounting practices used by Finnish firms. Both financial and non-financial performance measures, and recently developed techniques like employee attitudes and customer-satisfaction surveys are of special interest. The findings of the survey are compared to the results reported by Chenhall and Langfield-Smith (1998) who analysed management accounting practices in Australian firms. This makes it possible to compare differences and similarities in management accounting practices between these two countries.

A recent paper by Wijewardena and De Zoysa (1999) provides a comparative analysis of management accounting practices in Australia and Japan. They find, among other things, that while management accounting practices of Australian companies place an emphasis on cost control tools at the manufacturing stage, those of Japanese companies devote a much greater attention to cost planning and cost reduction tools at the product design stage. There have been several studies investigating the management accounting practices and their benefits in many countries (Bhimani in U.K. (1994), McKinnon & Bruns (1992) in the U.S. and Roberts (1995) in France). Bhimani (1996) reports evidence on management accounting practices in different European countries. Brierley, Cowton, and Drury (2001) investigate product costing practices in Europe. Lukka and Granlund (1996) and Virtanen, Malmi, Vaivio, and Kasanen (1996) analyse the cost accounting practices in Finland by using a sample of industrial manufacturing firms. Malmi (1999) investigates the diffusion of ABC in Finnish firms. Cost accounting practices have been reported on earlier and certain newer techniques, like activity-based costing have been of interest in Finland but not management accounting practices on the whole and not even the emphasis that companies intend to place on those practices in the future.

This chapter contributes to the management accounting literature by providing a European perspective to management accounting systems. This study also provides evidence of the differences and similarities between Australia and another technology-intensive country, Finland.

BACKGROUND

Finland was in deep recession in the beginning of 1990s. Yet it managed to rise from the recession to an unforeseeable level in economy. Some Finnish companies have succeeded extremely well in global competition. Finland occupies the highest rankings in numerous international studies investigating competitiveness and innovation. The United Nations Human Development Report (2001) ranks Finland as the most technologically advanced country. Finland is also ranked high as an environment for innovation. The International Institute for Management Development (IMD) recognized Finland as the second most appealing place for research and development investment in 2002 (Cornelius, Schwab & Porter, 2002). Also, The World Economic Forum (WEF, 2002) ranked Finland second in 2002 in terms of competitiveness based upon the strength of Finnish technological innovation, effective public institutions and the extensive networking between companies and research institutes.

DATA AND RESEARCH DESIGN

The data used in the study were collected by sending a survey to 132 Finnish firms at the business unit level. The business unit was chosen because different business units may use different control systems. The design of the survey follows that used by Chenhall and Langfield-Smith (1998), De Meyer, Nakane, Miller, and Ferdows (1989), Miller, De Meyer, and Nakane (1992), Joye and Blayney (1990), and Innes and Mitchell (1995).

The survey was pilot tested by a group of managers from eight different companies before mailing the questionnaire. A total of 51 responses were received with a response rate of 39%. This is a fairly high rate given the number of total items (188) in the questionnaire and the fact that the terminology can be at least partly unfamiliar for the respondents. On the other hand, if the respondents are not familiar with the techniques presented in the questionnaire, then these techniques are not likely to be emphasized in their organization. So the large variety of questions is not likely to affect the reliability of the answers but it might affect the respondents' willingness to fill in the questionnaire. The sample consists mainly of large firms operating in three industries that are important for Finland, i.e. forest, metal and electronics industries. These were chosen because one would expect that leading companies use advanced management tools. Some of the companies are among the largest in their field in the world and simultaneously leading companies in their business lines. To examine for non-response bias, the first ten and last ten responses were compared to test whether the responses differ between the two groups. The results indicate that there are no statistically significant differences between the groups.

The questionnaire has 45 preselected management accounting practices. On the left-hand side of the questionnaire, the respondents are asked whether their businesses had adopted each management accounting practice. Then they were asked to indicate the degree of benefit the practice has had over the last 3 years using a seven-item scale. On the right-hand side of the questionnaire, the respondents were asked to indicate the emphasis the business unit will place on each practice over the next 3 years also on a seven-item scale.

The Chenhall and Langfield-Smith (1998) study investigated large Australian manufacturing companies. These companies were strategic business units or companies in their own right. By using 78 responses, they analysed the adoption of management accounting practices and their importance in the future. Machinery and equipment was the largest industry with 21 respondents; food and beverages had 13 respondents as well as the group other manufacturing. A majority of the respondents (67) were chief accountants or group controllers. The study reported in this chapter is also made mainly in big manufacturing companies and the background of the respondents is similar so these two data sets should be suitable for comparison.

Demographic Data

The target group of the questionnaire is a business unit. The main industries in the data are in the forest industry and metal industry with each group forming 35% of the sample. The electronics industry represents 16% and chemical industry 4% of the responses. The rest belong to a group of other industries (10%), which mainly consists of units providing different services.

The majority of the respondents (65%) belong to senior management, 27% to middle management and 8% are specialists. 74% represent the accounting function, 14% the production function, 8% research and development and one of the respondents belongs to the human resources function. 72.5% of the respondents have academic education and 27.5% have polytechnic or college education.

The unit size is measured by the number of personnel and the turnover of the unit. 15.7% of the respondents have 20–100 employees; 11.8% have 101–200; 27.5% have 201–500; 19.6% have 501–1000; and 25.5% more than 1000 employees. The units are big; 45% of the respondents have turnover of 160 million euros or more, and only five of the respondents have turnover of less than 20 million euros. Altogether their turnovers account for a considerable amount of the gross national product. Also majority of the companies responding to survey are consolidated companies. The demographic data are shown in Table 1.

RESULTS

Table 2 reports the results of the adoption of management accounting practices in Finland and Australia. This table is divided into three equal panels in order to help the discussion and is not meant to imply that adoption (or benefits) is either high or low in any absolute sense. Management accounting practices that belong to the first panel have relative high adoption, those that belong to the second panel have relative moderate and the last fifteen in the third panel have relative low adoption. Management accounting practices are divided into long-term planning, budgeting systems, product costing, performance evaluation and decision support systems.

Traditional techniques in management accounting refer to the use of budgeting systems for planning and control and performance measures such as ROI and divisional profit among other things. Recently developed contemporary techniques refer to practices like benchmarking, activity-based techniques, balanced performance measures, team-based measures, employee-based measures and strategic planning.

The results reported in Table 2 indicate that a high proportion of the respondents in the survey have adopted most of the practices. 20 out of 45 practices are adopted by at least 90% of the firms and 43 items are adopted

Table 1.   Demographic Data.

	Number	%
Position at work		
Senior management	33	64.7
Middle management	14	25.5
Specialist	4	7.8
Educational background		
Academic	37	72.5
Polytechnic or college	14	27.5
Annual sales in million euros		
2–10	2	3.9
11–40	6	11.8
41–80	8	15.7
81–160	12	23.5
>160	23	45.1
Function		
Production	7	13.7
Human resources	1	2.0
Finance	38	74.5
Research and development	4	7.8
Number of employees		
20–100	8	15.7
101–200	6	11.8
201–500	14	27.5
501–1000	10	19.6
>1000	13	25.5
Industry classification		
Forest industry	18	35.3
Metal industry	18	35.3
Electronics industry	8	15.7
Other	7	13.7

by at least 71% of the firms. The high adoption rates on management accounting practices may exist because the questionnaire asks for adoption over the last 3 years regardless of the level of adoption. However, the level of adoption is likely to vary across companies.

Budgeting for controlling costs is adopted by every business unit in the sample. Budgeting for cash flows and budgeting for evaluating managers' performance also have a relative high adoption rate. Among the budgeting practices, budgeting for planning financial position is ranked lowest, but still has an adoption rate of 84%. Chenhall and Langfield-Smith report similar results using data for Australian firms. In Australia, budgeting for financial position has the highest adoption rate (adopted by all units). That, however,

Table 2. Relative Adoption Rates of Management Accounting Practices in Finland and Australia.

Management Accounting Practice	Finland %	Finland Rank	CLS Rank	Management Accounting Practice	Finland %	Finland Rank	CLS Rank
Panel I: High Adoption Rate							
Budgeting for controlling costs	100	1	2	Budgeting for evaluating managers' performance	94	4	a
Performance evaluation: qualitative measures	98	2	12	Product costing: variable costing	94	4	4
Capital budgeting measures like ROI, payback	96	3	b	Performance evaluation: ROI	94	4	3
Budgeting for planning cash flows	96	3	2	Performance evaluation: production processes	94	4	a
Performance evaluation: employee attitudes	96	3	3	Performance evaluation: customer satisfaction surveys	94	4	4
Product profitability analysis	96	3	3	Long range forecasting	92	5	9
Formal strategic planning	94	4	4	Performance evaluation: divisional profit	92	5	9
Strategic plans developed together with budgets	94	4	12				
Panel II: Moderate Adoption Rate							
Performance evaluation: ongoing supplier evaluations	92	5	14	Budgeting for compensating managers	86	8	13
Budgeting for coordinating activities across the business units	90	6	5	Product costing: absorption costing	86	8	16
Performance evaluation: budget variance analysis	90	6	4	Activity-based management	86	8	21
Performance evaluation: cash flow ROI	90	6	15	Budgeting linking financial position, resources & activities	84	9	17
	90	6	6	ROI	84	9	1

Table 2. (*Continued*)

Management Accounting Practice	Finland %	Rank	CLS Rank
Benchmarking of operational processes			
Capital budgeting measures like IRR, NPV	88	7	b
Budgeting for planning day-to-day operations	88	7	2
Performance evaluation: non-financial measures	88	7	7
Panel III: Low Adoption Rate			
Strategic plans developed separate from budgets	82	10	20
Product costing: activity-based costing	80	11	24
Performance evaluation: team performance	80	11	12
Benchmarking of product characteristics	80	11	12
Benchmarking of strategic priorities	80	11	8
Benchmarking carried out within the wider organization	80	11	15
Target costing	78	12	27
Performance evaluation: balanced scorecard	73	13	11

Management Accounting Practice	Finland %	Rank	CLS Rank
Budgeting for planning financial position			
Benchmarking of management processes	84	9	8
Benchmarking carried out with outside organizations	84	9	18
Performance evaluation: controllable profit	71	14	10
Performance evaluation: residual income	71	14	23
Cost-volume-profit analysis	71	14	14
Product life-cycle analysis	71	14	20
Economic value or shareholder value analysis	71	14	22
Operations research techniques	69	15	25
Value chain analysis	51	16	26

CLS = ranking in the Chenhall and Langfield-Smith (1998) study of Australian firms.
[a] Not included in Chenhall and Langfield-Smith (1998) study.
[b] Capital budgeting tools is one practice in Chenhall and Langfield-Smith (1998) study. It is ranked 2.

is not among the highest adoption rates in Finland. The number one practise in Finland (budgeting for controlling costs) is ranked as number two in Australia. The importance of budgets in Finland is also confirmed by Ekholm and Wallin (2000) who conclude that the annual budget is not yet ready to be thrown away. Bruggeman, Slagmulder, and Waeytens (1996) report that activity-based budgeting has been adopted in 13.8% of Belgian companies. In Greece, the most frequent reply to how the budget was used was either as a framework to the firm's planning or a guide to expenditure during the year (Ballas & Venieris, 1996).

The most adopted long-term planning practice is capital budgeting measures (ROI and payback) which is ranked number three with an adoption rate of 96%. Formal strategic planning, strategic plans developed together with budgets, long-range forecasting are all adopted by at least 92%. Capital budgeting measures are divided into two groups, i.e. ROI and payback method forming one and measures like internal rate of return (IRR) and net present value (NPV) forming the other. Chenhall and Langfield-Smith use only one measure, i.e. capital budgeting tools. This practice is ranked number two by Australian firms.

The three measures for product costing are variable costing, absorption costing and activity-based costing. Variable costing has a relatively high adoption rate (ranked 4), absorption costing has a moderate adoption rate and activity-based costing has a relatively low adoption rate. Lukka and Granlund (1996) report the dominance of variable costing in Finland. Variable costing is frequently used for external reporting in Finland most probably due to the fact that Finnish firms still prefer to use variable costing. Lukka and Granlund (1996) point out that 5% of the respondents are currently implementing ABC and 25% are considering implementing it. Malmi (1996) provides empirical evidence about activity-based costing in Finnish metal and engineering industries. The results show that ABC is used in 13.7% of the units. Laitinen (1995) reports that in three different business categories 39%, 26.7% and 39.3% of the firms have considered or have implemented an ABC system. In Chenhall and Langfield-Smith study, all the above-mentioned three product costing measures have the lowest adoption rates and of these measures, absorption costing was ranked the highest (16).

Performance evaluation measures include both financial and non-financial ones. Some of the techniques are traditional and some are recently developed. The highest ranking performance evaluation measure in Finnish firms is qualitative measures (2) and the second highest is employee attitudes (3). The other performance evaluation measures with high adoption rates are return on investment (ROI) (4), production processes (4), customer satisfaction surveys (4) and divisional profit (5). These include conventional financial measures but many of them are non-financial. In the Chenhall and Langfield-Smith study, the non-financial performance measures like customer satisfaction and employee attitudes have a moderate adoption rate; measures like ROI, budget variance analysis and divisional profit have a relatively high adoption rate. Non-financial measures are ranked number seven in Australia. In Denmark, the most widely used traditional performance measures are material costs and labour costs per unit used in seven out of ten firms (Israelsen, Anderson, Rohde, & Sorensen, 1996). From non-financial measures, inventory turnover, percent on-time-deliveries and outgoing quality yield are the most widely used. Barbato, Collini, and Quagli (1996) report of little interest in Italy in adopting non-financial measures as part of performance-appraisal systems. He also reports that companies often keep track of non-financial measures but do not seem to integrate them into a total performance evaluation system. The Dutch evidence (Boons, Roozen, & Weerd de, 1994) also suggests the dominance of accounting-based indicators in performance evaluation.

Product profitability analysis is ranked highest (3) on decision support systems in Finnish firms. In fact, it is the only measure in the high adoption rate category. The second highest measure is benchmarking of operational processes, which has a relatively moderate adoption rate (90%). Benchmarking of operational processes was the highest ranked (6) decision support system in Chenhall and Langfield-Smith study. Benchmarking of strategic priorities is ranked 11 by Finnish firms and benchmarking of management processes is ranked 9. Many of these decision support systems are ranked in a category of low adoption rates both in Finland and Australia. For example, value chain analysis is ranked last in Finland with adoption rate of 51% and it is second last in Australia with adoption rate of 49%. Operations research techniques, shareholder value analysis and product life-cycle analysis are also in a category of low adoption rate.

Activity-based management (ABM) is ranked 8 and it has a moderate adoption rate. Virtanen et al. (1996) report that none of the 12 Finnish companies interviewed in their study have tried new cost accounting technologies other than ABC/ABM. A paper by Malmi (1996) points out that the ABM is used in 12.7% of the Finnish companies. In Belgium, 13.8% of the companies reported of ABM being in operation (Bruggeman et al., 1996). One of the newer practices, target costing, has a moderate adoption rate and this is also the case in the Lukka and Granlund (1996) study where only 1% of the respondents were implementing it and 6% were considering it.

Similar results are reported in Sweden (Ask, Ax, & Jönsson, 1996) where only 1% of the respondents indicated an interest in target costing. Israelsen et al. (1996) report that about half of the Danish companies systematically include target costs in the development of new products. Benchmarking is used by one of four companies. Half carry out systematic analyses of key processes, with only one-third of these having developed information sharing agreements with partners (Israelsen et al., 1996).

The Ask et al. (1996) survey also investigates the respondent's satisfaction with the received accounting information in general. On a scale from 1 (very satisfied) to 5 (very dissatisfied) the mean of all respondents is 2.4 and median 2 indicating that the firms are satisfied with the accounting information they receive. This does not vary across different functions. Mendoza and Bescos (2001) report the degree of satisfaction with all information managers receive in 11 French companies. On product costs, 44% of all managers express a high degree of satisfaction and 29% stated that they are dissatisfied. On operating costs, 47.5% are very satisfied and 23.3% dissatisfied.

Management Accounting Practices: Past Benefits

Tables 3–5 present the relative benefits of the management accounting practices included in Table 2 during the past 3 years and the relative future emphasis to be placed on these practices over next 3 years. Standard deviations are also shown in Tables 3–5 to express the diversity of responses. Divisional profit (performance measurement) is ranked number one when asked about the degree of benefit over last 3 years. Many of the companies in the survey are business units that are part of a consolidated group; that may explain the high rank. Other performance evaluation practices in the high benefit category are ROI, budget variance analysis, production processes, customer satisfaction surveys and employee attitudes. Budgeting for controlling costs is ranked number two and it is the only budgeting measure on the high benefit category. In product costing, the number one measure is variable costing which is ranked three. Absorption costing is also ranked high in tenth place. Quite many of the long-term planning practices are included in the high benefit category: capital budgeting measures like ROI and payback, strategic plans developed together with budgets, formal strategic planning and long-range forecasting. The only decision support system that is in the high benefit category is product profitability analysis.

The respondents seem to obtain low benefits from many of the decision support systems. They are also ranked low in adoption rates. The high

Table 3. Management Accounting Practices with High Benefit: Past Benefits and Future Emphasis.

Management Accounting Practice	Relative Benefits Past 3 Years				Relative Future Emphasis Next 3 Years			
	Finland			CLS Rank	Finland			CLS Rank
	Mean	SD	Rank		Mean	SD	Rank	
Performance evaluation: divisional profit	5.43	1.80	1	4	5.49	1.65	7	5
Budgeting for controlling costs	5.39	1.30	2	1	5.75	1.28	2	1
Product costing: variable costing	5.04	1.76	3	21	5.56	1.35	5	32
Performance evaluation: qualitative measures	4.86	1.44	4	24	5.72	0.90	3	26
Performance evaluation: ROI	4.86	2.02	5	2	5.53	1.37	6	4
Capital budget measures like ROI, payback	4.84	1.86	6	a	5.34	1.65	10	a
Performance evaluation: budget variance analysis	4.76	1.84	7	3	4.84	1.49	23	6
Strategic plans developed with budgets	4.74	1.64	8	6	5.31	1.53	11	9
Product profitability analysis	4.67	1.72	9	15	5.76	1.20	1	3
Product costing: absorption costing	4.63	2.22	10	9	5.46	1.68	8	25
Performance evaluation: production processes	4.47	1.83	11	b	5.23	1.31	12	b
Performance evaluation: customer satisfaction surveys	4.39	1.70	12	11	5.61	0.98	4	12
Performance evaluation: employee attitudes	4.34	1.66	13	34	5.44	0.99	9	31
Formal strategic planning	4.33	1.84	14	10	4.86	1.67	22	2
Long range forecasting	4.26	1.75	15	26	4.98	1.61	18	11

The Relative Benefits columns list management accounting practices in order of the average benefits derived from using each practice during the past 3 years and the Relative Future Emphasis columns show the future emphasis to be given to each practice.
CLS = relative rankings in the Chenhall and Langfield-Smith (1998) study of Australian firms.
[a]Capital budgeting tools is one measure in Chenhall and Langfield-Smith (1998) study. It is ranked 5 on past benefits and 7 on future emphasis.
[b]Not included in Chenhall and Langfield-Smith (1998) study.

Table 4. Management Accounting Practices with Moderate Benefit: Past Benefits and Future Emphasis.

Management Accounting Practice	Relative Benefits Past 3 Years				Relative Future Emphasis Next 3 Years			
	Finland			CLS Rank	Finland			CLS Rank
	Mean	SD	Rank		Mean	SD	Rank	
Budgeting for evaluating managers' perform	4.14	1.65	16	a	5.06	1.43	15	a
Benchmarking of operational processes	4.08	2.03	17	25	5.13	1.59	14	13
Budgeting for planning cash flows	4.06	1.68	18	12	4.63	1.63	27	10
Performance evaluation: cash flow ROI	4.02	2.00	19	17	4.89	1.39	20	22
Performance evaluation: ongoing supplier evaluations	3.90	1.91	20	18	5.04	1.35	17	19
Budge for compensating managers	3.86	2.08	21	23	4.73	1.62	24	33
Performance evaluation: non-financial measures	3.73	1.93	22	14	4.98	1.39	19	20
Strategic plans developed separately	3.63	2.29	23	13	4.33	1.99	34	34
Budgeting for coordinating activities	3.57	1.84	24	16	5.15	1.56	13	16
Budget for planning financial position	3.53	2.06	25	7	4.51	1.66	30	8
Performance evaluation: controllable profit	3.53	2.35	26	8	4.48	1.77	32	15
Budget for planning day-to-day operations	3.41	1.92	27	19	4.06	1.86	39	17
Benchmarking of product characteristics	3.35	2.16	28	27	4.54	1.59	29	28
Capital budget measures like IRR, NPV	3.33	1.85	29	b	4.00	1.65	41	b
Product costing: activity-based costing	3.32	2.12	30	38	5.07	1.45	16	29

The Relative Benefits columns list management accounting practices in order of the average benefits derived from using each practice during the past 3 years and the Relative Future Emphasis columns show the future emphasis to be given to each practice.
CLS = relative rankings in the Chenhall and Langfield-Smith (1998) study of Australian firms.
[a]Not included in Chenhall and Langfield-Smith (1998) study.
[b]Capital budgeting tools is one measure in Chenhall and Langfield-Smith (1998) study. It is ranked 5 on past benefits and 7 on future emphasis.

Table 5. Management Accounting Practices with Low Benefit: Past Benefits and Future Emphasis.

Management Accounting Practice	Relative Benefits Past 3 Years				Relative Future Emphasis Next 3 Years			
	Finland			CLS Rank	Finland			CLS Rank
	Mean	SD	Rank		Mean	SD	Rank	
Benchmarking of management processes	3.30	2.04	31	29	4.65	1.51	26	14
Cost-volume-profit analysis	3.27	2.21	32	31	4.26	1.71	36	35
Budget linking financial position, resources & activities	3.25	2.07	33	36	4.48	1.79	31	30
Benchmarking with outside organisations	3.22	1.87	34	35	4.61	1.31	28	27
Benchmarking of strategic priorities	3.16	2.00	35	33	4.46	1.59	33	24
Activity-based management	3.10	1.89	36	42	4.26	1.63	37	36
Benchmarking carried out within the wider organization	3.10	2.04	37	32	4.30	1.69	35	18
Performance evaluation: team performance	3.08	2.02	38	28	4.67	1.48	25	21
Target costing	2.94	2.00	39	30	4.07	1.62	38	40
Performance evaluation: balanced scorecard	2.80	2.29	40	22	4.89	2.05	21	23
Performance evaluation: residual income	2.67	2.35	41	20	4.03	2.06	40	39
Product life-cycle analysis	2.65	2.16	42	41	4.00	1.78	42	38
Operations research techniques	2.53	2.05	43	39	3.69	1.70	44	41
Economic or shareholder value analysis	2.34	1.91	44	37	3.82	1.87	43	37
Value chain analysis	1.41	1.65	45	40	3.61	1.87	45	42

The Relative Benefits columns list management accounting practices in order of the average benefits derived from using each practice during the past 3 years and the Relative Future Emphasis columns show the future emphasis to be given to each practice. CLS = relative rankings in the Chenhall and Langfield-Smith (1998) study of Australian firms.

benefit category includes many recently developed non-financial measures as well as traditional financial measures. One ranking worth noticing is shareholder value analysis, which is ranked as low as 44, since the Institute of Management Accountants (IMA, 1996) found in a survey that 35% of its respondents used EVA® or similar measures and 45% expected to use them in the future.

Finnish evidence is similar to the results reported by Chenhall and Langfield-Smith. Direct comparisons of *t*-tests between Finnish and Australian practices were also completed. No significant differences were found.

The results indicate that the respondents seem to obtain high benefits from the financial measures like budgeting for controlling costs, ROI (performance evaluation), divisional profit (performance evaluation), capital budgeting tools among others. On the other hand, some of the recently developed non-financial measures are ranked higher in Finland. Qualitative measures (performance evaluation) are ranked fourth in Finland, 24 in Australia and employee attitudes (performance evaluation) are ranked 13 in Finland and 34 in Australia.

Management Accounting Practices: Future Emphasis

Tables 3–5 also report the emphasis the firms intend to place on each management accounting practice over the next 3 years. The results show that product profitability is expected to be the most important practice in the future. Budgeting for controlling costs is ranked the next most important measure and qualitative measures (performance evaluation) is ranked number 3. The newer techniques like customer satisfaction survey (4) and employee attitudes (9) are going to be important in the future. Financial measures are also going to keep their status. Divisional profit, variable costing, ROI in performance evaluation and on capital budgeting, and absorption costing are all ranked high.

Budgeting seems to be focusing on controlling costs; the next most important measure is budgeting for coordinating activities across the business units, which rises from rank 24 to 13. The biggest change is use of the balanced scorecard, which rises from rank number 40 to number 21. As Roberts (1995) points out, tableau de bord (TB) is a similar instrument panel or dashboard for a business, which collects key information needed for steering or piloting the business. TB tends to emphasize physical numbers as these numbers are seen as fundamental – changes in them will be reflected later in accounting numbers. Fisher (1995) and Brancato (1995) have identified three principal reasons why firms are adopting non-financial measures: (1) perceived limitations in traditional accounting-based measures (2) competitive pressure and (3) outgrowth of other initiatives like TQM. One noticeable non-financial measure is customer satisfaction (rising from rank 12 to rank 4). Anderson, Fornell, and Lehmann (1994) point out that higher customer satisfaction improves financial performance by increasing the loyalty of existing customers, reducing price elasticities, lowering marketing costs through positive word-of-mouth advertising, reducing transaction costs and enhancing firm reputation.

Table 6 shows those managing accounting practices that have at least a six-point difference in ranking between past benefits and future emphasis. It shows those management accounting practices where the degree of emphasis is expected to change. Results indicate that relatively greater future emphasis will be placed on product profitability analysis, customer satisfaction surveys, budgeting for coordinating activities across business units, activity-based costing, benchmarking carried out with outside organizations, team performance and balanced scorecard. Practices that are expected to be given a decreased emphasis in the future are formal strategic planning, budgeting for planning cash flows, budgeting for planning day-to-day operations and capital budgeting measures like IRR and payback.

Discussion about Finnish Situation

The results reported so far indicate that the recently developed techniques are relatively more adopted in Finland than in Australia. This may be partly because of the different sample period in the studies: the Australian results reported by Chenhall and Langfield-Smith were made in 1998 and the development of new techniques has been quite recent. On the other hand, the organizations presented in this study are leading companies in their field in the world and one would expect that pioneer companies use the most advanced techniques. There has not been that much innovations in the management accounting practices in Finland until the last decade so organizations are quite easily motivated to try some of the new practices. Joining the European Union in 1995 changed the accounting legislation. The preference of variable costing might stem from the past. Contrary to many other countries, variable costing was allowed in external reporting in Finland. So far the change in legislation is not seen in product costing principles; variable costing still dominates.

Table 6. Management Accounting Practices with At Least Six-Point
Difference Between Ranking of Past Benefits and Future Emphasis.

Management Accounting Practice	Relative Rankings		
	Past benefits	Future benefits	Difference
Increased ranking			
Product profitability analysis	9	1	8[a]
Performance evaluation: customer satisfaction surveys	12	4	8[a]
Budgeting for coordinating activities across business units	24	13	11[a]
Product costing: activity-based costing	30	16	14[a]
Benchmarking carried out with outside organizations	34	28	6[a]
Performance evaluation: team performance	38	25	13[a]
Performance evaluation: balanced scorecard	40	21	19[a]
Decreased ranking			
Performance evaluation: divisional profit	1	7	6
Performance evaluation: budget variance analysis	7	23	16
Formal strategic planning	14	22	8[b]
Budgeting for planning cash flows	18	27	9[a]
Strategic plans developed separate from budgets	23	34	11
Budgeting for planning day-to-day operations	27	39	12[b]
Capital budgeting measures like IRR, payback	29	41	12[a]

All *t*-tests are two-tailed tests of significance.
[a]Significant at the 1% level.
[b]Significant at the 5% level.

A quality-focused management philosophy has been ruling in Finland for
some time now. Quite a few of the new management accounting innovations
are derivates from that philosophy. Lukka and Granlund (1996) also report
on the importance of the quality. Certification to quality standards is emphasized. Different kinds of supplier partnerships are going to be even more
important in the future.

The respondents participating in this study belong to large firms. Lukka
and Granlund (1996) find some support in their study for the statement, that
the larger the unit, the more willing it is to introduce activity-based costing.

Malmi (1996) reports that larger size differentiates ABC users from non-users. Virtanen et al. (1996) also find this to be true in Finland. Large organizations have the time, money and resources for experimenting with new tools. These companies need a lot of capital for running the business, so technology and manufacturing is also emphasized from the strategic point of view.

Finland is a technology-intensive economy. Technology innovations help organizations to achieve their goals in increasing competition. Different kinds of enterprise resource planning (ERP) systems have been implemented or are in the process of being implemented. Also other technologies, like supply chain management (SCM) or customer relationship management (CRM) technologies are going to be emphasized in the future in Finland. Dugdade (1994) also points out the importance of information technology in the U.K. Many of the companies in this sample are technology-driven and use manufacturing techniques like TQM. Different information technology systems provide opportunities to provide information according to needs.

The spread of the firms in terms of industry and size gives possibilities for comparisons. Table 7 shows the most beneficial management accounting practices by different industries. In the forest industry, the most beneficial practices have been traditional financial measures, but the future emphasis is also going to be on non-financial measures like customer satisfaction surveys (performance evaluation) and qualitative measures (performance evaluation). The respondents from the metal industry ranked divisional profit (performance evaluation) and budgeting for controlling costs number one and two respectively; the future emphasis is also going to be on these measures. The only non-financial measure in the top five for the metal industry is qualitative measures (performance evaluation), which is ranked number four at past benefits and also on future emphasis. The respondents in the electronics industry ranked the measures differently. Measures like ROI (performance evaluation), capital budgeting measures like ROI and payback or budget variance analysis are not among the most beneficial measures neither in the past nor in the future. On the other hand, there are measures like non-financial measures (performance evaluation), employee attitudes (performance evaluation) or strategic plans developed together with budgets that are not seen beneficial by forest or metal industry. Some of the measures are seen beneficial by all industries, i.e. variable costing (product costing), budgeting for controlling costs, qualitative measures (performance evaluation) and product profitability analysis.

Table 8 shows classification by the number of employees. In general, the larger the firm, the more relative benefits are derived from the practices.

Table 7. Management Accounting Practices: A Comparison of Most Beneficial Practices Between Industries.

Management Accounting Practice	Relative Benefits Past 3 Years						Relative Future Emphasis Next 3 Years					
	Industry											
	Forest		Metal		Electronics		Forest		Metal		Electronics	
	Mean	Rank	Mean	Rank	Mean	Rank	Mean	Rank	Mean	Rank	Mean	Rank
Performance evaluation: ROI	5.83	1	5.00	5	3.75	26	6.22	1	5.44	10	4.71	26
Performance evaluation: divisional profit	5.59	3	5.94	1	4.75	7	5.12	13	6.00	1	5.00	20
Product costing: variable costing	4.94	6	5.11	3	5.25	1	5.50	8	5.76	5	5.75	3
Capital budgeting measures like ROI, payback	5.61	2	4.94	6	3.50	30	6.00	2	5.33	13	4.43	31
Budgeting for controlling costs	5.44	4	5.44	2	4.63	8	5.61	6	5.89	2	5.75	3
Performance evaluation: non-financial measures	3.61	25	3.11	32	5.13	2	4.71	21	4.88	18	5.25	12
Performance evaluation: employee attitudes	4.11	16	4.35	15	5.00	3	5.17	11	5.50	9	5.88	2
Performance evaluation: qualitative measures	4.89	7	5.06	4	4.75	6	5.83	4	5.78	4	5.38	10
Product profitability analysis	4.67	8	4.39	14	4.88	4	5.88	3	5.65	6	5.75	3
Performance evaluation: budget variance analysis	5.06	5	4.06	18	4.50	11	5.03	14	4.56	27	4.88	22
Long range forecasting	3.53	28	4.50	11	4.75	5	4.50	28	5.17	15	5.50	8
Strategic plans development together with budgets	4.35	13	4.72	8	3.82	23	5.00	17	5.22	14	6.13	1
Product costing: absorption costing	4.28	15	4.61	9	4.63	10	4.88	19	5.81	3	5.25	13
Performance evaluation: customer satisfaction surveys	4.44	12	4.06	20	3.88	22	5.61	15	5.56	8	5.25	14

Table 8. Management Accounting Practices: A Comparison of Most Beneficial Practices by Number of Employees.

Management Accounting Practice	Relative Benefits Past 3 Years								Relative Future Emphasis Next 3 Years							
	Number of employees															
	20–200		201–500		501–1000		>1000		20–200		201–500		501–1000		>1000	
	Mean	Rank	Mean	Rank	Mean	Rank	Mean	Rank	Mean	Rank	Mean	Rank	Mean	Rank	Mean	Rank
Performance evaluation: divisional profit	5.27	4	5.71	1	5.60	1	6.00	1	5.15	12	5.43	7	5.70	3	5.75	9
Product costing: absorption costing	5.58	1	4.70	14	5.30	4	5.31	8	5.64	3	4.64	28	5.50	6	5.92	5
Performance evaluation: ROI	4.69	10	5.31	3	4.90	9	5.75	2	5.21	11	5.46	6	5.00	16	6.42	1
Product profitability analysis	4.21	26	4.42	17	5.60	2	5.38	7	5.07	16	5.83	1	5.90	1	6.31	2
Budgeting for controlling costs	5.43	2	5.50	2	5.20	5	5.38	6	6.00	1	5.36	10	5.50	5	6.08	4
Product costing: variable costing	5.36	3	4.83	10	5.40	3	5.42	4	5.79	2	5.08	15	5.50	7	5.83	7
Capital Budget measures like ROI, payback	4.85	6	4.93	8	4.70	13	5.67	3	4.93	17	5.29	13	5.00	15	6.17	3
Performance evaluation: budget variance analysis	5.09	5	5.07	5	5.11	17	5.42	5	5.13	8	4.57	29	4.50	29	4.92	30
Strategic plans developed with budgets	4.79	8	5.08	4	4.70	14	5.17	9	5.36	7	5.00	17	5.20	9	5.73	10
Performance evaluation: qualitative measures	4.69	11	5.00	7	5.10	8	5.08	10	5.62	4	5.71	2	5.80	2	5.77	8
Performance evaluation: customer satisfaction surveys	4.42	20	4.62	15	4.70	16	4.92	12	5.31	9	5.69	3	5.60	4	5.85	6
Product costing: activity-based costing	4.83	7	4.00	28	3.50	40	3.42	38	5.14	13	5.50	4	4.60	25	5.00	26
Performance evaluation: production processes	4.38	22	5.00	6	5.20	6	4.54	19	5.23	10	5.50	5	5.20	10	5.00	27
Performance evaluation: employee attitudes	4.17	27	4.07	27	4.60	18	4.92	11	5.46	5	5.21	14	5.50	8	5.62	11

Also, the emphasis on future management accounting practices is higher in larger firms. The largest firms (> 1,000 employees) in the sample obtain the most benefits from traditional financial measures and the emphasis is also going to be on those measures in the future. This also applies for the firms with the number of employees between 501 and 1000 except that their future emphasis also includes non-financial measures like qualitative measures (performance evaluation) and customer satisfaction surveys (performance evaluation). Product profitability analysis will be emphasized more in the future regardless of the size of the firm. All respondent groups see budgeting for controlling costs beneficial and it will keep its status also in the future. Non-financial measures like qualitative measures and customer satisfaction surveys will be emphasized even more in the future. The larger firms will no longer emphasize budget variance analysis. Divisional profit in performance evaluation will lose its status by all respondent groups.

CONCLUSIONS

The purpose of this chapter was to describe the relative adoption rates, received benefits and future emphasis of management accounting practices in Finland. All the management accounting variables have been adopted by the majority of the respondents. A common feature for all the categories is even greater future emphasis on highest ranked practices. Also, the relative benefits from the last 3 years and the future emphasis in next 3 years are generally bigger when the size of the firm increases. The increased emphasis on both financial and non-financial measures of all kinds has been reflected already in a 1991 Ernst and Young's study (IQS, 1991).

The three most beneficial practices in management accounting are traditional financial measures including divisional profit in performance evaluation, budgeting for controlling costs and variable costing. A lot of the companies in the survey are investment-intensive so controlling costs is important. The focus on costs may also be explained by the time of the survey; signals of a recession were seen during that time. Future emphasis is on product profitability analysis, budgeting for controlling costs and qualitative measures in performance evaluation. Financial measures are going to be important in the future but it was also seen that greater emphasis is going to be placed on newer practices. The results indicate that Finnish firms put greater emphasis to recently developed non-financial measures than the Australian firms reported by Chenhall and Langfield-Smith (1998).

When compared to other studies done in Europe, the differences in management accounting techniques are not distinct. Shields (1998), Macintosh (1998) and Lukka and Granlund (1998) also point out a certain homogeneity in Europe.

This study has certain limitations. The chosen sample is not random: it focused mainly on three different manufacturing industries and business units belonging to large firms. The findings should be seen as representing these firms and not as generally representative of Finnish firms. Large units are also more likely to be familiar with the latest concepts. Also the terminology in the questionnaire was difficult and the respondents might have been unable to understand some of the variables. Despite these facts, the results of the study provide some perspectives of the management accounting practices used in Finland and the differences between these practices in Finland and in Australia. Finally, the time of the survey is likely to be influencing the results of this survey. In certain economical situation, some of the practices are likely to be emphasized more and therefore further research of the management accounting practices is needed.

ACKNOWLEDGMENT

I am grateful for the valuable comments and suggestions by Professors Juha-Pekka Kallunki and Robert Chenhall.

REFERENCES

Anderson, E. W., Fornell, C., & Lehmann, D. R. (1994). Customer satisfaction, market share, and profitability: Findings from Sweden. *Journal of Marketing Research, 58*, 53–66.

Ask, U., Ax, C., & Jönsson, S. (1996). Cost management in Sweden: From modern to post-modern. In: A. Bhimani (Ed.), *Management accounting: European perspectives* (pp. 199–217). Oxford: Oxford University Press.

Ballas, A., & Venieris, G. (1996). A survey of management accounting practices in Greek firms. In: A. Bhimani (Ed.), *Management accounting: European perspectives* (pp. 123–139). Oxford: Oxford University Press.

Banerjee, J., & Kane, W. (1996). Report on CIMA/JBA survey. *Management Accounting, 74*, 30–37.

Barbato, M. B., Collini, P., & Quagli, A. (1996). Management accounting in Italy. In: A. Bhimani (Ed.), *Management accounting: European perspectives* (pp. 140–163). Oxford: Oxford University Press.

Bhimani, A. (1994). Monitoring performance measures in UK firms. *Management Accounting (UK), 72*, 34–36.

Bhimani, A. (1996). *Management accounting: European perspectives.* Oxford: Oxford University Press.

Boons, A. N. A. M., Roozen, R. A., & Weerd de, R. J. (1994). Kosteninformatie in de Nederlandse Industrie. In: *Relevantie, methoden en ontwikkelingen.* Rotterdam: Coopers & Lybrand.

Brancato, C. K. (1995). *New performance measures – A research report.* Report no. 1118-95-RR. New York, NY: The Conference Board.

Brierley, J. A., Cowton, C. J., & Drury, C. (2001). Research into product costing practice: A European perspective. *European Accounting Review, 10,* 215–256.

Bromwich, M., & Bhimani, A. (1994). *Management accounting: Pathways to progress.* London: The Chartered Institute of Management Accountants.

Bruggeman, W., Slagmulder, R., & Waeytens, D. (1996). Management accounting changes: The Belgian experience. In: A. Bhimani (Ed.), *Management accounting: European perspectives* (pp. 1–30). Oxford: Oxford University Press.

Bunce, P., Fraser, R., & Woodcock, L. (1995). Advanced budgeting: A journal to advanced management systems. *Management Accounting Research, 6,* 253–266.

Chenhall, R., & Langfield-Smith, K. (1998). Adoption and benefits of management accounting practices: An Australian study. *Management Accounting Research, 9,* 1–19.

Cornelius, P., Schwab, K., & Porter, M. E. (2002). IMD World Competitiveness Report. IMD, Lausanne.

De Meyer, A., Nakane, J., Miller, J., & Ferdows, K. (1989). Flexibility: The next competitive battle the manufacturing futures survey. *Strategic Management Journal, 10,* 135–144.

Dugdade, D. (1994). Theory and practice: The views of CIMA and students. *Management Accounting (UK), 72,* 56–59.

Ekholm, B-G., & Wallin, J. (2000). Is the annual budget really dead? *The European Accounting Review, 9,* 519–539.

Fisher, J. (1995). Use of nonfinancial performance measures. In: S. M. Young (Ed.), *Readings in management accounting* (pp. 329–335). Englewood Cliffs, NJ: Prentice-Hall.

Groot, T. L. C. M. (1996). Managing costs in Netherlands: Past theory. In: A. Bhimani (Ed.), *Management accounting: European perspectives* (pp. 164–179). Oxford: Oxford University Press.

Human Development Report (2001). *Making new technologies work for human development.* Oxford: Oxford University Press for the United Nations Development Programme (UNDP).

Innes, J., & Mitchell, F. (1995). A survey of activity-based costing in the UK's largest companies. *Management Accounting Research, 6,* 137–153.

Institute of Management Accountants (1996). *Are corporate America's financial measurements outdated?* Montvale, NJ: IMA.

IQS (1991). *International Quality Study: The definitive study of the best international quality management practises.* Cleveland, OH: Ernst & Young and American Quality Foundation.

Israelsen, P., Anderson, M., Rohde, C., & Sorensen, P. E. (1996). Management accounting in Denmark: Theory and practice. In: A. Bhimani (Ed.), *Management accounting: European perspectives* (pp. 31–53). Oxford: Oxford University Press.

Ittner, C. D., & Larcker, D. F. (1998). Are nonfinancial measures leading indicators of financial performance? An analysis of customer satisfaction. *Journal of Accounting Research, 36,* 1–35.

Joye, M. P., & Blayney, P. I. (1990). Cost and Management Accounting Practices in Australian Manufacturing Companies: Survey Results. Monograph no. 7, The Accounting and Finance Foundation, University of Sydney.

Kaplan, R. S., & Norton, D. P. (1996). *The balanced scorecard*. Boston: Harvard University Press.

Laitinen, E. K. (1995). Management Accounting Systems (MAS) in three types of Finnish firms: Challenges for management accounting. *Finnish Journal of Business Economics, 46*, 391–414.

Lebas, M. (1996). Management accounting practice in France. In: A. Bhimani (Ed.), *Management accounting: European perspectives* (pp. 74–99). Oxford: Oxford University Press.

Lukka, K., & Granlund, M. (1996). Cost accounting in Finland: Current practice and trends of development. *The European Accounting Review, 5*, 1–28.

Lukka, K., & Granlund, M. (1998). It's a small world of management accounting practices. *Journal of Management Accounting Research, 10*, 153–179.

Lynch, R. L., & Cross, K. F. (1992). *Measure up – Yardsticks for continuous improvement*. Cambridge, MA: Basil Blackwell.

Macintosh, N. B. (1998). Management accounting in Europe: A view from Canada. *Management Accounting Research, 9*, 495–500.

Malmi, T. (1996). ABC in Finnish metal and engineering industries. *The Finnish Journal of Business Economics, 45*, 243–264.

Malmi, T. (1999). Activity-based costing diffusion across organizations: An exploratory empirical analysis of Finnish firms. *Accounting, Organization and Society, 24*, 649–672.

McKinnon, S. M., & Bruns, W. J. (1992). Management information and accounting information: What do managers want. *Advances in Management Accounting, 1*, 55–80.

Mendoza, C., & Bescos, P-L. (2001). An explanatory model of managers' information needs: Implications for management accounting. *The European Accounting Review, 10*, 257–289.

Miller, J. G., De Meyer, A., & Nakane, J. (1992). *Benchmarking global manufacturing*. Homewood IL: Irwin.

Roberts, A. (1995). Management accounting in France. *Management Accounting (U.K.), March*, 44–46.

Shields, M. D. (1998). Management accounting practices in Europe: A perspective from the States. *Management Accounting Research, 9*, 501–513.

Virtanen, K., Malmi, T., Vaivio, J., & Kasanen, E. (1996). Drivers of management accounting in Finland. In: A. Bhimani (Ed.), *Management accounting: European perspectives* (pp. 54–73). Oxford: Oxford University Press.

WEF. (2002). *Global competitiveness report*. New York: Oxford University Press for the World Economic Forum.

Wijewardena, H., & De Zoysa, A. (1999). A comparative analysis of management accounting practices in Australia and Japan: An empirical investigation. *The International Journal of Accounting, 34*, 49–70.

INVESTMENTS IN HUMAN CAPITAL IN DIFFERENT INSTITUTIONAL ENVIRONMENTS

Juha-Pekka Kallunki, Pasi Karjalainen and Minna Martikainen

ABSTRACT

This chapter investigates the proportion of labor costs that represents investments in human capital, and the rate of amortization of this asset in all six countries for which the required data are available in the Compustat Global Vantage database. The sample includes countries with different financial and legal systems, which enables us to investigate how the growth and depreciation rates of human capital and the resulting human capital asset ratio differ in different institutional environments. The results indicate that the estimated proportion of labor expenses that represents investments in human capital is large in the so-called common-law countries with a market-based financial system. On the other hand, the depreciation rate of the estimated human capital assets is lower in these countries. The results, therefore, indicate that the human capital assets are high in equity-oriented financial reporting environments. The results also indicate that the estimated ratios of the human capital asset to market value of equity are reasonably related to firm characteristics that are

Advances in International Accounting
Advances in International Accounting, Volume 18, 121–140
ISSN: 0897-3660/doi:10.1016/S0897-3660(05)18006-4

hypothesized to be determinants of the human capital asset ratios. Finally, these results remain the same in different industries.

INTRODUCTION

As pointed out by Amir and Lev (1996), among others, investments in intangible assets such as brand development, research and development or human capital are of crucial importance for firms in the knowledge-based economy. Consequently, valuation of intangible assets is an important issue from equity holder's point of view, too. There is a large body of literature investigating the stock market valuation of firms' investments in intangible assets. Bublitz and Ettredge (1989), for instance, found that the slope co-efficient of regressing stock returns on R&D costs is positive suggesting that stock market values R&D expenditures as an asset rather than a cost. Similar results are reported by Chaucin and Hirschey (1993) and Green, Stark and Thomas (1996), among others. Ballester, Livnat, and Sinha (1998) use Ohlson's (1995) valuation approach to estimate the proportion of a firm's labor expenses that the market views as an investment in human capital.

This chapter investigates the proportion of labor costs that represents investments in human capital, and the rate of depreciation of this asset by using the Compustat Global Vantage data from all six countries in which firms voluntarily or obligatorily report labor costs in their published financial statements. Requirements for financial reporting are set by the legal and financial environment of the country. In the so-called common-law countries with the market-based financial system, financial reporting is aimed at providing the information needed by equity-investors. In these countries, the growth/depreciation rates of the human capital can be assumed to be high/low, because investors have broad information set available for their decision making. The uniform Compustat industry sector code is used to investigate the human capital in different industries aside from the country-specific effects. The economic relevance of the estimated human capital is assessed by examining its firm-specific determinants. The chapter contributes to the literature that investigates the market valuation of intangible assets, especially the paper by Ballester et al. (1998). While Ballester et al. (1998) investigate the market valuation of firms' labor expenditures in U.S. where some firms voluntarily disclose these costs in their financial reports; the current chapter investigates the degree and determinants of the human capital in different countries with different financial reporting environment.

HUMAN CAPITAL AND ITS DETERMINANTS

Valuing Human Capital in Ohlson (1995) Framework

Earlier studies estimating the value of human capital have mainly been focusing on the value of individual employees to the firm. For instance, Lev and Schwartz (1971) approximated the value of human capital as the present value of earnings of all employees for the remaining active service life. Flamholtz (1971) improved this approach by allowing the possibility of employees' career movements within the firm or the possibility of employees leaving the firm before retirement or death.

Jaggi and Lau (1974) developed a stochastic model that used groups of employees as the basis for the valuation of human capital. This approach is based on the fact that it is much easier to predict patterns of group behavior than those of individual behavior. More recently, Rosett (2000) used data from union contracts to estimate labor stock for firms with a relatively large fraction of unionized work force. He defines the firm's labor stock as the present value of the expected cost of compensating employees.

Ballester et al. (1998) used an equity valuation model to estimate the growth and depreciation rates of the human capital. This approach is motivated by the literature that investigates the stock market valuation of R&D expenditures. For instance, Hirschey and Weygandt (1985) estimated the market valuation and the amortization rate for advertising and R&D expenditures. They found that advertising and R&D expenditures have a positive impact on a firm's Tobin Q (ratio of market value and replacement cost of assets) suggesting that the market treats these expenditures as intangible capital investments.

As Ballester et al. (1998) points out, the equity valuation model based on the so-called residual income can be used to explicitly measure the investments in the human capital asset and the depreciation rate of this asset. Residual income valuation is based on the assumption that a firm's market value is given by the present value of its expected dividends. Assuming the clean surplus in accounting, Ohlson (1995) shows that its market value can also be computed as the sum of its reported book value and the infinite sum of discounted residual income as follows:

$$\text{MV}_t = \text{BV}_t \sum_{i=1}^{\infty} E\left[\frac{E_{t+i}^{\text{R}} - r_{\text{f}}\text{BV}_{t+i-1}}{(1 + r_{\text{f}})^i}\right] \tag{1}$$

where BV_t is the book value (as reported) at time t, E [.] the expectations based on information at time t, E_t^R the reported earnings for period t and r_f the cost of equity capital (risk-free interest rate given risk neutrality).

It can be demonstrated that under additional assumptions of risk neutrality and an autoregressive structure on the time series of residual income, the market value (MV) is a function of current book value (BV) and current abnormal earnings (see Ohlson, 1995 and also Myers, 1999) as follows:

$$MV_t = \alpha_1 BV_t + \alpha_2(E_t^R - r_f BV_{t-1}) + \gamma v_t \tag{2}$$

Abnormal earnings are calculated as current earnings minus the risk-free rate times the beginning of period book value. The variable v_t captures information other than that pertaining to abnormal earnings, and α and γ are functions of the risk-free rate and the time series properties of abnormal earnings and other information.

Suppose a fraction β (where $0 < \beta < 1$) of the labor expenses (w_t) in each period represents increase in the human capital of the firm.

Moreover, it is assumed that labor expenses grow at a certain rate of g percent every year, such that $w_t = (1 + g)w_{t-1}$. Further, if the rate of depreciation for this asset is δ (where $0 < \delta < 1$), then the value of the human capital asset at the end of period t (L_t) is given by the following:

$$L_t = \beta w_t + (1 - \delta)L_{t-1} \tag{3}$$

After incorporating the value of L_{t-1}, L_t can be written as

$$L_t = \beta w_t \left[1 + \left(\frac{1-\delta}{1+g}\right) + \left(\frac{1-\delta}{1+g}\right)^2 + \left(\frac{1-\delta}{1+g}\right)^3 + \cdots + \left(\frac{1-\delta}{1+g}\right)^t\right]$$

$$= \beta w_t \left(\frac{1+g}{\delta+g}\right) \equiv \beta \phi w_t \tag{4}$$

where the second equality is the sum of the series as t approaches infinity and ϕ is defined as $(1 + g)/(\delta + g)$.

Similarly, for large t,

$$L_{t-1} = \beta \phi w_{t-1} \tag{5}$$

Reported earnings (E_t^R) are based on a full expensing of labor costs. Alternatively, an accounting system that capitalizes the investment in human capital will report earnings (E_t), which, after making adjustments for additions to and depreciation of the human capital asset, are given by

$$E_t = E_t^R + \beta w_t - \delta L_{t-1} \tag{6}$$

The accounting system will show book value of equity that is equal to the full-expensing book value plus the human capital asset L_t. By inserting these adjusted values (under capitalization of some labor costs) of earnings and book values in Eq. (2) we get the following:

$$MV_t = \alpha_1(BV_t + L_t) + \alpha_2(E_t^R + \beta w_t - \delta L_{t-1} - r_f(BV_{t-1} + L_{t-1})) + \gamma v_t \quad (7)$$

Eqs. (2) and (7) represent valuation equations which are based on two different accounting systems – one that has full expensing of labor costs, and another that capitalizes some of these costs. Both these valuation equations will provide the same value if each follows the clean surplus relationship. Moreover, it is assumed that the abnormal earnings follow the Markovian process. However, the two systems may have different valuation consequences if some further assumptions about the earnings generating process are made to obtain less complicated valuation equation.

In particular, the Markovian process assumes that the expected abnormal earnings in the current period are equal to abnormal earnings in the prior period multiplied by a persistence coefficient. This particular coefficient is assumed to be less than one. Under full expensing of labor costs book value is consistently understated. Moreover, book value will be more grossly understated to the extent that the investment in human capital grows over time. Therefore, under full expensing, abnormal earnings are actually expected to increase period by period, instead of declining as assumed by the Markovian process. The accounting system that is based on capitalization of some labor costs is likely to generate abnormal earnings that better fit the underlying Markovian assumptions for valuation process. This holds at least until the human capital asset stops growing.

The application of the valuation equation that is based on a partial capitalization of labor expenses for a subset of firms that experienced a positive growth in labor expenses is described. Such firms can be assumed to be at the stage where the investment in human capital is growing.

Assume that the dynamics of the human capital asset can be described as in Eqs. (3) and (4). After substituting the values of L_t and L_{t-1} and some manipulation, Eq. (7) can be written as follows:

$$\begin{aligned}
MV_t &= \alpha_1 BV_t + \alpha_2(E_t^R - r_f BV_{t-1}) + (\alpha_1\beta\phi + \alpha_2\beta)w_t \\
&\quad - (\alpha_2\delta\beta\phi + r_f\alpha_2\beta\phi)w_{t-1} + \gamma v_t \\
&\equiv A_0' + A_1 BV_t + A_2(E_t^R - r_f BV_{t-1}) + A_3 w_t + A_4 w_{t-1} \quad (8)
\end{aligned}$$

where

$$A_0' \equiv \gamma v_t$$
$$A_1 \equiv \alpha_1$$
$$A_2 \equiv \alpha_2$$
$$A_3 \equiv (\alpha_1\beta\phi + \alpha_2\beta) = (A_1\beta\phi + A_2\beta)$$
$$A_4 \equiv -A_2\beta\phi[\delta + r_f]$$

and

$$\phi \equiv (1 + g)/(\delta + g)$$

The parameters of interest in the above relationship are A_1, A_2, β (the investment portion of labor expenditures) and δ (the amortization rate for human capital). Although the above relationship is linear in the dependent variables, it is not linear in these parameters. Therefore, the non-linear regression technique is needed to estimate the model.

Firm-Specific Factors Affecting the Human Capital Asset

It can be hypothesized that there are certain firm-specific factors that affect the proportion of labor costs that is regarded as investments in human capital by the stock market. In other words, the estimated human capital is likely to be affected by certain economic characteristics of the firm. Ballester et al. (1998) suggest that the following firm characteristics should be linked to the ratio of the human capital asset to the market value of equity.

1. *Average salary* (the ratio of labor expense to the number of employees). Firms employing quality and skilled labor are likely to invest more in training and developing their human capital, and a skilled labor force commands higher salaries. Therefore, this type of firms should have higher ratios of human capital to market value, and it can be hypothesized that there exists a positive relationship between average salary and the estimated human capital asset.
2. *Labor intensity* (the ratio of labor expense to sales). The labor-intensive firms can be assumed to invest intensively in retention and training of personal. It is, therefore, hypothesized that there exists positive relation between the ratio of labor expense to sales and human capital.
3. *Operating uncertainty* (the standard deviation of the return on equity measured over the sample period). It is hypothesized that there exists a positive relationship between operating uncertainty, measured by the

standard deviation of the return on equity, and the ratio of human capital to market value. This is because firms are expected to make larger investments in human capital in order to prepare employees to fast changes in business environment.

4. *Profitability* (return on asset). It is hypothesized that profitable firms do not need to make investments in human capital. Therefore, the negative relation is expected to exist between investments in human capital and profitability measured by the return on assets (income before extraordinary items divided by total assets).

5. *Growth* (the average growth rate of sales during the sample period). It is hypothesized that there would exist a negative relation between the growth and the investments in human capital. This is because it is expected that a growing firm needs to have all its available resources to sustain its growth, and no extra assets are assumed to be used in human capital investments.

6. *Size* (the log of total assets). It is hypothesized that there would exist a negative relation between size of the firm and the investments in human capital. This is because it is assumed that larger firms do not need to have employees to carry out more than the limited amount of tasks.

Factors Creating International Differences in the Human Capital Asset

It can be hypothesized that there are certain country-specific factors that are likely to influence the estimated human capital asset. These factors include the financial and legal systems of the country. Countries are often classified into bank- and market-based financial systems based on the relative importance of the stock market and banking sector in the financing of firms (see, for instance, Demirgüç-Kunt & Maksimovic, 2002). In a market-based financial system, firms have to disclose accounting and other value-relevant information to get the financing from the public stock market. In a bank-based system, firms can finance their investments through private negotiations with banks, and they do not necessarily need to disclose additional financial information except that required by the legislation. Therefore, it can be assumed that the firms need for disclosing labor-related information is greater in a market-based system than in a bank-based system. It is, however, an empirical question as to what extent these differences in disclosing the labor-related costs create differences in a degree of the human capital assets in different countries. This is due to the fact that stock prices should reflect all value-relevant information in an efficient stock market regardless of the financial system of the country.

The U.K. and the U.S. are typical examples of countries with market-based financial system, whereas Germany is an example of a country with a clear bank-based system.

Ball, Kothari, and Robin (2000) and Leuz, Nanda, and Wysocki (2003), among others, argue that the information content of financial reports across countries is affected by certain institutional factors. The most important institutional variable causing differences in accounting income across countries is the legal system. In the so-called code-law countries, setting and enforcement occur under codified law in which the role of governmental processes is vital. In the so-called common-law countries, the role of the market is more important. In common-law countries the shareholders' point of view comes first, while in code-law countries the other stakeholders' needs are more important. Given these differences in the legal environments of countries, it can be assumed that the value-relevance of labor-related costs is greater in common-law countries than in code-law countries.

RESEARCH DESIGN

The Data

The sample consists of all active industrial firms from six countries, i.e. Germany, Finland, France, Switzerland, the U.K. and the U.S. The sample covers all firms in which the necessary data of labor costs are available for a 9-year or longer period during the sample period from 1991 to 2001. All variables used in the study are retrieved from the Compustat Global Vantage Database. The Compustat data item 'Labor and related expense' are used as a labor costs variable for the U.S. firms where the staff expense is not reported separately by the company but is reported in a note to the financial statements. The Compustat data item 'Staff expense-total' is used as a labor costs variable for other countries because the staff expense is reported separately by the company on the financial statements.

The parameters of the human capital valuation model are estimated for each firm in non-linear time-series regressions. These estimates are then used to calculate the ratios of human capital asset to the market value of equity for each firm. The economic relevance of the resulting human capital asset ratios is then tested by using the sample of whole panel data and the sample of different countries and industries. The observations that are higher than 95% decile or lower than 5% decile are eliminated to exclude outliers.

Finally, the observations where the ratios of human capital asset to the market value of equity exceed 0.9 are deleted.

Methods and Preliminary Data Analysis

Following Ballester et al. (1998), this paper uses the Ohlson (1995) framework to estimate the proportion of labor costs that represents investments in human capital and the rate of amortization of this asset. Eq. (8) in the previous section is estimated in the following form in time-series regressions (see Ballester et al., 1998):

$$\frac{MV_t}{BV_{t-1}} = A_0 + A_1 \frac{BV_t}{BV_{t-1}} + A_2 \frac{E_t}{BV_{t-1}} + A_3 \frac{w_t}{BV_{t-1}} + A_4 \frac{w_{t-1}}{BV_{t-1}} \qquad (9)$$

where MV_t is the market value of equity in the end of the year t, BV_{t-1} is the book value of equity in the end of year $t-1$, E_t is the earnings for year t, w_t is the extent of the labor costs in year t, and w_{t-1} is the extent of the labor costs in year $t - 1$.

In addition, the following non-linear dependencies exist between the slopes ($A_0 - A_4$) of the model as described in the previous section:

$$A_0 \equiv \alpha_0$$
$$A_1 \equiv \alpha_1$$
$$A_2 \equiv \alpha_2$$
$$A_3 \equiv \alpha_1 \beta \phi + \alpha_2 \beta$$
$$A_4 \equiv -\alpha_2 \beta \phi (\delta + r_f)$$

and

$$\phi \equiv \frac{1 + g}{\delta + g}$$

The average growth rate in labor expenses (g) is calculated as the average growth rate over the estimation period. The risk-free interest rate is calculated as the average value of 1-month short-term interest rate over the period of 1991–2001 in each country. The parameters of model (9) are estimated by using the non-linear estimation procedure. The parameters β and δ are restricted to fall between 0 and 0.5. The estimated parameters are used to calculate the value of the human capital (HU) and the ratio of the human capital asset to the market value of equity (HU/MV) for each firm-year observation in the period 1991–2001 as follows:

$$HU_{it} = \beta_i \delta_i w_{it} \tag{10}$$

$$\frac{HU_{it}}{MV_{it}} = \frac{\beta_i \delta_i w_{it}}{MV_{it}} \tag{11}$$

The ratio of the human capital asset to the market value of equity (HU/MV) describes the importance of the human capital asset to the market valuation of the firm i.e. it tells how investments in human capital are reflected in the market value of the firm. If the value of the ratio is low, the stock market considers the human capital as a value-increasing activity and vice versa. In other words, if the human capital is expected to produce future benefits for the firm, these expectations should be reflected also as an increasing market value of equity and vice versa.

The study uses the firm-specific mixed panel estimation procedure to investigate if the different firm-specific characteristics can be used to explain the ratio of the human capital asset to the market value of equity.

The estimation procedure includes the ARMA (1,1) model to consider the possible first-order autocorrelation of dependent variable. At first, each firm-specific characteristic is regressed separately against the ratio of the human capital asset to the market value of equity. The model is estimated for whole panel data, i.e. over different years and countries as follows:

$$\frac{HU_{it}}{MV_{it}} = \mu + \alpha_i + \beta_1 X_{it} + \varepsilon_{it} \tag{12}$$

where X is the following firm-specific characteristics:

WATEMP the labor cost divided by the number of employees, LABORINT the labor cost divided by the sales, ROA the income before extraordinary items divided by 2-year average of total asset, Log(assets) the log of total assets, Std. Dev. ROE the standard deviation of ratio ROE calculated over period 1991–2001 where ROE is income before extraordinary items divided by the book value of equity, Msalesgrowth the average growth rate of sales over the whole period 1991–2001. μ an intercept term, α_i the firm-specific random effect, β_1 the estimated regression coefficient of the X_{it} and ε_t an error term.

The effect of the firm-specific characteristic on the ratio of the human capital asset to the market value of equity is also investigated by estimating the model where all independent variables are in the same model. The model is estimated for both the whole panel data and different countries as follows:

$$\frac{HU_{it}}{MV_{it}} = \mu + \alpha_i + \beta_1 WATEMP_{it} + \beta_2 LABORINT_{it} + \beta_3 ROA_{it}$$

$$+ \beta_4 Log(assets)_{it} + \beta_5 Std. Dev. ROE_{it} + \beta_6 Msalesgrowth_{it} + \varepsilon_{it}$$

$$(13)$$

where the dependent and independent variables are the same as described in Eq. (12), μ is an intercept term, α_i the firm-specific random effect, β_i are the estimated regression coefficients, and ε_t is an error term.

The industry-specific regression coefficients are estimated to investigate how different firm-specific characteristics are associated with the ratio of human capital asset to the market value of equity in different industries. The following model is estimated:

$$\frac{HU_{it}}{MV_{it}} = \mu + \alpha_i + \sum \gamma_k I_k WATEMP_{it} + \sum \gamma_k I_k LABORINT_{it}$$

$$+ \sum \gamma_k I_k ROA_{it} + \sum \gamma_k I_k Log(assets)_{it}$$

$$+ \sum \gamma_k I_k Std. Dev. ROE_{it}$$

$$+ \gamma_k I_k Msalesgrowth_{it} + \varepsilon_{it} \qquad (14)$$

where the dependent and independent variables are the same as described in Eq. (12), subscript k refers to the industry, γ_k refers to the industry-specific regression coefficients for the different firm-specific variables, I is an industry dummy variable taking a value of one for industry k, zero otherwise, μ an intercept term, α_i the firm-specific random effect, and ε_t is an error term.

As a preliminary data analysis, Table 1 reports country-specific descriptive statistics of the variables used in the empirical analysis. The results indicate that the human capital asset constitutes an essential part of the market value of firms in all countries. The estimated proportion of human capital asset is more than 20% of the market value of equity in all countries. In the U.S., where the firms are allowed to report labor costs voluntarily, the average value of the ratio of human capital asset to the market value of equity is the lowest. The highest means of this ratio are reported in Germany and Switzerland. As a whole the preliminary results indicate that the estimated proportion of labor costs that represents investments in human capital is large in all countries but there are no distinct differences in the intensity of human capital investments or the stock market valuation of the human capital asset in different countries.

Table 1.   Descriptive Statistics of Variables for Sample
Period – 1991–2001.

Variable	Statistics	Countries						
		Germany	Finland	France	Switzerland	U.K.	U.S.	All
HU/MV	Mean	0.283	0.244	0.237	0.286	0.263	0.224	0.255
	Min	0.000	0.000	0.000	0.000	0.000	0.000	0.000
	Max	0.898	0.840	0.875	0.898	0.854	0.899	0.899
WATEMP	Mean	42.430	33.903	33.887	55.674	30.266	51.005	42.516
	Min	20.557	17.450	20.521	29.229	12.199	10.274	10.274
	Max	68.398	47.114	58.168	85.448	46.342	82.773	85.448
LABORINT	Mean	0.236	0.222	0.235	0.273	0.215	0.316	0.258
	Min	0.050	0.116	0.108	0.108	0.110	0.129	0.050
	Max	0.434	0.448	0.426	0.438	0.373	0.571	0.571
ROA	Mean	4.185	5.382	3.389	4.372	7.369	7.680	5.706
	Min	−3.836	−0.301	−0.979	−3.287	−1.412	−1.852	−3.953
	Max	12.839	12.581	8.424	12.559	13.954	16.819	16.820
Log(assets)	Mean	13.028	13.314	14.014	13.492	13.621	14.441	13.735
	Min	7.343	10.317	11.162	11.904	9.825	9.787	7.343
	Max	18.286	16.615	18.310	15.115	16.854	17.706	18.310
Std.Dev.ROE	Mean	9.861	9.173	6.557	8.383	7.712	9.275	8.795
	Min	1.726	4.196	1.533	2.433	1.648	2.070	1.533
	Max	59.140	32.959	16.781	22.409	33.717	29.619	59.140
Msalesgrowth	Mean	0.088	0.121	0.106	0.082	0.110	0.123	0.108
	Min	0.002	0.038	0.048	−0.033	0.042	0.027	−0.033
	Max	0.229	0.342	0.283	0.239	0.164	0.279	0.342

HU/MV is the ratio of the estimated human capital asset to the market value of equity.
WATEMP is the ratio of labor expense to the number of employees.
LABORINT is the ratio of labor expense to the sales.
ROA is the income before extraordinary items divided by the average of most recent two years
of assets.
Log(assets) is the log of total assets.
Std.Dev.ROE is the standard deviation of return on equity measured over whole sample period.
Msalesgrowth is the average growth rate of sales during the whole sample period.

EMPIRICAL RESULTS

Table 2 reports the results of estimating the non-linear time-series regressions as described in model (9). The estimated proportion of labor costs that
represents investments in human capital, β, and the estimated depreciation
rate of the human capital, δ, from these regressions will be used to calculate

Table 2. Non-Linear Regression Results Based on Time-Series Data (Model 9).

Variable	Statistics	Country					
		Germany	Finland	France	Switzerland	U.K.	U.S.
Intercept (α_0) (A_1)	Mean	−0.645	−1.147	0.839	−0.363	−0.754	−1.550
	Median	−0.221	−0.543	0.338	−0.149	−0.419	−0.589
	Min	−119.615	−15.782	−44.988	−11.825	−10.736	−72.973
	Max	19.231	6.534	33.085	10.995	4.951	13.057
Book value (α_1) (A_2)	Mean	1.456	1.283	0.881	0.652	0.858	1.396
	Median	0.353	0.559	0.453	0.496	0.572	1.037
	Min	−20.036	−5.827	−19.138	−2.997	−2.495	−11.751
	Max	107.874	17.541	18.327	5.784	5.085	50.801
Earnings (α_2)	Mean	4.976	5.363	5.872	5.780	5.646	6.834
	Median	1.497	2.524	4.482	4.941	4.193	3.667
	Min	−76.610	−19.148	−32.042	−0.912	−3.544	−84.783
	Max	216.844	56.230	71.220	22.644	46.051	72.612
Beta (β)	Mean	0.284	0.134	0.245	0.286	0.325	0.291
	Median	0.424	0.061	0.118	0.417	0.500	0.327
	Min	0.000	0.000	0.000	0.000	0.000	0.000
	Max	0.500	0.500	0.500	0.500	0.500	0.500
Delta (δ)	Mean	0.145	0.180	0.150	0.189	0.128	0.179
	Median	0.000	0.015	0.000	0.046	0.000	0.012
	Min	0.000	0.000	0.000	0.000	0.000	0.000
	Max	0.500	0.500	0.500	0.500	0.500	0.500
N		893	141	311	236	415	805

α_1 (A_1) is the coefficient of book value of equity.
α_2 (A_2) is the earnings valuation coefficient.
Beta (β) is the proportion of current labor costs that represents investment in the human capital asset of a firm.
Delta (δ) is the rate of depreciation in the human capital asset of a firm.

the amount of the human capital asset for each firm. As predicted, the signs of the estimated slope coefficients of earnings, α_2, are positive in all countries. The estimated proportion of labor costs that represents investments in human capital, β, varies across countries. The highest βs are reported in the U.K. and U.S., indicating that a relatively large proportion of labor costs is regarded as investments in human capital in countries that can be described as common-law countries with a market-based financial system.

The results reported in Table 2 also indicate that, in all countries, the estimated depreciation rate of the human capital asset, δ, is smaller than the proportion of labor costs that represents investments in the human capital,

β. This means that the human capital asset increases faster than it decreases. In the U.K., which is a clear common-law country with a market-based financial system, the estimated δ gets the lowest (0.13) and the estimated β gets the highest (0.33) value of all countries in the sample. This indicates that the human capital asset of the British firms increases clearly faster than it depreciates. These results are consistent with Hirschey and Weygandt (1985) who report a depreciation rate of 10–20% for research and development costs, but are clearly smaller than those reported by Ballester et al. (1998) who found an average depreciation rate of 34% for human capital.

Table 3 reports the results of testing whether the estimated growth and depreciation rates of the human capital, i.e. the estimated β and δ differ across countries. The numbers reported in the table are the values of the t-test statistics for testing whether the sample means of the estimated β and δ coefficients are significantly different in different countries. The results reported in Panel B of Table 3 confirm those reported in Table 2. The mean values of the estimated βs are significantly different in different countries suggesting that the proportion of current labor costs that represent investment in human capital differs across countries. To illustrate, the results reported in Table 2 indicate that the estimated growth rate in human capital is the highest for the British firms (the mean β equals to 0.325), and the results reported in panel A of Table 3 confirm that the differences in the growth rates between the British firms and the firms from other countries are statistically significant. Panel B of Table 3 also reports the results of testing whether the estimated depreciation rates of human capital asset, δ, are significantly different across countries. The results indicate that the estimated δs are significantly different across countries in many cases, but the differences are not as clear as they were in the case of the estimated βs. It, therefore, seems that the human capital assets grows at clearly different rates, but vanishes about at the same rate in different countries.

Table 4 reports the results of investigating, whether the different firm-specific characteristics are related to the ratio of human capital asset to the market value of equity. The signs of the estimated coefficients are as expected, and the statistically significant slopes are reported for the average salary, labor intensity and profitability. These results indicate that the estimated human capital asset makes economic sense, because it is reasonably related to the firm characteristics that can be assumed to be the determinants of the human capital asset. The positive relation between the average salary and the ratio of human capital asset to the market value of equity indicates that firms that employ quality skill labor are likely to invest more in training and developing their human capital. The positive relation between the ratio of

Table 3. Results of Testing whether Mean Values for Estimated Growth Rates (β) and Depreciation Rates (δ) in Table 2 Differ across Countries.

Country	Finland	France	Switzerland	U.K.	U.S.
Panel A: t-Values for Beta Coefficients					
Germany	9.74	2.67	−0.08	−3.11	−0.62
	(0.001)*	(0.008)*	(0.935)	(0.002)*	(0.534)
Finland		−5.94	−7.66	−11.14	−10.23
		(0.001)*	(0.001)*	(0.001)*	(0.001)*
France			−2.11	−4.86	−3.12
			(0.035)*	(0.001)*	(0.002)*
Switzerland				−2.22	−0.33
				(0.027)	(0.740)
U.K.					2.71
					(0.007)*
Panel B: t-Values for Delta Coefficients					
Germany	−1.78	−0.39	−2.76	1.37	−3.23
	(0.075)	(0.699)	(0.006)*	(0.170)	(0.001)*
Finland		1.30	−0.37	2.42	0.05
		(0.195)	(0.712)	(0.016)*	(0.963)
France			−1.99	1.42	−1.94
			(0.047)*	(0.156)	(0.052)
Switzerland				3.46	0.60
				(0.001)*	(0.548)
U.K.					−4.11
					(0.001)*

The mean differences of Beta and Delta coefficients are compared between two countries, one at a time, and *t*-values for the null hypothesis that the variance across two countries are equal, are as reported.

The *p*-values are presented in parentheses below the *t*-values.

*Represents the mean differences of Beta and Delta coefficients that are statistically significant at the 5% level or better.

labor intensiveness and the ratio of human capital asset to the market value indicates that the labor-intensive firms invest intensively in retention and training of personnel. The negative relation between the profitability of the firm and the ratio of human capital asset to the market value reveals that the profitable firms do not necessarily need to invest heavily in the human capital.

When all independent variables are included into the same model, the signs of the estimated coefficients for the average salary, labor intensity and

Table 4. Regression Results Based on Firm-Specific Mixed Panel Estimation Procedure (Models 12 and 13).

Variable	Exp sign	Intercept	(1) WATEMP	(2) LABORINT	(3) ROA	(4) Log(asset)	(5) Std.Dev.ROE	(6) Msales growth	N	−2 res log likelihood
Eq. (12): HU/MV $= \mu + \alpha + \beta_1 X + \varepsilon$										
1	+	0.235 (0.001)*	0.002 (0.009)*						918	−1331.3
2	+	0.167 (0.001)*		0.537 (0.001)*					918	−1353.2
3	−	0.353 (0.001)*			−0.008 (0.001)*				918	−1355.3
4	−/+	0.464 (0.001)*				−0.012 (0.176)			918	−1331.7
5	−/+	0.273 (0.001)*					0.003 (0.136)		919	−1329.5
6	−	0.318 (0.001)*						−0.107 (0.752)	919	−1337.4
Eq. (13): HU/MV $= \mu + \alpha + \beta_1 \text{WATEMP} + \beta_2 \text{LABORINT} + \beta_3 \text{ROA} + \beta_4 \text{Log(asset)} + \beta_5 \text{Std.Dev.ROE} + \beta_6 \text{Msalesgrowth} + \varepsilon$										
All		0.443 (0.001)*	0.002 (0.002)*	0.369 (0.004)*	−0.008 (0.001)*	−0.021 (0.02)*	0.002 (0.395)	−0.063 (0.858)	915	−1348.3

WATEMP is the ratio of labor expense to the number of employees.

LABORINT is the ratio of labor expense to the sales.

ROA is income before extraordinary items divided by the average of assets in most recent 2 years.

Log(assets) is the log of total assets.

Std.Dev.ROE is the standard deviation of return on equity measured over whole sample period.

Msalesgrowth is the average growth rate of sales during the whole sample period.

Random intercept statement used to relax the assumption of a common intercept and coefficients across firms.

−2 res log likelihood is the likelihood maximum of the estimated regression equation.

The significance levels are presented in parentheses below the estimated coefficient.

*Represents coefficients that are statistically different from zero at the 5% level or better.

profitability remain as expected and statistically significant. The sign of the size coefficient becomes negative and statistically significant. The signs of the operating uncertainty and growth are as expected but remain insignificant.

Table 5 reports the results of the industry-specific regression, where the ratio of human capital asset to the market value of equity is regressed on its firm-specific determinants. The results indicate that the signs of the estimated slopes of the firm-specific characteristics are as predicted. This supports the results reported in Table 4.

The results also indicate that there exists a positive relation between the average salary and the ratio of human capital asset to the market value of

Table 5. Regression Results Based on Firm-Specific Mixed Panel
Estimation Procedure (Model 14).

				All Countries ($n = 879$)			
Industry	Intercept	WATEMP	LABORINT	ROA	Log(asset)	Std.Dev.ROE	Msales growth
Intercept	0.486						
	$(0.002)^*$						
I_{1000}		0.005	−0.021	−0.012	−0.025	−0.002	1.146
		$(0.031)^*$	(0.967)	$(0.011)^*$	(0.140)	(0.766)	(0.308)
I_{2000}		0.003	0.393	−0.006	−0.028	−0.003	0.178
		(0.115)	(0.269)	$(0.057)^*$	$(0.066)^*$	(0.682)	(0.880)
I_{3000}		−0.003	0.329	−0.009	−0.010	0.003	−0.766
		(0.370)	(0.653)	(0.299)	(0.659)	(0.722)	(0.641)
I_{3500}		0.008	1.342	−0.018	−0.060	−0.003	1.011
		$(0.093)^*$	$(0.059)^*$	$(0.008)^*$	(0.108)	(0.881)	(0.686)
I_{6000}		0.000	0.211	−0.010	−0.019	0.004	0.212
		(0.729)	(0.322)	$(0.001)^*$	$(0.098)^*$	(0.384)	(0.749)
I_{8000}		0.004	0.590	−0.021	−0.066	0.021	0.350
		$(0.099)^*$	(0.248)	$(0.002)^*$	$(0.045)^*$	$(0.068)^*$	(0.765)
I_{9000}		0.003	0.901	−0.004	−0.013	−0.010	−2.697
		$(0.068)^*$	$(0.062)^*$	(0.510)	(0.484)	(0.548)	$(0.078)^*$

Using Model 14, HU/MV is regressed with firm-specific variables, i.e. WATEMP, LABORINT, ROA, Log(asset), Std.Dev.ROE and Msalesgrowth accross different industries. The industry dummies are as follows:
I_{1000} = Basic Materials.
I_{2000} = Consumer Discretionary.
I_{3000} = Consumer Staples.
I_{3500} = Health Care.
I_{6000} = Capital Goods.
I_{8000} = Information Technology.
I_{9000} = Utilities.
*Represents coefficients that are statistically different from zero at the 10% level or better.

equity in four industries. The statistically significant relationships between
the labor intensity and the ratio of human capital asset to the market value
of equity are reported in two industries. The results also clearly indicate that
almost in all industries the profitability of the firm is significantly negatively
related to the ratio of human capital asset to the market value of equity. It,
therefore, seems that the profitability of the firm has an important role to
play in all industries when explaining the estimated human capital assets.
The size of the firm is significantly related to the ratio of human capital asset
to the market value of equity in three industries, whereas the operating

Table 6. Regression Results Based on Firm-Specific Mixed Panel
Estimation Procedure (Model 13).

Variables	Exp sign	Country					
		Germany	Finland	France	Switzerland	U.K.	U.S.
Intercept		0.234	0.940	0.587	1.200	−0.269	1.173
		(0.347)	(0.222)	(0.257)	(0.018)*	(0.448)	(0.001)*
WATEMP	+	−0.001	−0.004	−0.001	0.006	0.005	0.003
		(0.441)	(0.273)	(0.665)	(0.001)*	(0.009)*	(0.005)*
LABORINT	+	0.499	0.608	0.328	0.130	0.936	0.105
		(0.059)*	(0.248)	(0.491)	(0.772)	(0.002)*	(0.648)
ROA	−	−0.006	−0.026	−0.018	−0.025	−0.005	−0.004
		(0.055)*	(0.001)*	(0.023)*	(0.001)*	(0.094)*	(0.080)*
Log(Assets)	−/+	−0.002	−0.048	−0.008	−0.144	0.011	−0.054
		(0.908)	(0.352)	(0.797)	(0.002)*	(0.666)	(0.001)*
Std.Dev.ROE	−/+	0.002	0.005	−0.014	−0.000	0.006	−0.005
		(0.545)	(0.728)	(0.439)	(0.995)	(0.388)	(0.408)
Msalesgrowth	−	0.272	0.373	−0.359	0.750	0.446	−1.544
		(0.717)	(0.740)	(0.790)	(0.632)	(0.788)	(0.036)*
N		227	56	118	77	143	272

Using Model 13, HU/MV is regressed with the six different firm-specific variables, i.e.
WATEMP, LABORINT, ROA, Log(asset), Std.Dev.ROE and Msalesgrowth in different
countries.
WATEMP is the ratio of labor expense to the number of employees.
LABORINT is the ratio of labor expense to the sales.
ROA is income before extraordinary items divided by average of most recent 2 years of assets.
Log(assets) is the log of total assets.
Std.Dev.ROE is the standard deviation of return on equity measured over whole sample period.
Msalesgrowth is the average growth rate of sales during the whole sample period.
Random intercept statement used to relax assumption of a common intercept and coefficients
across firms.
The significance levels are presented in parentheses below the estimated coefficient.
*Represents coefficients that are statistically different from zero at the 10% level or better.

uncertainty and the growth of the firm have no effect on the ratio of human capital asset to the market value of equity.

Table 6 reports the results of regressing the ratio of human capital asset to the market value of equity on the firm-specific characteristics in different countries. A strong relation between the estimated human capital assets and its economic determinants is observed in the U.K. and, especially, in the U.S., which both can be regarded as countries with the market-based financial system. In countries with a clear bank-based financial system, i.e. Germany and France, the relation between the estimated human capital assets and its economic determinants is somewhat lower. Therefore, it seems that the economic relevance of the estimated human capital asset is about the same in countries with a different financial system.

CONCLUSIONS

This chapter applies the Ohlson's (1995) framework to estimate the proportion of labor costs that represents investments in human capital, and the rate of depreciation of this asset by using international data. The results indicate that the estimated proportion of labor expenses that represents investments in human capital is large in the so-called common-law countries with a market-based financial system. On the other hand, the depreciation rate of the estimated human capital assets is lower in these countries.

For the whole panel data, the results of testing whether the estimated parameters and the resulting human capital asset ratios make economic sense indicate that the average salary, the labor intensity and the profitability seem to be the economic determinants of the human capital asset ratio as predicted by the theory. Industry-specific results also confirm the findings that different firm-specific characteristics can be used to explain the ratio of human capital asset to the market value of equity in some sense. Country-specific regression results strongly support the hypothesis that the negative association between the profitability and the human capital asset ratio makes economic sense.

ACKNOWLEDGMENT

We thank OKO Bank of Finland, Jenny ja Antti Wihurin Rahasto, Liikesivistysrahasto, Kaupallisten – ja Teknisten Tieteiden Tukisäätiö, Marcus Wallenbergin Liiketaloudellinen Tutkimussäätiö and Oulun yliopiston Tukisäätiö for their financial support.

REFERENCES

Amir, E., & Lev, L. (1996). Value-relevance of non-financial information: The wireless communications industry. *Journal of Accounting and Economics, 22*, 3–30.

Ball, R., Kothari, S. P., & Robin, A. (2000). The effect of international institutional factors on properties of accounting earnings. *Journal of Accounting and Economics, 29*, 1–51.

Ballester, M., Livnat, J., & Sinha, N. (1998). Labor costs and investments in human capital. Manuscript.

Bublitz, B., & Ettredge, M. (1989). The information in discretional outlays: Advertising, research and development. *Accounting Review, 64*, 108–124.

Chaucin, K. W., & Hirschey, M. (1993). Advertising, R&D expenditures and the market value of the firm. *Financial Management, 22*, 231–258.

Demirgüc-Kunt, A., & Maksimovic, V. (2002). Funding growth in bank-based and market-based financial systems: Evidence from firm-level data. *Journal of Financial Economics, 65*, 337–363.

Flamholtz, E. (1971). A model for human resource valuation: A stochastic process with service rewards. *The Accounting Review, 46*, 253–267.

Green, J. P., Stark, A. W., & Thomas, H. M. (1996). U.K. evidence on the market valuation of research and development expenditures. *Journal of Business Finance and Accounting, 23*, 191–216.

Hirschey, M., & Weygandt, J. J. (1985). Amortization policy for advertising and research and development expenditures. *Journal of Accounting Research, 23*, 326–335.

Jaggi, B., & Lau, H.-S. (1974). Toward a model for human resource valuation. *The Accounting Review, 49*, 321–329.

Leuz, C., Nanda, D., & Wysocki, P. D. (2003). Earnings management and investor protection: An international comparison. *Journal of Financial Economics, 69*, 505–527.

Lev, B., & Schwartz, A. (1971). On the use of the economic concept of human capital in financial statements. *The Accounting Review(January), 46*, 103–111.

Myers, J. N. (1999). Implementing residual income valuation with linear information dynamics. *The Accounting Review(January), 74*, 1–28.

Ohlson, J. A. (1995). Earnings, book values, and dividends in security valuations. *Contemporary Accounting Research, 11*, 661–687.

Rosett, J. G. (2000). *Equity risk and the labor stock: The case of union contracts.* Working Paper, Tulane University.

RISK IN AUDIT PRICING: THE ROLE OF FIRM-SPECIFIC DIMENSIONS OF RISK

Jussi Nikkinen and Petri Sahlström

ABSTRACT

This chapter investigates the impact of the firm-specific dimensions of risk suggested in the finance literature, the financial risk, operating leverage and business risk on audit fees. It is hypothesized that audit fees are related to these three dimensions of risk, size, audit complexity and a set of the agency theory based control variables. The hypothesis is empirically tested using a sample from the U.K. audit market. The results of the study show that audit fees as hypothesized are positively related to financial leverage, operating leverage and business risk of a firm and that the control variables behave according to expectations. This implies that the three dimensions of the firm-specific risk are taken into account in audit pricing decisions and should therefore be incorporated into models when investigating the audit pricing issues.

INTRODUCTION

Many studies recognize the role of risk inherent in audit pricing.[1] For example, Simunic and Stein (1987) point out that auditing is a business in

Advances in International Accounting
Advances in International Accounting, Volume 18, 141–151
Copyright © 2005 by Elsevier Ltd.
All rights of reproduction in any form reserved
ISSN: 0897-3660/doi:10.1016/S0897-3660(05)18007-6

which the auditor must assume the risk of an uncertain rate of returns and consequently the auditor's pricing decision should reflect this risk. Similarly, Menon and Williams (2001) note that a litigation risk measure (leverage) is often included in the audit pricing models. Thus, various risk measures are used as control variables for audit risk in the audit pricing models.[2] The finance literature (see, e.g., Hamada, 1972; Lev, 1974; Gahlon & Gentry, 1982) shows, however, that the firm-specific risk is a function of three dimensions of risk, which are the financial leverage, operating leverage and business risk of a firm. Consequently, according to the finance literature all of these risk dimensions should be taken into account in audit pricing decisions.

The purpose of this chapter is to investigate the impact of the three dimensions of risk, i.e. the financial risk, operating leverage and business risk, on the audit fee determination. Since the risk of a firm consists of these dimensions, the auditor's cost function should include these factors. Consequently, the auditor's pricing decision should reflect all these dimensions of firm-specific risk. It is therefore hypothesized that audit fees are related to these three dimensions of risk, audit complexity and, as suggested by Gul (1999) and Gul and Tsui (2001), to a set of control variables based on the agency theory. While all the dimensions of risk are expected to affect the audit pricing decisions, the different dimensions, i.e. business risk, operating leverage and financial leverage may not, on the other hand, be equally important for the auditor's pricing decision. To empirically investigate these issues, the determination of audit fees is investigated using a large sample from the U.K. audit market.

This chapter contributes to the body of audit pricing literature (for a review see, Cobbin, 2002) by investigating the impact of the three dimensions of the firm-specific risk, i.e. the financial risk, operating leverage and business risk, on the audit fee determination. While various risk measures are typically used as control variables in the audit pricing-models, the finance theory suggests that the firm-specific risk is a function of the risk dimensions investigated in this study. Consequently, all of these risk dimensions should be taken into account in audit pricing decisions.

The results of the study have an important implication for auditing companies. Since the auditing business has grown increasingly complex at both the national and international levels, auditors need better tools for assessing audit risks. Consequently, a better understanding of the role of risk in audit pricing is likely to lead to more accurate audit pricing decisions.

IMPACT OF RISK ON AUDIT PRICING

Auditing is a business in which the final income of an audit project is unknown since an auditor faces the possibility that the financial statements contain undetected material misstatements, which may be observed after an audit report has been published. Such a revelation may result in loss of auditor reputation, loss of the client or in the worst case in costly litigation. As a consequence, the auditor's cost function consists of two components, which are the amount of work hours used and the expected future loss (see Simunic & Stein, 1987). The client's risk affects both of these components. The expected future loss increases as the probability of bankruptcy increases, since the probability that the firm will be re-audited and misstatements revealed is higher in a case of bankruptcy. Moreover, to avoid litigations in a case of bankruptcy, it can be expected that auditors will increase their effort to detect misstatements for firms with a high probability of bankruptcy. The auditors should take this into account when pricing their services. As a result, a positive relationship should pertain between audit fees and client's risk. The previous empirical evidence supports this argument (see, e.g., Simunic & Stein, 1987; Cobbin, 2002 for a review).

The theoretical framework for the use of firm characteristics in the risk measurement is based on studies according to which certain firm-specific characteristics are connected to risk. Hamada (1972), Lev (1974), and Gahlon and Gentry (1982), among others, show that the firm risk is a positive function of the financial leverage, operating leverage and business risk of a firm. Since the audit fee is a positive function of risk, it should be positively related to these risk dimensions. Therefore, it can be hypothesized that positive relationships pertain between audit fees and financial leverage, operating leverage and business risk of a firm. If these hypotheses are confirmed, it implies that all of these risk dimensions should be used in the modeling of the audit pricing.

While the dimensions of risk are hypothesized to have an impact on audit fees, several other factors affecting the audit fees have to be taken into account in the model construction. Firm size and the complexity of the auditing process are the most important among these factors (see, e.g., Bamber, Bamber, & Schoderbek, 1993). The size of the client has a positive impact on the auditing fees. The complexity of the auditing process increases the level of auditor effort, thereby raising the auditing fee.

Moreover, according to agency theory, audit fees represent monitoring cost, as proposed by Jensen and Meckling (1976) and therefore factors affecting the agency costs should be taken into account, as suggested by Gul and Tsui (2001). Jensen (1986) suggests that the agency costs are lower for firms with high levels of management ownership since managers' interests are more likely to be similar with those of shareholders when they own a larger proportion of the shares. Consequently, it can be hypothesized that monitoring costs, including audit fees, will be higher for firms with lower manager ownership as argued by Agrawal and Jayaraman (1994). Moreover, based on the theory of Jensen and Meckling (1976); and Jensen (1986, 1989), the agency problem is more severe in firms with higher free cash flow (FCF). The reason for this is the fact that if a firm has a large amount of cash reserves then managers have more flexibility to choose where to use the funds. To reduce this problem, owners use auditors to inspect managers' behavior. Therefore, it can be hypothesized that there is a positive relationship between FCF and audit fees.

On the basis of the framework of risk dimensions, a positive relationship should exist between the audit fee and the three dimensions of risk. Moreover, factors affecting the audit fees, i.e. firm size and the complexity of the auditing process, and also the agency costs should be incorporated into a model investigating the role of risk in audit pricing.

DATA

The hypotheses are tested using data from the U.K. The variables used are retrieved from the publicly available Worldscope database. The sample consists of all listed firms during the period 1992–2000. Firms belonging to the financial services industry (SIC codes 6000–6999) are excluded from the sample due to their unique characteristics.

The variables are defined as follows: Audit fee, the dependent variable, is defined as a natural logarithm of audit fees (FEE). Debt to equity ratio is used to measure financial leverage (FLEV). Operating leverage (OLEV) is measured by the change in sales divided by the change in operating income. This measure can be interpreted so that if all costs are variable then the value of OLEV is one, and as the fraction of fixed costs increases, i.e. operating leverage increases, so OLEV also increases. This definition is used since it is impossible to measure the ratio of fixed costs to variable costs using information from the financial statements. The problem of this measure is that it is not defined if the denominator is zero. Moreover, as the denominator approaches zero, the variable approaches infinity. To avoid these problems, an observation is omitted if the change in operating income is zero and the natural logarithm of the variable is used in the analyses.

Business risk can be measured using the market beta when the other dimensions of risk, i.e. FLEV and OLEV, are included in the model as in our case (see Kallunki, 1996). The beta is estimated using monthly stock and FTSE 100 index returns over a 2-year period before the end of the fiscal year applying the market model of Sharpe (1964).

On the basis of the earlier literature (see, e.g., Gul, 1999; O'Sullivan, 1999; Gul & Tsui, 1997, 2001) the following control variables are used. FCF is a measure of free cash flow and it is defined as free cash flow from operating activities minus interest payments. The variable is deflated by the total assets (see Lehn & Poulsen, 1989). The management ownership (MANA) is measured by the percentage of shares owned by insiders of the firm. Firm size (SIZE) is measured by the natural logarithm of total assets and the complexity of the auditing process (COMPLEX) is measured using the percentage of foreign sales to total sales. In addition to these variables, in the robustness check QR, ROI and PBV are added in the model (see, e.g., Gul & Tsui, 1997, 2001). QR is quick ratio, i.e. the ratio of current assets less inventories to current liabilities. ROI is return on investments and PBV is the market price to book value ratio. The beginning of year values are used for the balance sheet items and market values in the variable construction. Table 1 presents descriptive statistics of the sample used in the study with and without outliers detected using the Weisberg (1985) test. At the 5% significance level the test detects eight outliers.

METHODOLOGY

To investigate the importance of different dimensions of risk in audit pricing the following regression equation is estimated:

$$\text{FEE}_{i,t} = \alpha_0 + \sum_{k=92}^{99} \alpha_1^k D_k^{\text{year}} + \alpha_2 \text{FLEV}_{i,t} + \alpha_3 \text{OLEV}_{i,t} + \alpha_4 \text{BR}_{i,t}$$
$$+ \alpha_5 \text{FCF}_{i,t} + \alpha_6 \text{MANA}_{i,t} + \alpha_7 \text{SIZE}_{i,t} + \alpha_8 \text{COMPLEX}_{i,t} + e_{i,t} \quad (1)$$

where FEE is the logarithm of audit fee, D_k^{year} denotes a dummy variable having a value of one at year k and otherwise zero, FLEV the financial leverage, OLEV the operating leverage, BR the business risk, FCF the free cash flow, MANA the percentage of shares own by insiders of the firm, SIZE the logarithm of total assets, COMPLEX the percentage of foreign sales to total sales, and i and t denote, respectively, firm and year.

Table 1. Descriptive Statistics.

Variable	Raw Data		Outliers Removed	
	Mean	S. D.	Mean	S. D.
FEE	0.993	2.375	0.979	2.288
ASSETS	1.147	5.266	1.146	5.269
FLEV	0.568	0.759	0.568	0.759
OLEV	1.888	1.508	1.886	1.508
BR	0.704	0.808	0.704	0.808
FCF	0.034	0.968	0.033	0.968
MANA	0.250	0.203	0.249	0.203
COMPLEX	26.824	29.285	26.847	29.290
Number of observations		3,141		3,133

Notes:
Outliers are removed based on the Weisberg (1985) test.
FEE = audit fee in millions.
ASSETS = total assets in billions.
FLEV = financial leverage.
OLEV = operating leverage.
BR = business risk, i.e. market beta.
FCF = free cash flow divided by total assets.
MANA = percentage of shares owned by insiders of the firm.
COMPLEX = percentage of foreign sales to total sales.

To avoid the dummy variable trap, no dummy variable is used for the year 2000. The possibility of multicollinearity is detected using the variance inflation factors (see, e.g., Judge, Hill, Griffiths, Lütkepohl, & Lee, 1988, pp. 868–871). White's test and the Breusch–Pagan test are performed. Based on these tests, it is concluded that the error variances are heteroscedastic. Consequently, the White (1980) heteroscedasticity consistent covariance matrix is used.

Eq. (1) allows the intercepts to vary over years since according to Menon and Williams (2001) audit fees have varied in the long run. However, the F-test used to detect the equality of the coefficients of the dummy variables indicates that they are not significantly different when this particular sample is used ($F = 1.60$, $p = 0.131$). Therefore, Eq. (1) is re-estimated without the year dummies as suggested, for example, by Baltagi (1995). These results are reported.

According to the theory outlined in the Section second, the audit fee should be positively related to the dimensions of risk, i.e. the coefficients of FLEV, OLEV, and BR should be positive. Based on the agency theory, the coefficient of FCF should be positive and the coefficient of MANA negative.

In addition, the coefficients of control variables SIZE and COMPLEX are expected to be positive.

The robustness of the results is examined in two ways. First, the Weisberg (1985) test is used to identify the outliers in the data. After identification, the outliers are removed and Eq. (1) is re-estimated. Second, three additional control variables, which may also reflect risk, are included. These variables are the QR measured as the ratio of current assets less inventories to current liabilities, profit before interest and tax to total equity (ROI), and PBV. Thus, the following regression model is estimated:

$$FEE_{i,t} = \alpha_1 + \alpha_2 FLEV_{i,t} + \alpha_3 OLEV_{i,t} + \alpha_4 BR_{i,t} + \alpha_5 FCF_{i,t} + \alpha_6 MANA_{i,t}$$
$$+ \alpha_7 SIZE_{i,t} + \alpha_8 COMPLEX_{i,t} + \alpha_9 QR_{i,t} + \alpha_{10} ROI_{i,t}$$
$$+ \alpha_{11} PBV_{i,t} + e \tag{2}$$

The coefficients of QR and ROI should be negative and the coefficient of PBV-positive.

RESULTS

Table 2 presents the results of explaining audit fees with the firm-specific risk dimensions and control variables, i.e. the estimation results of Eq. (1). The F-test for fixed effects ($p = 0.13$) indicates that intercepts are equal over time and therefore the estimation is done without yearly dummies (see Baltagi, 1995). The variance inflation factors (VIF) show that multicollinearity does not cause problems (see, e.g., Judge, Hill, Griffiths, Lütkepohl, & Lee 1988, pp. 868–871). Consequently, FLEV, OLEV, and BR measure the individual components of risk.

The explanatory power of the model is rather high, 0.75. Regarding the estimates of the risk measures, all coefficients have expected signs and they are highly significant indicating that audit fees are positively related with financial leverage, operating leverage and business risk of a firm. This result implies that these risk measures capture different aspects of firm's risk and that these risk dimensions are taken into account in pricing of auditing services. The coefficients of the control variables are also highly significant having expected signs. This is in accordance with the previous literature showing that the agency theory, firm size and complexity of auditing process affect audit pricing.

To test the robustness of the results, the effect of possible outliers on the results is investigated. Outliers are detected by using Weisberg's (1985) test.

Table 2.   Different Components of Risk in Explaining Audit Fees.

Variable	Measure	Prediction	Coefficient	Prob. of *t*-stat.
Intercept		?	−1.8986	0.000
FLEV	Financial leverage	+	0.1044	0.000
OLEV	Operating leverage	+	0.0321	0.000
BR	Business risk	+	0.0626	0.000
FCF	Control variable	+	0.3380	0.009
MANA	Control variable	−	−0.3566	0.000
SIZE	Control variable	+	0.6067	0.000
COMPLEX	Control variable	+	0.0103	0.000
Number of observations			3,141	
Adjusted R^2			0.75	
F-statistic			1,403.64	
Prob.			0.000	

Notes:
The White (1980) heteroscedasticity consistent covariance matrix is used.
Possibility of multicollinearity is detected using the variance inflation factors.
FEE = audit fee in millions.
ASSETS = total assets in billions.
FLEV = financial leverage.
OLEV = operating leverage.
BR = business risk, i.e. market beta.
FCF = free cash flow divided by total assets.
MANA = percentage of shares owned by insiders of the firm.
COMPLEX = percentage of foreign sales to total sales.

The test detects eight outliers at the 5% level of significance. Moreover, the effect of additional explanatory variables, suggested in the previous literature, on the results is investigated by adding QR, ROI and PBV as explanatory variables in Eq. (2) (see, e.g., Simunic & Stein, 1987; Gul & Tsui, 1997, 2001). The estimation results after removing the possible outliers indicate that the explanatory power is higher than with the outliers. However, the coefficients are virtually unchanged. The results of the extended model indicate that the additional explanatory variables are highly significant, having the expected signs. Moreover, the results show that the coefficients of risk dimensions are slightly lower in the extended model estimation. This may be due to the fact that the additional variables measure, at least to some extent, some risk characteristics of a firm and therefore, they affect the effect of measures of FLEV, OLEV and BR of a firm even though the coefficients remain highly significant. Generally, the results of the study support the hypotheses Table 3.

Table 3. Robustness Check.

Variable	Measure	Prediction	Outliers Removed		Extended Model	
			Coeff.	Prob.	Coeff.	Prob.
Intercept		?	−1.8066	(0.000)	−1.8486	(0.000)
FLEV	Financial leverage	+	0.1091	(0.000)	0.0727	(0.000)
OLEV	Operating leverage	+	0.0371	(0.000)	0.0301	(0.000)
BR	Business risk	+	0.0711	(0.000)	0.0515	(0.002)
FCF	Control variable	+	0.3274	(0.005)	0.3658	(0.015)
MANA	Control variable	−	−0.3670	(0.000)	−0.3469	(0.000)
SIZE	Control variable	+	0.5965	(0.000)	0.6063	(0.000)
COMPLEX	Control variable	+	0.0105	(0.000)	0.0105	(0.000)
QR	Control variable	−			−0.0417	(0.000)
ROI	Control variable	−			−0.1596	(0.019)
PBV	Control variable	+			0.0137	(0.000)
Number of observations			3133		3141	
Adjusted R^2			0.79		0.76	
F-statistic			1,671.33		1,000.23	
Prob.			0.000		0.000	

Notes:

The White (1980) heteroscedasticity consistent covariance matrix is used.

Outliers are removed based on the Weisberg (1985) test.

FEE = audit fee in millions.

ASSETS = total assets in billions.

FLEV = financial leverage.

OLEV = operating leverage.

BR = business risk, i.e. market beta.

FCF = free cash flow divided by total assets.

MANA = percentage of shares owned by insiders of the firm.

COMPLEX = percentage of foreign sales to total sales.

QR = quick ratio, i.e. ratio of current assets less inventories to current liabilities.

ROI = return on investments, i.e. profit before interest and tax to total invested capital.

PBV = market price to book value ratio.

SUMMARY AND CONCLUSIONS

This chapter investigates the impact of the firm-specific dimensions of risk on the audit fee determination. Since, according to the finance literature, the risk of a firm consists of three dimensions, which are FLEV, OLEV and BR, all these characteristics should be reflected in audit pricing. Thus, it is hypothesized that audit fees are related to these three dimensions of risk, size, audit complexity and a set of the agency theory based control variables. To empirically investigate these issues, the determination of audit fees is investigated using a large sample from the U.K. audit market. The results of the study show that audit fees are positively related to FLEV, OLEV and BR of a firm as hypothesized. Moreover, it is found that agency theory, firm size and the complexity of auditing process explain audit fees. The result implies that these risk dimensions capture different aspects of a firm's risk and are therefore taken into account in audit pricing.

NOTES

1. For example, Simunic and Stein (1987) report that the single most significant explanatory variable was financial leverage.
2. The existing audit pricing literature such as Simunic (1980), Palmrose (1986), Francis and Simon (1987), Pong and Whittington (1994), Simon (1995), Collier and Gregory (1996), Adams, Sherris, and Hossain (1997), Gul (1999), O'Sullivan (1999), Gul and Tsui (2001) and Menon and Williams (2001) has focused on an important area, namely the determination of audit fees, i.e. audit pricing.

ACKNOWLEDGMENTS

The authors gratefully acknowledge financial support from the Emil Aaltonen Foundation and the Ostrobothnia Chamber of Commerce foundation.

REFERENCES

Adams, M., Sherris, M., & Hossain, M. (1997). The determinants of external audit costs in the New Zealand life insurance industry. *Journal of International Management and Accounting, 8*, 69–86.
Agrawal, A., & Jayaraman, N. (1994). The dividend policies of all-equity firms: A direct test of the free cash flow theory. *Managerial and Decision Economics, 15*, 139–148.
Baltagi, B. (1995). *Econometric analysis of panel data.* New York: Wiley.
Bamber, E. M., Bamber, L. S., & Schoderbek, M. P. (1993). Audit structure and other determinants of audit report lag: An empirical analysis. *Auditing: A Journal of Practice & Theory, 12*, 1–23.
Cobbin, P. E. (2002). International dimensions of the audit fee determinants literature. *International Journal of Auditing, 6*, 53–77.
Collier, P., & Gregory, A. (1996). Audit committee effectiveness and the audit fee. *European Accounting Review, 5*, 177–198.

Francis, J. R., & Simon, D. T. (1987). A test of audit pricing in the small-client segment of the U.S. audit market. *Accounting Review, 62*, 145–157.

Gahlon, J. M., & Gentry, J. A. (1982). On the relationship between systematic risk and the degrees of operating and financial leverage. *Financial Management, 11*, 15–23.

Gul, F. A. (1999). Audit prices, product differentiation and economic equilibrium. *Auditing: A Journal of Practice & Theory, 18*, 90–100.

Gul, F. A., & Tsui, J. S. L. (1997). A test of the free cash flow and debt monitoring hypotheses: Evidence from auditing pricing. *Journal of Accounting and Economics, 24*, 219–237.

Gul, F. A., & Tsui, J. S. L. (2001). Free cash flow, debt monitoring, and audit pricing: Further evidence on the role of director equity ownership. *Auditing: A Journal of Practice & Theory, 20*, 72–84.

Hamada, R. S. (1972). The effect of the firm's capital structure on the market efficiency. *Journal of Finance, 27*, 435–458.

Jensen, M. C., & Meckling, W. (1976). A theory of the firm: Managerial behavior, agency costs and ownership structure. *Journal of Financial Economics, 3*, 305–360.

Jensen, M. C. (1986). Agency costs of free cash flow, corporate finance and takeovers. *American Economic Review, 76*, 323–329.

Jensen, M. C. (1989). Eclipse of the public corporation. *Harvard Business Review, 5*, 61–74.

Judge, G., Hill, R. C., Griffiths, W. E., Lütkepohl, H., & Lee, T. C. (1988). *Introduction to the theory and practice of econometrics.* New York: Wiley.

Kallunki, J. P. (1996). Stock returns and earnings announcements in Finland. *European Accounting Review, 5*, 199–216.

Lehn, K., & Poulsen, A. (1989). Free cash flow and stockholder gains in going private transactions. *Journal of Finance, 44*, 771–787.

Lev, B. (1974). On the association between operating leverage and risk. *Journal of Financial and Quantitative Analysis, 9*, 627–641.

Menon, K., & Williams, D. D. (2001). Long-term trends in audit fees. *Auditing: A Journal of Practice & Theory, 20*, 116–136.

O'Sullivan, N. (1999). Board characteristics and audit pricing post-Cadbury: A research note. *European Accounting Review, 8*, 253–263.

Palmrose, Z. (1986). Audit fees and auditor size: Further evidence. *Journal of Accounting Research, 24*, 97–110.

Pong, G. M., & Whittington, G. (1994). The determinants of audit fees: Some empirical models. *Journal of Business Finance and Accounting, 21*, 1071–1095.

Sharpe, W. F. (1964). Capital asset prices: A theory of market equilibrium under conditions of risk. *Journal of Finance, 19*, 425–442.

Simon, D. T. (1995). The market for audit services in South Africa. *International Journal of Accounting Education and Research, 30*, 356–365.

Simunic, D. A. (1980). The pricing of audit services: Theory and evidence. *Journal of Accounting Research, 18*, 161–190.

Simunic, D. A., & Stein, M. T. (1987). The impact of litigation risk on audit pricing: A review of the economics and the evidence. *Auditing: A Journal of Practice & Theory, 15*, 120–134.

Weisberg, S. (1985). *Applied linear regression.* New York: Wiley.

White, H. (1980). A heteroscedasticity-consistent covariance matrix estimator and a direct test for heteroscedasticity. *Econometrica, 48*, 817–838.

IAS VERSUS U.S. GAAP: ASSESSING THE QUALITY OF FINANCIAL REPORTING IN SOUTH AFRICA, THE UNITED KINGDOM, AND THE UNITED STATES

Jenice Prather-Kinsey and Sandra Waller Shelton

ABSTRACT

In this study, we investigate whether financial reporting, using International Accounting Standards (IAS) results in quality disclosures, given differences in institutional and market forces across legal jurisdictions. This study contributes to the global accounting debate by utilizing U.S.-based companies complying with U.S. Generally Accepted Accounting Principles (U.S. GAAP) as a benchmark for measuring the quality of IAS as applied by South Africa (S.A.) and United Kingdom (U.K.) companies. Although South Africa, United Kingdom, and the United States are common law countries with strong investor protection, South Africa's institutional factors and market forces vary from that of the U.K. and the U.S. South Africa's financial market is less developed than that of the U.K. and the U.S. We compare the discretionary accruals of firms complying with U.S. GAAP to the discretionary accruals of U.K. and S.A. firms complying with IAS. This allows a comparison between

Advances in International Accounting
Advances in International Accounting, Volume 18, 153–168
Copyright © 2005 by Elsevier Ltd.
All rights of reproduction in any form reserved
ISSN: 0897-3660/doi:10.1016/S0897-3660(05)18008-8

companies (S.A. and U.K.) operating under different institutional factors and market forces that have adopted IAS versus U.S. companies that report under U.S. GAAP. Our sample, consisting of U.S., S.A., and U.K. listed firms, contains 3,166 firm-year observations relating to the period 1999–2001. The results of our study indicate that S.A firms utilizing IAS report absolute values of discretionary accruals that are significantly greater than absolute values of discretionary accruals of U.S. firms utilizing U.S. GAAP. In contrast, U.K. firms utilizing IAS report discretionary accruals that are significantly less than the discretionary accruals of companies in the United States reporting under U.S. GAAP. This study contributes to the literature by providing evidence of the quality of financial information prepared under IAS and its dependency on the institutional factors and market forces of a country.

INTRODUCTION

The purpose of this study is to examine whether financial reporting, using International Accounting Standards (IAS) results in quality disclosures, given differences in institutional factors and market forces.[1] This study examines the quality of financial statements prepared in accordance with IAS by concentrating on discretionary accruals as a measure of earnings management. In this study, earnings management is viewed as having an inverse relationship to earnings quality (i.e. high earnings quality is synonymous with low earnings management).

Recent interest in global accounting standards has resulted in considerable debate as to whether IAS results in high-quality financial reporting. U.S. Generally Accepted Accounting Principles (U.S. GAAP) is frequently viewed as the benchmark for high-quality global standards (Levitt, 1998; McGregor, 1999). Moreover, the Financial Accounting Standards Board (FASB) has published a comparison on the differences in U.S. GAAP and IAS and finds significant differences between them. Prior studies examining the quality of financial information prepared using IAS compared to U.S. GAAP have presented mixed results (Leuz, 2003; Harris & Muller, 1999; Ashbaugh & Olsson, 2002).

Ball, Robin, and Wu (2003) suggest that the global accounting debate focuses too much on the choice of accounting standards and too little on market forces and institutional factors. This study contributes to the global accounting debate by utilizing U.S.-based companies complying with U.S.

GAAP as a benchmark for measuring the quality of IAS as applied by South Africa (S.A.) and United Kingdom (U.K.) companies. Although South Africa, the United Kingdom, and the United States are common law countries with strong investor protection, South Africa's institutional factors and market forces vary from that of the U.K. and the U.S. For example, South Africa's financial market is less developed than that of the U.K. and the U.S. Appiah-Kusi and Menyah (2003) find that investors are less informed as a result of inadequate disclosures and the existence of insider trading in the South African market. Furthermore, the inefficiency of the South African market is reflected in the fact that stock market prices do not adjust rapidly to the arrival of new information, hence, future prices can be predicted from lagged prices. There is also less credible firm-specific information available to individuals for the pricing of individual stocks.

Given these differences in institutional and market forces for South Africa, versus the U.K. and the U.S., management's incentives to engage in earnings management may outweigh the costs. Ball, Kothari and Robin (2000) argue that when the costs of complying with IAS are viewed as exceeding the costs of non-compliance, substantial non-compliance will occur. In our study, earnings management (quality) is determined by examining discretionary accruals for U.S., S.A., and U.K.-based firms. We compare the discretionary accruals of firms complying with U.S. GAAP to the discretionary accruals of U.K. and S.A. firms complying with IAS. This allows a comparison between companies operating under different institutional factors and market forces that have adopted IAS versus companies that report under U.S. GAAP.

The results of our study indicate that S.A. firms utilizing IAS report absolute values of discretionary accruals are significantly greater than absolute values of discretionary accruals of U.S. firms utilizing U.S. GAAP. In contrast, U.K. firms utilizing IAS report discretionary accruals that are significantly less than the discretionary accruals of companies in the United States reporting under U.S. GAAP. This study contributes to the literature by providing evidence of the quality of financial information prepared under IAS and its dependency on the institutional factors and market forces of a country.

LITERATURE AND HYPOTHESES

Prior market-based comparison studies examining the quality of financial information prepared under IAS with financial information prepared under U.S. GAAP have presented mixed results. Harris and Muller (1999) find that U.S. GAAP earnings reconciliation adjustment is value-relevant and that U.S. GAAP amounts are valued differently for market value and return models than IAS amounts. Similarly, Ashbaugh and Olsson (2002) in an examination of non-U.S./non-U.K. firms find that the earnings capitalization model is the dominant accounting-based valuation model when cross-listed firms report under IAS. However, the residual income model is the dominant accounting-based valuation model for cross-listed firms reporting under U.S. GAAP. Leuz (2003) examined firms in Germany's "New Market" for growth firms, which are required to choose between IAS and U.S. GAAP in preparing their financial statements. Leuz findings do not indicate that U.S. GAAP is of higher quality than IAS. Differences in the bid-ask spread and share turnover across IAS and U.S. GAAP firms are statistically insignificant. Similarly, Leuz and Verrecchia (2000) find in a cross-sectional analysis that firms which commit to either IAS or U.S. GAAP exhibit lower percentage bid-ask spreads and higher share turnover than firms following German GAAP.

Few studies have examined earnings management practices in non-U.S. countries. Darrough, Pourjalali, and Saudagaran (1998) examined the choices of accounting accruals using a large sample of Japanese companies. The results of the study indicate that similar to managers of U.S. firms, managers of Japanese companies chose income-increasing accounting accruals to increase their bonuses and to increase the amount of outside funding. Management's incentive to manage earnings may significantly affect the quality of earnings in cross-listed firms reporting financial information under IAS. Management has incentives to adjust accounting earnings to maximize firm and/or manager wealth. The more the discretion given to management in financial reports, the greater the opportunity for more manipulated and thus less-quality reported financial disclosures.

Francis, Khurana, and Pereira (2003) in an examination of 31 countries found that financial disclosures are more transparent and national accounting standards require timelier (accrual-based) reporting in countries with stronger investor protection (common law countries). The authors address the debate regarding international accounting standards by suggesting that in the absence of a change in market forces and institutional factors, simply transplanting accounting rules from one country to another is futile. Similarly, Ball et al. (2003) debate that the global accounting debate focuses too much on the choice of accounting standards and too little on market forces and institutional factors. Although, Francis et al. (2003) found that common law countries have higher-quality accounting and auditing standards and the enforcement of such standards through higher-quality auditing is more likely to exist than in civil law countries, differences existed in values for variables within common law countries. Although, S.A., the U.K., and the U.S. are common law countries with the strongest legal protection of investors (compared to civil law countries), the development of the financial market in South Africa is much less than that of the financial markets in the U.K. and the U.S. Furthermore, Appiah-Kusi and Menyah (2003) in an examination of return predictability in African markets conclude that the South African market is inefficient; stock prices do not adjust rapidly to the arrival of new information, hence, future prices can be predicted from lagged prices.

Given the differences in institutional and market forces for South Africa, versus the U.K. and the U.S., management's incentives to engage in earnings management in South Africa may outweigh the costs. Ball et al. (2000) argue that when the costs of complying with IAS are viewed as exceeding the costs of non-compliance, substantial non-compliance will occur. In this study, earnings management (quality) is determined by examining discretionary accruals for the U.S., S.A., and U.K.-based firms. We compare the discretionary accruals of S.A. firms (IAS) and U.K. firms (IAS) with discretionary accruals of U.S. firms (U.S. GAAP). Based on these arguments and results, we hypothesize as follows:

H1. S.A.-based firms report relatively higher discretionary accruals compared to U.S. firms.

H2. U.K.-based firms report discretionary accruals that are not significantly different from that of U.S. firms.

This study examines the quality of financial statements under IAS by comparing management's use of discretionary accruals under IAS with management's use of discretionary accruals under U.S. GAAP, given differences in institutional and market forces.

FINANCIAL REPORTING IN S.A. AND THE U.K.

We select S.A. and the U.K. to study because the former is an emerging stock exchange that permits application of IAS to list, and the latter is a developed stock exchange that permits application of IAS of its foreign registrants to list. Some argue that application of GAAP may vary between countries because of the varying business environments and literal translation of standards. For example, the types of business transactions of a developed country may be less susceptible to management's discretionary reporting than in a less-developed country (see Choi, Frost, & Meek, 2003). The U.K. is an industrialized country where management is faced with determining significant amounts of intangibles/amortization and depreciation of tangible assets. In S.A., a less-developed country, management may be more concerned with managing its human capital as it represents the greatest percentage of production/mining cost, which is not measured in the financial reports. Hence, when discussing the quality of IAS, it seems relevant to measure its quality across two levels of economic development. Below we discuss the regulatory bodies and financial reporting requirements in S.A. and the U.K.

The Johannesburg Stock Exchange (JSE), located in Johannesburg, S.A., became privately owned after the end of apartheid in 1995. The JSE is an emerging stock exchange, the third largest emerging market. The Council of the South Africa Institute of Chartered Accountants (SAICA) and the Accounting Practices Board promulgate S.A. Accounting Standards. The SAICA adopts IAS with occasional minor modifications, and listed companies may follow S.A. GAAP or IAS. S.A. GAAP is almost identical to IAS except that S.A. eliminates some of the alternative treatments permitted by IAS. Hence, compliance with S.A. GAAP is compliance with IAS, but compliance with IAS may not be in compliance with S.A. GAAP. The JSE requires all listed firms to provide annual financial statements that are in English, and audited by an independent accountant (McDonald & Prather-Kinsey, 2002).

In contrast, the London Stock Exchange (LSE) is a developed stock market. The Accounting Standards Board (ASB) promulgates U.K. accounting standards. Like S.A. and the U.S., the ASB is an independent not-for-profit regulatory body. The ASB statements of Standard Accounting Practice and Financial Reporting Standards are very similar to IAS. In fact, the LSE now allows foreign registrants to present their financial statements in accordance with IAS (Larson & Kenny, 1994). Listed companies must provide audited annual and half-year interim reports (Choi et al., 2002).

JSE, LSE, and U.S. stock exchanges are similar in that accounting standards are promulgated by the accountancy profession, and the accounting regulatory structure is of British origin. Both the LSE and JSE may have markets that respond less to financial disclosures than the U.S. (see Frost & Pownall, 1994; Appiah-Kusi & Menyah, 2003). U.S. managers may manage their discretionary accruals more than the U.K. and S.A. firms because of the U.S. market's sensitivity to disclosures. Hence, we use the U.S. as a benchmark for measuring the quality of IAS reporting in S.A. and the U.K.

RESEARCH METHODOLOGY

Research Design

Prior studies have documented discretionary accruals as a measure of earnings management (Healy, 1985; DeAngelo, 1986; Jones, 1991; DeFond & Jiambalvo, 1991; Dechow, Sloan, & Sweeney, 1995; Becker, DeFond, Jiambalvo, & Subramanyam, 1998). Becker et al. (1998) examined the effect of audit quality on earnings management by utilizing discretionary accruals as a measure of earnings quality. This study measures earnings quality by examining discretionary accruals for U.S. firms, S.A. firms, and U.K.-based firms. We compare the discretionary accruals of firms complying with U.S. GAAP and IAS. Discretionary accruals are estimated using a cross-sectional version of a model developed in Jones (1991). Specifically, discretionary accruals are estimated from the following model:

$$TA_{ijt}/A_{ijt-1} = a_{jt}[1/A_{ijt-1}] + \beta_{1jt}[\Delta REV_{ijt}/A_{ijt-1}] + \beta_{2jt}[PPE_{ijt}/A_{ijt-1}] + e_{ijt}$$

$$(1)$$

where TA_{ijt} = total accruals for sample firm i in industry j for year t;

A_{ijt-1} = total assets for sample firm i in industry j for year $t - 1$;
ΔREV_{ijt} = change in net revenues for sample firm i in industry j for year t;
PPE_{ijt} = gross property plant and equipment for sample firm i in industry j for year t;
e_{ijt} = error term for sample firm i in industry j for year t.

Total accruals are measured using COMPUSTAT data and defined as income before extraordinary items minus operating cash flows. Standard Industrial Classification (SIC) codes are used to assess company industry. As in Becker et al. (1998), Subramanyam (1996), and DeFond and Park (1997), discretionary accruals are defined as the error term from the regression above.

Sample Selection

We selected firms for this study and obtained descriptive statistics based on data for the years 1999, 2000, and 2001. The sample consists of 1,583 U.S. firms complying with U.S. GAAP, 154 S.A. firms complying with IAS and

1,429 U.K. firms complying with IAS for the years 1999, 2000, and 2001. The S.A. and U.K. firms listed on the JSE and LSE, respectively, were selected from Global Vantage. The U.S. firms were selected, without replacement, based on those with the closest sales and in the same industry classification as the S.A. and U.K. sample. The 1,583 U.S.-based firms were selected from COMPUSTAT.

Total accruals, measured using COMPUSTAT and Global Vantage data, are defined as income before extraordinary items minus operating cash flows. SIC codes are used to assess company industry. As in Becker et al. (1998), Subramanyam (1996), and DeFond and Park (1997), discretionary accruals are defined as the error term from the regression model (see regression model (1)). The control variables include size (total assets), market capitalization, country of domicile, size of the home equity market, and the number of exchanges on which a company lists. We exclude multinationality and leverage as control variables because prior research (Street & Nichols, 2002) has not found these variables useful in explaining the extent of accounting disclosures.

Prior studies have found that compliance with IAS standards and type of auditor influence the level of IAS compliance. This study controls for these factors by including only companies whose financial reports are prepared in compliance with IAS standards and are audited by Big 5 firms. Street, Nichols, and Gray (2000) found that size of home equity market and country of domicile may also affect the degree of compliance with IAS. We control for size of home equity market and country of domicile by testing each market, S.A., U.K., and U.S. separately.

Descriptive Statistics

Table 1 presents financial variables describing S.A. IAS, United Kingdom IAS, and U.S. firms' U.S. GAAP, respectively. Panels A, B, and C present variables for S.A., U.K., and U.S. firms, respectively, with the results of parametric and non-parametric tests comparing S.A. firms to U.S. firms, U.K. firms, to U.S. firms, and both S.A. and U.K. firms to U.S. firms. Specifically, assets, earnings, operating cash flows, and absolute value of total accruals are not significantly different for S.A. firms and U.S. firms in the sample. However, mean total accruals are significantly different between S.A. and U.S. firms ($p = 0.02$). Similarly, mean total accruals are significantly different between U.K. firms and U.S. firms in the sample ($p = 0.000$). Furthermore assets, earnings, and operating cash flows are

Table 1. Descriptive Statistics for 1999, 2000, 2001 – All Firm Years (*n* = 3,166).

Variable Name	Mean	Median	Standard Deviation	t-Statistic (p-value)	Z-Statistic (p-value)
Panel A: South African Stock Exchange (*n* = 154)					
Natural log of assets	6.234	6.226	1.242	0.507	0.952
Income before extraordinary items/total assets	0.136	0.084	0.273	0.100	0.219
Operating cash flows/total assets	0.134	0.115	0.145	0.265	0.113
Total liabilities/total assets	0.580	0.539	0.310	0.671	0.712
Total accruals/total assets	−0.002	−0.040	0.274	0.020	0.019
Absolute value of total accruals/total assets	0.116	0.065	0.249	0.189	0.585
Panel B: London Stock Exchange (*n* = 1,429)					
Natural log of assets	5.688	5.456	1.753	0.000	0.000
Income before extraordinary items/total assets	0.091	0.071	0.128	0.020	0.809
Operating cash flows/total assets	0.152	0.135	0.123	0.053	0.000
Total liabilities/total assets	0.632	0.585	0.349	0.093	0.000
Total accruals/total assets	−0.062	−0.069	0.165	0.000	0.000
Absolute value of total accruals/total assets	0.096	0.077	0.147	0.357	0.000
Panel C: New York Stock Exchange (*n* = 1,583)					
Natural log of assets	5.985	5.796	1.618	0.000	0.000
Income before extraordinary items/total assets	0.105	0.067	0.211	0.115	0.523
Operating cash flows/total assets	0.139	0.117	0.247	0.095	0.000
Total liabilities/total assets	0.605	0.546	0.440	0.131	0.000
Total accruals/total assets	−0.033	−0.050	0.242	0.004	0.000
Absolute value of total accruals/total assets	0.101	0.065	0.223	0.626	0.000

Note: Tests are two-tailed. *t*-Statistics are from *t*-tests of the differences in the means and Wilcoxon *Z*-statistics are from Wilcoxon two-sample tests.

significantly different between U.K. firms and U.S. firms. The median for log of assets for U.S. firms is $5.8 million compared to $5.4 million for U.K. firms and median cash flows are 11.7% of total assets for U.S. firms compared to 13.5% of total assets for U.K. firms. In conclusion, Table 1 reports differences between U.S. firms' U.S. GAAP and South African firms' and United Kingdom firms' IAS with respect to size and total accruals across the three samples. Additionally, non-parametric tests indicate differences in cash flows and absolute value of discretionary accruals. Therefore, in addition to a univariate test of our hypothesis, we also perform a multivariate test that includes control variables of log of assets, operating cash flows, and total accruals.

RESULTS

Univariate Results

Table 2 presents the univariate analysis of discretionary accruals. Mean and median discretionary accruals and the absolute value of discretionary accruals are presented for the S.A., U.K., and U.S. firms in panels A, B, and C, respectively. Panel D presents the differences from subtracting the means for matched pair samples for S.A. and U.S. firms, U.K. and U.S. firms, and U.K. and S.A. firms (combined) versus U.S. firms, along with the results of t-tests of the differences between the groups. Panel A indicates that U.S., firms report mean (median) discretionary accruals of 0.2% (-0.9%) of total assets. The t-tests indicate that the mean discretionary accrual is significantly different from zero for U.S. firms in the sample. As indicated in panel B, S.A. firms have mean (median) discretionary accruals of 2% (-2%) of total assets. The mean central tendency measure is significantly different from zero. Sections A–C indicate that the mean values of discretionary accruals are largest among S.A. firms. As indicated in panel C, U.K. firms have mean (median) discretionary accruals of -2.0% (-2.2%) of total assets. The t-tests indicate that the mean central tendency is significantly negative. Panel D indicates that the difference in absolute value of discretionary accruals for South African versus U.S. firms is statistically significant ($p = 0.031$). The absolute value of discretionary accruals is one way of measuring management's discretion in accounting choices that result in both increases in income, as well as, decreases in income. Panels A–C indicate that the mean values of absolute value of discretionary accruals are largest among South African firms. This finding is consistent with managers of South

Table 2. Discretionary Accruals for Sample Firms from South Africa, United Kingdom, and United States during 1999, 2000, 2001.

Panel A: Observations from Firms on **New York** Stock Exchange ($n = 1,583$)

	Mean	Median	*p*-value
Discretionary accruals	0.002	−0.009	0.000
Absolute value of discretionary accruals	0.088	0.048	0.000

Panel B: Observations from Firms on **South African** Stock Exchange ($n = 154$)

	Mean	Median	*p*-value
Discretionary accruals	0.019	−0.017	0.024
Absolute value of discretionary accruals	0.108	0.055	0.000

Panel C: Observations from Firms on **London** Stock Exchange ($n = 1,429$)

	Mean	Median	*p*-value
Discretionary accruals	−0.020	−0.022	0.000
Absolute value of discretionary accruals	0.078	0.054	0.000

Panel D: Differences Across Samples

	(B−A) Mean (*p*-value)	(C−A) Mean (*p*-value)	(B+C)−A Mean (*p*-value)
Discretionary accruals	0.0269	−0.022	−0.015
	0.248	0.004	0.045
Absolute value of discretionary accruals	0.0454	−0.009	−0.006
	0.031	0.189	0.343

Note: In Panel A–C, *p*-values for means are from *t*-tests to measure central tendencies from zero. Panel D represents the differences from subtracting the means for matched pair samples for South African and U.S. firms, U.K. and U.S firms, U.K. and S.A. firms versus U.S. firms. In Panel D, *p*-values for means are from *t*-tests.

African firms having greater flexibility in the choice of discretionary accruals. In contrast, panel D indicates that U.K. firms report discretionary accruals that are on average 2.2% of assets lower than the discretionary accruals reported by U.S. firms. This difference is statistically significant ($p = 0.004$).

MULTIVARIATE RESULTS

A limitation of the univariate analysis is that it ignores a number of variables that potentially confound the results. Accordingly, we conduct a multivariate analysis that controls for differences across the sample groups that may confound simple univariate comparisons. The descriptive data in Table 1 indicates differences in the size of firms across the three groups (U.S., U.K., and S.A.). Therefore, we include log of assets to control for the potential effects of size on the choice of discretionary accruals. Table 1 also indicates differences in operating cash flows across the countries. Accordingly, operating cash flows are included in the multivariate regression. Table 1 indicates differences in the total accruals across countries. Therefore, since total accruals differ across countries, and to control for the possibility that firms with larger total accruals also have larger discretionary accruals, we include total accruals as control variables in our multivariate analysis.

In the multivariate analysis, discretionary accruals are estimated as described in Model 1 of the research design section. In the multivariate analysis, discretionary accruals are regressed on a dummy variable indicating country type (U.S., U.K., or S.A.) and the control variables noted above. The multivariate analysis is performed by estimating the coefficients in the following regression model:

$$DA_{it} = \beta_0 + \beta_1 OCF_{it} + \beta_2 Assets_{it} + \beta_3 ToAccr_{it} + \beta_4 NumExchs_{it}$$
$$+ \beta_5 SACtyInc_{it} + \beta_6 LCtyInc_{it} + \beta_7 ShareIncr_{it} + \beta_8 ShareDecr_{it} + e_{it} \quad (2)$$

where DA_{it} = estimated discretionary accrual from regression model 1;

OCF = operating cash flows;
Assets = natural log of total assets;
ToAccr = total accruals;
NumExchs = number of stock exchanges on which a company lists;
SACtyInc = country of location of listing equals 1 if it is S.A., 0 otherwise;
LCtyInc = country of location of listing equals 1 if it is London, 0
   otherwise;
ShareIncr = dummy variable equal to 1 when there is a increase of $<10\%$
   of shares outstanding during the a year, 0 otherwise;
ShareDecr = dummy variable equal to 1 when there is a decline of $>10\%$ of
   shares outstanding during the a year, 0 otherwise.

Table 3 presents the results of a multivariate analysis with the control variables discussed earlier in this section. In Table 3, the coefficient on the South African location dummy variable indicates that South African firms report discretionary accruals that are higher than the U.S. and U.K. firms by an average of 3.0% of assets. In Table 2, mean absolute value of discretionary accruals for South African firms exceeded those of U.S. firms by 4.5%. In Table 3, the coefficient on the United Kingdom location dummy variable indicates that United Kingdom firms report discretionary accruals that are lower than U.S. and South African firms by an average of 1.6% of

Table 3. OLS Regression of Discretionary Accruals on U.S., U.K., and S.A. Firms and Control Variables.

Variable	Pooled Estimate	*t*-Statistic	*p*-Value
Intercept	0.177	12.33	0.000
OCF	0.120	7.42	0.000
Assets	−0.018	−8.31	0.000
ToAccr	0.000	7.51	0.000
NumExchs	−0.007	−1.70	0.089
SACtyInc	0.031	1.28	0.040
LCtyInc	−0.016	−2.54	0.011
ShareIncr	0.038	3.97	0.000
ShareDecr	0.013	0.72	0.471

total assets. This is consistent with Table 2 that indicates that mean discretionary accruals for U.K. firms are 2.2% less than those of U.S. firms. Thus, the results of the multivariate analysis are consistent with those of the univariate analysis.

The control variables, operating cash flow, total assets, and total accruals in Table 3 are significantly associated with discretionary accruals. Discretionary accruals are positively associated with operating cash flows and total accruals. Discretionary accruals are negatively associated with total assets (log of assets). Furthermore, discretionary accruals of firms that list on more than one stock exchange are not significantly different than the discretionary accruals of firms that only list on one stock exchange. The discretionary accruals for firms with more than a 10% increase in the number of outstanding shares during the year were 3.8% higher than the discretionary accruals for firms with no increase in the number of shares outstanding.

SUMMARY AND CONCLUSIONS

This study is motivated by the global accounting debate about IAS and U.S. GAAP. The debate focuses primarily on the quality of financial reporting using IAS versus U.S. GAAP. There is little empirical evidence regarding the affect of market forces and institutional factors on the quality of financial reporting. This study contributes to the global accounting debate by utilizing U.S.-based companies complying with U.S. GAAP as a benchmark for measuring the quality of IAS as applied by S.A. (South Africa) and U.K. (United Kingdom) companies. Although, S.A., U.K., and U.S. are common law countries with the strongest of legal protection for investors (compared to civil law countries), the development of the financial market in South Africa is much less than that of the financial markets in the U.K. and the U.S. Earnings quality is determined by examining discretionary accruals for the U.S. firms, S.A. firms, and U.K.-based firms. We compare the discretionary accruals of firms complying with U.S. GAAP with the discretionary accruals of firms complying with IAS, given differences in institutional factors and market forces.

The results of our study indicate that S.A. firms utilizing IAS report absolute values of discretionary accruals that are significantly greater than the absolute values of discretionary accruals of U.S. firms utilizing U.S. GAAP. Given the institutional factors and market forces, evidenced by an emerging market with market inefficiency and inadequate disclosure (Appiah-Kusi & Menyah, 2003) in South Africa, management's incentives to engage in earnings management may outweigh the costs. In contrast, U.K. firms utilizing IAS report discretionary accruals that are significantly less than the discretionary accruals of companies in the United States reporting under U.S. GAAP. These results imply that managers in the U.K. are more conservative in reporting earnings than in the U.S. That is, the quality of IAS is dependent on the institutional factors and market forces of a country.

In this study, we investigate whether the quality of financial statements prepared in accordance with IAS are consistent with the quality of financial statements prepared in accordance with U.S. GAAP. This study contributes to the literature by providing evidence of the quality of financial information prepared under IAS, and its dependency on the institutional factors and market forces of a country.

NOTE

1. We realize that International Accounting Standards (IAS) are now referred to as International Financial Reporting Standards (IFRS). However, when we began this study the International Accounting Standards Board's (IASB's) pronouncements were referred to as IAS and when the core project standards, which are used in this study, were completed, they were referred to as IAS.

REFERENCES

Appiah-Kusi, J., & Menyah, K. (2003). Return predictability in African stock markets. *Review of Financial Economics, 12,* 247–270.

Ashbaugh, H., & Olsson, P. (2002). An exploratory study of the valuation properties of cross-listed firms' IAS and U.S. GAAP earnings and book values. *The Accounting Review, 77*(January), 107–126.

Ball, R., Kothari, S., & Robin, A. (2000). The effect of international institutional factors on properties of Accounting Earnings. *Journal of Accounting and Economics, 29*(February), 1–51.

Ball, R., Robin, A., & Wu, J. (2003). Incentives versus Standards: Properties of accounting income in four Asian countries and implications for acceptance of IAS. *Journal of Accounting and Economics, 36*, 235–270.

Becker, C., DeFond, M. L., Jiambalvo, J., & Subramanyam, K. R. (1998). The effect of audit quality on earnings management. *Contemporary Accounting Research, 15*(1), 1–24.

Choi, F. D. S., Frost, C. A., & Meek, G. K. (2002). *International Accounting* (4th ed.). Upper Saddle River, NJ: Prentice-Hall.

Darrough, M. N., Pourjalali, H., & Saudagaran, S. (1998). Earnings management in Japanese companies. *The International Journal of Accounting, 33*(3), 313–334.

DeAngelo, L. (1986). Accounting numbers as market valuation substitutes: A study of management buyouts of public stockholders. *Accounting Review, 61*(July), 400–420.

Dechow, P., Sloan, R., & Sweeney, A. (1995). Detecting earnings management. *Accounting Review, 70*(April), 193–225.

DeFond, M. L., & Jiambalvo, J. (1991). Incidence and circumstances of accounting errors. *Accounting Review, 66*, 643–655.

DeFond, M. L., & Park, C. W. (1997). Smoothing income in anticipation of future earnings. *Journal of Accounting and Economics, 23*, 115–140.

Francis, J., Khurana, I. K., & Pereira, R. (2003). The role of accounting and auditing in corporate governance and the development of financial markets around the world. *Asia-Pacific Journal of Accounting & Economics, 10*, 1–30.

Frost, C., & Pownall, G. (1994). A comparison of the stock price response to earnings disclosures in the United States and the United Kingdom. *Contemporary Accounting Research, 11*, 59–83.

Harris, M., & Muller, K. (1999). The market valuation of IAS versus U.S. GAAP accounting measures using form 20-F reconciliations. *Journal of Accounting and Economics, 26*, 285–312.

Healy, P. M. (1985). The effect of bonus schemes on accounting decisions. *Journal of Accounting and Economics, 7*(April), 85–107.

Jones, J. (1991). Earnings management during import relief investigations. *Journal of Accounting Research, 29*(Autumn), 193–228.

Larson, R. K., & Kenny, S. (1994). Raising capital overseas: International accounting standards may facilitate the process. *The CPA Journal, 64*, 64–67.

Leuz, C. (2003). IAS versus U.S. GAAP: Information asymmetry-bases evidence from Germany's New Market. *Journal of Accounting Research, 41*(June)(3), 445–473.

Leuz, C., & Verrecchia, R. (2000). The economic consequences of increased disclosure. *Journal of Accounting Research, 38*(Suppl 2000), 91–124.

Levitt, A. (1998). The importance of high quality accounting standards. *Accounting Horizons, 12*(1), 79–82.

McDonald C., & Prather-Kinsey, J. (2002). *The usefulness of developed country accounting standards in emerging stock markets: South Africa and Mexico.* Working paper, University of Missouri.

McGregor, W. (1999). An insider's view of the current state and future direction of International Accounting Standards Setting. *Accounting Horizons, 13*(2), 159–168.

Street, D. L., & Nichols, N. B. (2002). LOB and geographic segment disclosures: An analysis of the impact of IAS 14 revised. *Journal of International Accounting, Auditing and Taxation, 11*, 91–114.

Street, D. L., Nichols, N. B., & Gray, S. J. (2000). Assessing the acceptability of international accounting standards in the US: An empirical study of the materiality of US GAAP reconciliations by non-U.S. companies complying with IASC standards. *The International Journal of Accounting, 9*(1), 27–63.

Subramanyam, K. R. (1996). The pricing of discretionary accruals. *Journal of Accounting and Economics, 22*, 249–282.

USING "STATEMENT OF INTERMEDIATE BALANCES" AS TOOL FOR INTERNATIONAL FINANCIAL STATEMENT ANALYSIS IN AIRLINE INDUSTRY

C. Richard Baker, Yuan Ding and Hervé Stolowy

ABSTRACT

Since September 11, 2001 and during the ensuing economic slowdown, a number of airline companies have experienced significant financial difficulties, including bankruptcies and near bankruptcies. In an economic setting where many airlines are struggling to achieve or maintain profitability, it is important for accountants, auditors, and financial analysts to be able to analyze the relative performance of such companies. In this industry, income statements are normally prepared "by nature" rather than "by function." This differs from the usual presentation found in the income statements of many companies around the world, in particular most American companies. This paper demonstrates how to perform a comparative financial statement analysis when an income statement is prepared "by nature," through application of a tool called the "Statement

Advances in International Accounting

Advances in International Accounting, Volume 18, 169–198
ISSN: 0897-3660/doi:10.1016/S0897-3660(05)18009-X

of Intermediate Balances." This tool is illustrated using three companies chosen from different continents: Southwest Airlines, a low cost U.S. air carrier, Air France, the leader in Europe, and China Eastern Airlines, one of the biggest Chinese air carriers.

INTRODUCTION

Income statements (also known as "statements of operations" or "profit and loss accounts") can be presented in a manner that reflects two possible classifications of expenses, that is: "by nature" or "by function." In the first case, expenses are organized into categories like purchases, salaries, depreciation, rent, etc. In the second case, expenses are divided into "functions" like: selling and marketing, administration and general, research and development, etc. By tradition, or following local regulations, different countries may be more comfortable or more familiar with one of these two methods. For example, the "by function" form of presentation is well known in North America, while the "by nature" presentation is practiced in several European countries such as Italy, Spain, and France. In a particular country where one format is more practiced, the "alternative" format may not be familiar to the "financial community" (not only to financial analysts and investors, but also to academics and students). The main objective of this paper is to present a tool, called the "Statement of Intermediate Balances" (SIB), which is especially tailored to analyze an income statement presented "by nature." Despite a common belief that there is essentially one format for the income statement, an analysis of financial statements and annual reports on an international basis indicates that income statements presented "by nature" are widespread and are found, even in countries where the format "by function" is the general rule (or practice).

The airline industry provides particular evidence of the usefulness of the SIB because, in this sector, income statements are normally prepared "by nature" rather than "by function." In this paper, we will illustrate the use of the SIB by studying three companies chosen from different continents: Southwest Airlines Co. ("Southwest" in the rest of the chapter), a low cost U.S. air carrier, Air France, the leader in Europe (and now in the world, after completion of the merger with KLM), and China Eastern Airlines ("China Eastern"), one of the biggest Chinese air carriers.

INCOME STATEMENTS "BY NATURE" AND "BY FUNCTION"

Presentation

An income statement is intended to report how a company's financial and operating performance was achieved during a particular period. Such statements reflect the revenues and expenses of an enterprise during a period and display the net income for the period. Net income is typically the remainder after all expenses have been deducted from revenues and is a measure of the wealth generated by an economic entity (i.e. the net increase to stockholders' equity) during an accounting period.

An income statement can be organized in different ways with respect to its format (e.g. horizontal vs. vertical format), its degree of fineness, and the manner of classifying expenses (see Fig. 1).

Formats
An income statement includes a list of revenue and expense account balances, usually in aggregate form. The list of account balances can be presented as a continuous list (vertical format) or as two lists side by side (horizontal format).

Degree of Fineness
Expenses in an income statement are usually grouped into homogeneous categories and then subtracted step-by-step from revenues. With regard to the degree of fineness, the choice is between a single- or a multiple-step format.

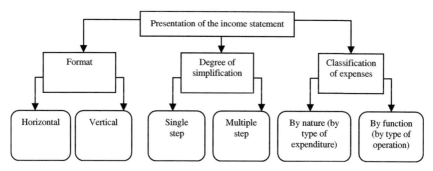

Fig. 1. Choices Regarding the Presentation of Income Statements.

Single step. This is the simplest version for an income statement. All revenues are grouped into one category and all expenses are grouped into another category. Expenses are then subtracted from revenues. A variation of this format can be seen, whereby all operating revenues are followed by all operating expenses. This permits the determination of operating income. Afterward, several sub levels of earnings may be presented (e.g. income before income tax, net income). This type of format is still considered to be a single-step format because the essential elements of the income statement (i.e. operating revenues and operating expenses) are presented separately.

Multiple step. In a multiple-step format, the revenue and expense categories are paired in a manner that highlights various sub components of net income (e.g. gross profit, operating income, income from continuing operations). The multiple-step format is the most common format used in business reporting because it is considered to be more informative than the single-step approach (see for more details, Kieso, Weygandt, & Warfield, 2001, p. 132).

Classification of Expenses

The distinction between classifying expenses "by nature" or "by function" is not addressed in U.S. GAAP (Generally Accepted Accounting Principles), even though U.S. government regulations do address this distinction. The International Accounting Standards Board (IASB) has specifically addressed the distinction between "by nature" and "by function" expense classification, by stating that:

> Expenses are subclassified to highlight components of financial performance that may differ in terms of frequency, potential for gain or loss and predictability. This analysis is provided in one of two forms ["by nature" or "by function"] (IASB, 2003, par. 90).

Classification by Function (or "Cost of Sales Method"). This type of income statement format classifies expenses according to their role in the determination of net income. Cost of goods sold, commercial, distribution, and administrative expenses are common categories employed in the "by function" format (see Fig. 2).

Classification by Nature (or "Nature of Expenditure Method"). In using the "by nature" format, expense accounts are combined in a way that reflects their nature (e.g. purchases of raw materials, transportation costs, taxes other than income tax, salaries and related costs, depreciation, etc.) (see

Income Statement by Function (Vertical Presentation)		Income Statement by Nature (Vertical Presentation)	
	Net sales revenue		Net sales
-	Cost of goods sold (cost of sales)	+	Other operating revenues
=	Gross margin	-	Cost of merchandise and raw materials sold and consumed
-	Commercial and distribution expenses	-	Labor and Personnel expenses
-	Administrative expenses	-	Other operating expenses
-	Other operating expenses	-	Depreciation expense
=	Operating income	=	Operating income

Fig. 2. Function of Expense Versus Nature of Expense Presentations.

Fig. 2). This format is relatively easy to use, even for small enterprises because no allocation or partitioning of expenses is required.

Choice of a Classification Approach

The multiple-step format, organized by function, is the most common format used by American companies (AICPA, 1999). In comparing the different approaches to income statement presentation, several remarks can be made

- A preference for classification "by nature" may reflect the requirements of governmental agencies that need such information to prepare national income accounts (this is often the case in European countries). A "by nature" presentation allows the calculation of the value added by an enterprise to the overall economy of a country. The "value added" concept is important for countries that have a value added tax system. In essence, the value added concept[1] measures the amount of value created by a firm beyond what it acquired from outside the economic entity (see Haller & Stolowy, 1998).
- Preference for a "by function" presentation often reflects an emphasis on the needs of capital markets. The "by function" format is the preferred method in North America, and it is used by most firms listed on the New York Stock Exchange.

The IASB has indicated that presentation of income statements "by function" "provides more relevant information to users than the classification of expenses by "nature" (IASB, 2003, par. 92). However, the IASB also points out that: "allocating costs to functions may require arbitrary allocations and involve considerable judgment." Paragraph 94 of the same standard recognizes that: "the choice between the function of expense method and the nature of expense method depends on historical and industry factors and the nature of the entity" (IASB, 2003). The IASB states that "each method of presentation has merit for different types of entities" (IASB, 2003, par. 94).

Compared to the classification "by function," the format "by nature" is a disaggregated format, with more items disclosed, and the related risk of revealing potential inside information to competitors. The trade-offs between positive and negative aspects of disaggregation are an issue. However, as the format of the income statement is highly standardized in the airline industry (see below), competitors are on a more even playing field.

Reasons for Adoption of "By Nature" Format in Airline Industry

The search for explanations concerning the prevalence of the "by nature" format in the U.S. airline industry is difficult because the origin of this format is not stated explicitly in companies' annual reports. Some explanations for the "by nature" format have been obtained by contacting the investor relations departments at several U.S. airline companies and by performing a search of regulations issued by the U.S. Department of Transportation (DOT).

Airline accounting in the U.S. is determined in part by the Uniform System of Accounts and Reports (USAR) issued by the U.S. DOT (DOT, 2002). Pursuant to DOT regulations: "all profit and loss elements are accounted for within specific objective accounts, which are descriptive of both basic areas of financial activity, or functional operation, and objective served" (DOT, 2002, USAR, part 241, sections 1–3). The USAR envisions two types of classification; one by function (or financial activity) and one by nature (or objective). Section 7 of the USAR includes a "chart of profit and loss accounts" employing an "objective classification of profit and loss elements," including:

- Transport revenues (passenger, mail, property, charter, other),
- Transport-related revenues and expenses (in-flight sales, restaurant and food service (ground), rents, limousine service...),
- Transport expenses (pilots and copilots, other flight personnel, maintenance labor..., traffic commissions, general services purchased, landing fees, maintenance materials, passenger food expense, provisions for obsolescence and deterioration...).

The USAR states that: "The profit and loss accounts are designed to reflect, *through natural groupings*, the elements entering into the derivation of income or loss" (our emphasis) (USAR, part 141, section 8). This regulation provides some explanation of why U.S. airlines report their income statement "by nature." However, we have been unable to locate an official explanation concerning why the "by nature" format has arisen in the U.S. in the airline industry. We hypothesize that this choice was made because the "by nature" format provides a higher degree of detail by disclosing more expense items and is therefore more useful for decision making.

In France, regulations relating to consolidated financial statements (Anonymous, 1999, par. 410) allow companies to choose between the "by nature" and "by function" models. However, for non-consolidated financial statements (all legal entities in France are required to prepare separate financial statements prepared in accordance with the General Accounting Plan – "Plan Comptable Général"), the presentation "by nature" is required, given the influence of the national income accounting in France. The requirement of the "by nature" format for non-consolidated financial statements may explain why this format is the most commonly used in France for consolidated financial statements. In the case of Air France, despite the choice mentioned above regarding consolidated financial statements, the income statement is presented "by nature." This might be explained by the tradition in favor of this format and also by a sort of mimetic behavior, given the fact that virtually all airline companies in the world have adopted the "by nature" format for their income statements (see below).

In China, after the accounting reforms of 1992, the income statement format for all Chinese companies (whether listed or not) is very close to the U.S. one, i.e. a multiple-step format organized "by function." However, companies with listed shares on exchanges outside of China are required to prepare their financial statements in accordance with IASB, which, as mentioned above, authorize both formats. In the case of China Eastern Airlines, the choice of "by nature" presentation for their expenses could also be a mimetic practice in order to follow foreign competitors in the airline industry.

While our analysis of the financial statements of airline companies is not comprehensive, if we exclude the three studied companies, we did find that in the U.S., American Airlines, Continental Airlines, Delta Air Lines, Northwest Airlines, and United Airlines have adopted the "by nature" format. In other countries, Air Canada, Japan Airlines, and LanChile, to mention a few examples, also prepare their income statements "by nature." This format is therefore the dominant practice in the air transport industry on a worldwide basis.

PRESENTATION OF STATEMENT OF INTERMEDIATE BALANCES

Principles

When an income statement is presented "by nature," it is often useful to adjust the statement to highlight the key intermediate balances that determine the value creation process of the enterprise. In preparing a SIB, the following balances can be highlighted: "commercial margin," "value added," "gross operating income," and Earnings from Operations Before Interest, Taxes, Depreciation and Amortization "EBITDA." Fig. 3 demonstrates the structure of a SIB.

Essentially, the SIB dissects the income statement into meaningful blocks of data to help the user understand and interpret the firm's economic activity. The intermediate balances can be presented in monetary terms, or as percentage variations from one period to the next (trend analysis), or as percentages of some relevant basis (common-size analysis). The SIB can be particularly useful if a company has manufacturing operations combined with merchandising (i.e. wholesale or retail) activities.

Definition of Terms

Commercial Margin
The commercial margin expresses the difference between the sales of merchandise and the cost of merchandise sold.

Current Period Production
The company's industrial output during the period is the total of production sold plus the cost of self-produced fixed assets.

Value Added
The term "value added" is a concept used in National Income accounting. It refers to the amount contributed by a particular enterprise to the national wealth. Value added is defined as the increase in value resulting from the enterprise's activities over and above that of goods and services provided by third parties and consumed by the firm. The concept is used in a number of countries; especially Australia, France, Germany, South Africa, and the United Kingdom (see Haller & Stolowy, 1998). Value added represents the

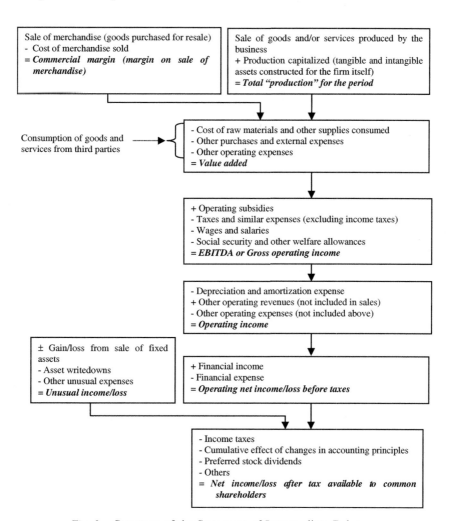

Fig. 3. Structure of the Statement of Intermediate Balances.

wealth created by the enterprise that will be distributed to various stake-holders including employees, lenders, governments, and shareholders.

EBITDA or Gross Operating Income

The EBITDA or Gross Operating Income measures the wealth created by the enterprise from its operations, independent of its financial income and expenses, and charges for depreciation and amortization. This indicator helps in evaluating the firm's short-term ability to create wealth since it is not affected by long-term strategic decisions regarding financing (i.e. capital structure) and capital investment policies. The ratio of EBITDA to sales (or accounting "production") is often considered to be a measure of the "business profitability" of the firm, thereby allowing inter-company comparisons. EBITDA is also considered to be a proxy for cash flow generated by operations.

Operating Income

Operating income or profit represents the results of the firm's normal and current activity without taking into account financial and unusual elements.

Net Operating Income before Income Taxes

Operating net income before taxes indicates economic and financial performance before consideration of unusual items and taxes.

Unusual Income (Loss)

Unusual income (loss) is the profit or loss from activities that are not related to the firm's usual operations. This "income" is shown as a separate item on the SIB.

Net Income (Loss)

The last line of the SIB is the Net Income (Loss), which is self-explanatory. This figure serves as a check on the equality between the adjusted SIB and the original income statement.

Income Statement "By Nature" Versus "By Function"

One of the features of income statements prepared "by nature" is that they allow the calculation of intermediate balances before the net income figure. The calculation of intermediate balances is a useful tool for financial statement analysis, particularly for comparative analyses of company performance. When an income statement is organized "by function," the calculation of intermediate balances such as commercial margin, value added, gross operating profit, and operating income are often difficult to perform. However, in the "by function" income statement, some other useful intermediate balances may be reported, such as: gross margin, operating income, etc. Consequently, neither format is necessarily superior to the other, and nor the format provides a complete understanding of the firm. One practical difficulty that arises in comparing income statements "by nature" with income statements "by function" is that the transformation of an income statement "by nature" to an income statement "by function" (and vice-versa) is a very difficult exercise because it requires knowledge of information (concerning inventory, detail of personnel expenses, etc.) that is typically not available to the financial analyst. In this context, one of the primary purposes of this paper is to argue that, when an income statement is presented "by nature," users of financial statements need to be trained to analyze this type of format because they will generally have less familiarity with it and there may be no way to convert the "by nature" format to the more familiar "by function" format. The preparation of a SIB can help analysts to understand the utility of the income statement prepared "by nature."

APPLICATION OF THE STATEMENT OF INTERMEDIATE BALANCES TO SOUTHWEST, AIR FRANCE, AND CHINA EASTERN

In an economic setting where a number of airline companies have experienced serious financial difficulties (e.g. in the U.S., Chapter 11 bankruptcy for U.S. Airways on August 11, 2002; financial restructuring of Continental Airlines in summer of 2002; Chapter 11 bankruptcy for United Airlines on December 9, 2002), it is important to be able to analyze and measure the relative performance of such companies. The following sections demonstrate how to perform, in an international setting, a comparative financial statement analysis when an income statement is prepared "by nature." The three companies studied in this case (Southwest, Air France, and China Eastern) were chosen for the following reasons. First, they are based in three different continents: North America, Europe, and Asia. Southwest is a U.S. based, "low-cost" carrier. Southwest experienced some financial difficulties after September 11th, but generally remained profitable. Air France is currently the largest airline in Continental Europe, and has become the largest airline in the world after completion of its merger with the Dutch company KLM. China Eastern is one of the largest Chinese air carriers.

Presentation of the Companies

The Management's Discussion and Analysis of Financial Position and Results of Operations (MD&A) in the annual report of United Airlines for the year 2001 summarized the state of the U.S. airline industry in particular, and the situation of world airline industry, as follows:

> Beginning in 2001, the weakening U.S. economy had a significant impact on the airline industry as corporations reduced their business travel budgets and changed their travel behavior. During the first six months of 2001, the industry began experiencing significant revenue declines as a result of the decrease in business traffic (…), particularly in the domestic markets. (…) United's revenues (…) were significantly impacted by the events of September 11 and the resulting reduction in the Company's operations."

In light of the continuing problems in the airline industry, and to better understand how the industry operates, we present financial statements prepared by nature for Southwest, Air France, and China Eastern.

Southwest is a major U.S. domestic airline that primarily provides short-haul, high frequency, point-to-point, low-fare service. Southwest carried 65.7 million passengers in 2003. Its fleet includes 388 aircraft at the end of 2003 (Southwest Air Lines Annual Report). By contrast, Air France is third worldwide in terms of transportation of international passengers and first in Europe in terms of traffic (before the merger with KLM). Air France carried 43.7 million passengers during fiscal 2003–2004. Its fleet included 372 aircraft as of March 31, 2004 (Air France Annual Report). China Eastern was established in the People's Republic of China in 1995. It is headquartered in Shanghai. Its shares are listed in Shanghai, Hong Kong, and New York. In 2003, China Eastern carried 12 million passengers. As at May 31, 2004, the Group operated a fleet of 102 aircraft (China Eastern Airlines Annual Report).

Appendix A contain the following:

• Consolidated Statements and statements of Income for the fiscal years ended December 31, 2000 through December 31, 2003 for Southwest (source: Annual Reports 2001, 2002, and 2003) (see Table A.1).
• Consolidated Income Statement for the fiscal years ended March 31, 2001 through March 31, 2004 for Air France (source: Annual Reports 2001–2002, 2002–2003, and 2003–2004) (see Table A.2).
• Consolidated Statements of Income for the fiscal years ended December 31, 2000 through December 31, 2003 for China Eastern (source: Annual Reports 2001, 2002, and 2003) (see Table A.3).

These consolidated financial statements have been respectively prepared in accordance with accounting principles generally accepted in the United States (Southwest), in France (Air France) and with International Financial Reporting Standards and the disclosure requirements of the Hong Kong Companies Ordinance (China Eastern). For simplification purposes, the term "income statement" is used to refer to the "consolidated statements of income" or "consolidated income statements" of the three companies studied.

From the previous annual reports of the three companies, we extracted the following comparative data:

	Southwest	Air France	China Eastern
	1999 (in $m)	1999–2000 (in €m)	1999 (in RMBm)
Passenger	4,563	8,377	8,031
Freight	103	1,240	1,730
Other	70	533	402
Maintenance		174	
Total	4,736	10,324	10,163

In the Southwest 2001, 2002, and 2003 Annual reports, the following additional information is provided:

- Agency commissions decreased primarily due to a change in the Company's commission rate policy.
- Depreciation expense increased due to the growth in the Company's aircraft fleet prior to September 11.
- "Other operating expenses" increased until 2002 due to a significant increase in passenger liability, aircraft hull, and third-party liability insurance costs following the terrorist attacks.
- In 2001, the "other gains/losses, net" include the Company's share of government grant funds under the Stabilization Act, arising from the terrorist attacks. On April 16, 2003, as a result of the United States war with Iraq, the Emergency Wartime Supplemental Appropriations Act (Wartime Act) was signed into law. Among other items, the legislation included a $2.3 billion government grant for airlines. Southwest received a share of the grant during second quarter 2003. This amount is included in "Other (gains) losses" in the accompanying Consolidated Income Statement for 2003.

In Air France's MD&A and notes to the financial statements for the year ended March 31, 2004, the following information is also included:

- Other operating revenues consist of the catering activities.
- Other external expenses include namely insurance premiums, professional fees, and aircraft engine rental costs.
- In 2003–2004, other operating income and charges, net mainly represents income linked to financial compensation on slot swaps at Heathrow airport.

From the China Eastern annual reports 2001, 2002, and 2003, we notice some changes in the presentation of the "Other income, net" and "Other operating income". The data disclosed in Table A.4 will allow restating some elements of the income statement in order to ensure comparability throughout the period (see Table A.4).

Additionally, the items "Aircraft depreciation and operating leases" and "Other depreciation and operating leases" mix depreciation and leases. In order to separate these two expenses, we found the amount of operating leases in the notes (see Table A.4).

Office and administration expenses mainly include training expenses, and expenses relating to overseas sales. Other operating expenses include maintenance expenses of other fixed assets, computer and telecommunications expenses, and other (unspecified) expenses. On December 31, 2002, the Group's fixed assets were revalued. The impact was charged to the income statement under the caption "Revaluation deficit of fixed assets."

Analysis of Format of Income Statements

Southwest, Air France, and China Eastern all use the vertical format for their income statements. Additionally, the first part of the income statement (up to the point "operating income" for Southwest and Air France, and "operating profit" for China Eastern), follows the single-step format, whereby operating expenses are subtracted from operating revenues. Following operating income, several sub-level earnings numbers are presented. This format corresponds to the variation of the single-step format discussed previously above.

More important, the three companies have clearly adopted the "by nature" format. Interestingly, China Eastern had a real choice because it follows the International Financial Reporting Standards which allow both formats. It appears likely that China Eastern adopted the format "by nature" in order to be consistent with international reporting practices in the airline industry.

Preparation of Statements of Intermediate Balances

Preliminary Indications

- The income statements for the three airline companies are presented "by nature," which is a necessary condition to the preparation of SIB.
- In a SIB, percentage figures usually do not appear following the year to which they relate because it is more important to have the percentages figures adjacent to one another. This allows the analyst to compare the evolution of the enterprise over the periods investigated. In practice, the percentages are as important, if not more important, than the absolute currency values.
- Common-sized SIB offer the advantage of allowing comparisons to be made between financial statements presented in different currencies, i.e. U.S. dollars (Southwest), Euros (Air France), and Renminbi (China Eastern).
- Common-sized SIB offer the additional advantage of allowing comparisons to be made between periods of unequal length (which is not the case here).
- If there is a difference between companies in the treatment of certain specific revenues or expenses, it is important to adjust these items so that they are treated in the same manner. For instance, the operating leases are included in China Eastern in the same caption with depreciation expenses. With the help of the notes, this amount has been restated (see Table A.4 and below). In the same vein, the "Share in net income of equity affiliates" in Air France has been restated to be included in the financing section, to be consistent with China Eastern and with the general definition of the SIB.
- The location of the sub-elements of the income statement can be different in the SIB from the income statement itself. For example, in Southwest, the "Other (gains) losses, net," which primarily relates to a Government grant, are treated as "unusual items" in the SIB.
- In the income statement of Southwest, the "other expenses (income)" line is presented with a sign opposite to that which would be considered to be a normal presentation (i.e. plus for expenses and minus for income).
- In the China Eastern SIB, the "Other income, net" and "Other operating income" have been restated to ensure comparability throughout the period (see Table A.4). Gain on disposal of aircraft and engines is reported under unusual items. This treatment is consistent with the two other airlines where the gains from sale of fixed assets are shown as unusual items.

- In the China Eastern SIB, the operating leases included in the items "Aircraft depreciation and operating leases" and "Other depreciation and operating leases" (see Table A.4) have been separated and reported in the consumption from third parties.
- In the China Eastern SIB, because office and administration expenses mainly include training expenses, and expenses relating to overseas sales, they have been included in the "Consumption from third parties."
- In the China Eastern SIB, other operating expenses include maintenance expenses of other fixed assets, computer and telecommunications expenses, and other (unspecified) expenses. They fit well in the "Consumption from third parties."
- In the China Eastern SIB, the "Revaluation deficit of fixed assets" has been considered as an unusual item.

Statement of Intermediate Balances
SIBs for Southwest (see Tables A.5 and A.6), Air France (see Tables A.7 and A.8), and China Eastern (see Tables A.9 and A.10), are presented both in absolute currency terms and in percentage terms (i.e. common-sized).

Comparative Analysis of Statements of Intermediate Balances

Revenues/Production[2]
Even though the common-sized SIBs are based on the principle of dividing all other figures in the statement by the total production for the year, we have added to the statement a line showing the change in revenues for each year as compared with the previous year. It can be seen that before the events of September 11, 2001, Southwest had the greatest growth in revenues (+19.3% in 2000), ahead of Air France (+18.9%), and China Eastern (+10.4%). After September 11th, the decrease in revenues was the greatest for Southwest (−1.7%). In contrast, Air France realized an increase (+2.0%) and China Eastern an even higher rise of 8.3%. In 2003, Southwest and China Eastern experienced an increase (7.5 and 9.2%, respectively) while the other company suffered a decrease (−2.8% for Air France).

The activities of the three companies are relatively different: China Eastern's revenues are more diversified (less passenger oriented) than Air France and significantly more diversified than Southwest. Seventy-two percent (71.9%) of China Eastern's revenues were derived from passengers versus 83.2% for Air France and 96.7% for Southwest in 2003.

Consumption from Third Parties

The ratio of Consumption from Third Parties to Total Production is lower for Southwest (47.9% in 2003) than for Air France (54.7% in 2003) and in particular as compared with China Eastern (72.5% in 2003). This ratio decreased for Air France and for Southwest in comparison with 2002 and 2001, indicating an ability to pass on increased costs to airline passengers. Looking at the breakdown of Consumption from Third Parties, we see that Fuel Cost represents the greatest expense for each of the companies (except for "Other Operating Expenses" for Southwest), especially for China Eastern. Fuel Cost as a percent of Total Production decreased for Air France over the period but increased for China Eastern from 2002 to 2003. This development can be explained by a decrease in consumption of fuel and a decrease in the average cost per gallon. For Southwest, the weight of fuel cost remained stable over the period (~14%).

Southwest was able to reduce the impact from Consumption from Third Parties because of a reduction in the amount of Commissions (i.e. fees paid to travel agents) (from 2.8% in 2000 to 0.8% in 2003). (The Company modified its system of paying commissions in 2001, which reduced this cost.) China Eastern experienced an even greater reduction in Commissions (from 5.7% in 2000 to 3.3% in 2003). For Air France, commissions decreased from 9.8% in 2000 to 8.5% in 2003. While Southwest was able to decrease its Aircraft Rental cost (at 3.1% in 2003), China Eastern increased its cost (from 6.9% in 2000 to 7.3% in 2003), and Air France faced a similar increase (from 3.3% in 2000 to 3.7% in 2003).

China Eastern reports the highest take off and landing charges (15.8% in 2003, versus 14.0% in 2000), compared to Air France (7.4% in 2003) and Southwest (6.3% in 2003).

We can also easily compare the maintenance costs expensed by the three companies. China Eastern comes first with 9.3% in 2003 (increasing from 7.3% in 2000), before Southwest (7.2% in 2003, 6.7% in 2000) and Air France (3.1% in 2003, 4.9% in 2000).

The composition of the category "Other operating expenses" or "Other" or "Other external expenses" may not be entirely comparable between the companies. The annual report of Southwest provides little specific information concerning the make up of Other Operating Expenses. The only information provided is that the category includes insurance premiums and advertising expenses. We learn that "Other operating expenses" increased due to a significant increase in passenger liability, aircraft hull, and third-party liability insurance costs following the terrorist attacks. For Air France, "Other external expenses" include insurance premiums, professional fees, and aircraft engine rental costs. As regards China Eastern, "Other operating expenses" include maintenance expenses of other fixed assets, computer and telecommunications expenses, and other (unspecified) expenses. These fit well in the "Consumption from third parties".

In general, it can be seen that Southwest generally has a lower cost structure than Air France and even lower than China Eastern. However, this relationship deteriorated throughout the period until 2002, with an increase in these costs for Southwest; while the other two companies were decreasing their consumption from third parties (this is especially true for Air France). The situation improved again for Southwest in 2003.

Value Added
While not widely used in North America, the Value Added figure shows the extent to which an enterprise contributes to the national wealth of the country (see Haller & Stolowy, 1998). The Value Added figure for Southwest declined sharply from 2000 to 2001 following the events of September 11th. This was because the cost of consumption from third parties increased in relation to total production. This trend shows that Southwest has been unable to pass along the increased cost to its customers. However, the situation improved for Southwest in 2003 and for Air France.

Gross Operating Income
The ratio of Salaries, Wages, and Benefits to Total Production for Southwest is generally much higher than for Air France and especially for China Eastern (37.5% in 2003 versus 33.1% for Air France and 10.1% for China Eastern). The increase recorded by Southwest was due in part to increased security requirements following the events of September 11th. Consequently, this increase explains why Southwest recorded a decrease in its Gross Operating Profit from 2000 (23%) to 2003 (14.6%). However, the Gross Operating Profit of Southwest is still higher than that of Air France (10.7% in 2003). China Eastern has by far the highest gross operating profit (17.3% in 2003), due to its low level of salaries.

As discussed previously, Gross Operating Income reflects the return derived from the core activities of the enterprise. The different Gross Operating Income figures indicate the relative performances of China Eastern and Southwest. A negative gross operating income (i.e. a Gross Operating Loss), which is not the case for any of our studied companies, is a sign of financial distress.

Operating Income
For Air France and Southwest, Depreciation and Amortization expense rose in 2003 in comparison with 2002, 2001, and 2000 because of the acquisition of additional aircraft and ground equipment. The ratio of Depreciation and Amortization to Total Production differs between the companies: 6.5% for Southwest in 2003, 9.6% for Air France in 2003, and 12.6% for China Eastern in 2003. The difference in the ratio of Depreciation and Amortization expense to Total Production slightly magnifies the gap between the Operating Income (Loss) of Southwest and China Eastern versus Air France. Air France has a very low operating income ("Earnings from operations") (1.1% in 2003, compared to 2.9% in 2000). Southwest posted very high but decreasing Operating income (8.1% in 2003, 18.1% in 2000). China Eastern has a decreasing operating income (1.8% in 2003).

Operating Net Income before Taxes
China Eastern's ratio of Interest Expense (Net) to Total Production is the highest in our sample (5% in 2003), but it decreased from 2000 (7.3%), which is a good sign. China Eastern must have a high level (although decreasing) of outstanding debt. Southwest recorded an increase in the Interest Expense ratio (from 1.2% in 2000 to 1.5% in 2003). Air France reports a very low level of interest expense (net) (0.5% in 2003). However, the comparison between the three studied companies should be made with caution as Southwest reports a gross interest expense when Air France and China Eastern disclose a net amount.

After adjustments for Interest Expense and other items, the Operating Net Income of Southwest remained positive in 2003 (7.6%) but decreasing (as compared with 18% in 2000). Air France a low ratio (1% in 2003) and China Eastern has a negative operating net income before taxes (−3.9% in 2003).

Unusual Income (Loss)
A special charge was recorded by Southwest in 2001 in relation to the September 11 terrorist attacks and the resulting impact on the companies' schedules and operations. However, the Company also received compensation under the Airline Stabilization Act, which partially offset their losses. The impact from unusual items was positive for Southwest (3.7% in 2001 and 4.4% in 2003). Air France also recorded a positive unusual item from gains on the disposal of fixed assets. China Eastern, conversely, recorded a loss on such items (−0.2% in 2003).

Net Income (Loss)
Southwest had the highest positive Net Income number at 7.4% of its Total Production in 2003. Air France disclosed a low net income percentage (0.8% in 2003), while China Eastern faced a loss in 2003 (−6.6% of Total Production).

Synthesis
The preparation of an SIB indicates that studying net income figures alone is not sufficient. If we look at the Value Added, Southwest has the highest amount. At the level of the gross Operating Income of the companies, it is clear that the situation of China Eastern is the best. At the level of Operating Income (Loss) before Taxes, the situation is once again better for Southwest. The situation for Southwest remained satisfactory because of its generally lower costs. However, it can be seen that there was deterioration even in Southwest's performance in 2002.

CONCLUSION

This chapter has demonstrated how to perform a comparative financial statement analysis when an income statement is prepared "by nature," through application of a tool called the "Statement of Intermediate Balances." This tool has been illustrated using three airline companies: Southwest, Air France, and China Eastern. It is particularly useful in a comparative and international setting. However, we should not forget that when working with the airline industry, the investment community also uses non-financial indicators (i.e. revenue passenger miles[3] or kilometers, revenue seat miles, passenger load factor, etc.) in addition to the information contained in financial statements. This non-financial information is not specifically dealt with in this chapter, but it can provide a useful complement to the preparation of a SIB (see Liedtka, 2002; Riley, Pearson, & Trompeter, 2003). From another perspective, we should remember that the SIB can be used outside the airline industry, if the income statement is reported by nature.

NOTES

1. "Value added" should not be confused with "economic value added," a term which is usually defined as operating income minus cost of capital employed.

2. All companies have no reselling activity. Consequently, there is no commercial margin to compute.

3. The term "revenue passenger mile" is defined as a mile flown on each flight stage multiplied by the number of "revenue passengers" on that stage. A "revenue passenger" is a person receiving air transportation from the air carrier for which remuneration is received by the air carrier.

ACKNOWLEDGMENT

Yuan Ding would like to acknowledge the financial support of the Research Center at the HEC School of Management (project A0306). Yuan Ding and Hervé Stolowy acknowledge the financial support of the Research Center in Financial Information (HEC Foundation). Both are Members of the GREGHEC, unité CNRS, FRE-2810.

REFERENCES

AICPA (1999). *Accounting trends and techniques – 1999.* New York: American Institute of Certified Public Accountants.

Air France Annual Report. http://www.airfrance-finance.com.

China Eastern Airlines Annual Report. http://www.ce-air.com/cea/en_U.S./investor/report

DOT (2002). *Uniform system of accounts and reports for large certificated air carriers.* Washington, DC: Department of Transportation, http://www.bts.gov/lawlib/docs/Part241-cy2000.pdf.

Haller, A., & Stolowy, H. (1998). Value added in financial accounting: A comparative study of Germany and France. *Advances in International Accounting, 11,* 23–51.

IASB (2003). *International accounting standard (IAS) No. 1: Presentation of financial statements (revised).* London: International Accounting Standards Board.

Kieso, D., Weygandt, J., & Warfield, T. (2001). *Intermediate accounting* (10th ed.). NY: Wiley.

Liedtka, S. L. (2002). The information content of nonfinancial performance measures in the airline industry. *Journal of Business Finance and Accounting, 29*(7–8), 1105–1121.

Riley, R. A., Pearson, T. A., & Trompeter, G. (2003). The value relevance of non-financial performance variables and accounting information: The case of the airline industry. *Journal of Accounting and Public Policy, 22*(3), 231–254.

Southwest Air Lines Annual Report. http://www.southwest.com

Anonymous (1999). *Règles et méthodes relatives aux comptes consolidés, arrêté du 22 juin 1999 portant homologation du règlement 99-02 du 29 avril 1999 du comité de la réglementation comptable (rules and methods relating to consolidated accounts – arrêté of june 22, 1999, approving the regulation No. 99-02 of april 29, 1999, of the accounting regulation committee).* Paris: Accounting Regulation Committee.

APPENDIX A

Consolidated income statements and statements of intermediate balances of Southwest, Air France and China Eastern.

Table A.1.   Southwest Airlines Consolidated Statements of Income for Years ended December 31, 2003, 2002, 2001, and 2000.

(In Millions of U.S. $)	2003	2002	2001	2000
Operating revenues				
Passenger	5,741	5,342	5,379	5,468
Freight	94	84	91	111
Other	102	96	85	71
Total operating revenues	5,937	5,522	5,555	5,650
Operating expenses				
Salaries, wages, and benefits	2,224	1,992	1,856	1,684
Fuel and oil	830	762	771	805
Maintenance materials and repairs	430	390	397	378
Agency commissions	48	55	103	160
Aircraft rentals	183	187	192	196
Landing fees and other rentals	372	345	311	265
Depreciation	384	356	318	281
Other operating expenses	983	1,017	976	860
Total operating expenses	5,454	5,104	4,924	4,629
Operating income	483	418	631	1,021
Other expenses (income)				
Interest expense	91	106	70	70
Capitalized interest	(33)	(17)	(21)	(28)
Interest income	(24)	(37)	(43)	(40)
Other (gains) losses, net	(259)	(27)	(203)	2
Total other expenses (income)	(225)	25	(197)	4
Income before income taxes and cumulative effect of change in accounting principle	708	393	828	1,017
Provision for income taxes	266	152	317	392
Income before cumulative effect of changes in accounting principles	442	241	511	625
Cumulative effect of changes in accounting principles, Net of income tax	0	0	0	(22)
Net income	442	241	511	603
Preferred stock dividends	0	0	0	0
Net income (loss) available to common shareowners	442	241	511	603

Table A.2. Air France Consolidated Income Statements for Years ended March 31, 2004, 2003, 2002, and 2001.

(In Millions of EUR)	2003–2004	2002–2003	2001–2002	2000–2001
Operating revenues				
Passenger	10,260	10,527	10,378	10,022
Cargo	1,412	1,479	1,448	1,491
Maintenance	508	540	548	566
Other	157	141	154	201
Total operating revenues	12,337	12,687	12,528	12,280
Operating expenses				
Aircraft fuel	(1,302)	(1,369)	(1,443)	(1,625)
Chartering costs	(414)	(415)	(639)	(741)
Aircraft operating lease costs	(458)	(522)	(489)	(410)
Landing fees and en route charges	(913)	(934)	(882)	(814)
Catering	(296)	(319)	(329)	(323)
Handling charges and other operating costs	(756)	(768)	(747)	(697)
Aircraft maintenance costs	(381)	(477)	(652)	(598)
Commercial and distribution costs	(1,051)	(1,157)	(1,133)	(1,199)
Other external expenses	(1,183)	(1,213)	(1,152)	(1,083)
Salaries and related costs	(4,079)	(3,856)	(3,738)	(3,436)
Taxes other than income tax	(186)	(187)	(163)	(154)
Total operating expenses	(11,019)	(11,217)	(11,367)	(11,080)
Gross operating result	1,318	1,470	1,161	1,200
Charge to depreciation/amortization, net	(1,184)	(1,195)	(972)	(915)
Charge to operating provisions, net	(46)	(115)	(39)	62
Gain on disposal of flight equipment, net	7	30	78	88
Other operating income and charges, net	44	2	7	8
Operating income	139	192	235	443
Restructuring costs	(22)	(13)	(11)	(5)
Net financial charges	(60)	(85)	(112)	(137)
Gains on disposals of subsidiaries and affiliates, net	5	4	24	96
Pretax income (loss)	62	98	136	397
Share in net income of equity affiliates	53	29	31	45
Amortization of goodwill	(15)	(16)	(16)	(62)
Income (loss) before income tax and minority interests	100	111	151	380
Income tax	(2)	13	5	45
Income (loss) before minority interests	98	124	156	425
Minority interests	(5)	(4)	(3)	(4)
Net income (loss)	93	120	153	421

Table A.3.   China Eastern Airlines Consolidated Statements of Income
for Years ended December 31, 2003, 2002, 2001, and 2000.

(In Millions of RMB)	2003	2002	2001	2000
Traffic revenues				
Passenger	10,261	10,038	9,587	8,644
Cargo and mail	3,187	2,445	2,092	2,124
Other operating revenues	829	596	474	452
Turnover	14,277	13,079	12,153	11,220
Other operating income	2	226	128	0
Operating expenses				
Wages, salaries, and benefits	(1,449)	(1,036)	(773)	(798)
Take off and landing charges	(2,254)	(1,988)	(1,703)	(1,572)
Aircraft fuel	(3,045)	(2,564)	(2,613)	(2,327)
Food and beverages	(542)	(606)	(567)	(499)
Aircraft depreciation and operating leases	(2,851)	(2,455)	(2,404)	(2,168)
Other depreciation and operating leases	(495)	(400)	(358)	(321)
Aircraft maintenance	(1,329)	(1,078)	(967)	(820)
Commissions	(465)	(380)	(487)	(645)
Office and administration	(1,058)	(1,044)	(849)	(724)
Revaluation deficit of fixed assets	0	(171)	0	0
Other	(570)	(520)	(563)	(568)
Total operating expenses	(14,058)	(12,242)	(11,284)	(10,442)
Operating profit	221	1,063	997	778
Finance costs, net	(712)	(731)	(814)	(814)
Exchange (loss)/gain, net	(70)	(38)	126	0
Other income, net	0	0	0	341
Share of results of associates before tax	(29)	(32)	5	0
Profit before taxation	(590)	262	314	305
Taxation	(247)	(54)	261	(100)
Profit after taxation	(837)	208	575	205
Minority interests	(112)	(122)	(33)	(29)
Profit attributable to shareholders	(949)	86	542	176

Table A.4. China Eastern Airlines Additional Information for Years ended December 31, 2003, 2002, 2001, and 2000.

	2003	2002	2001	2000
Net exchange gain/(loss)			126	120
Gain on disposal of aircraft and engines			2	112
Rental income from operating subleases of aircraft			126	111
Other, net			(5)	(2)
Other income, net			249	341
Gain on disposal of aircraft and engines	(29)	116	2	
Rental income from operating subleases of aircraft	31	110	126	
Other operating income	2	226	128	
Operating lease rentals (aircraft)	1,048	1,026	925	769
Operating lease rentals (land and buildings)	46	99	90	83

Table A.5. Southwest Airlines Statement of Intermediate Balances (in $ Millions).

For the Years Ended December 31	2003	2002	2001	2000
Passenger	5,741	5,342	5,379	5,468
Freight	94	84	91	111
Other	102	96	85	71
Total production for the period	5,937	5,522	5,555	5,650
Fuel and oil	(830)	(762)	(771)	(805)
Agency commissions	(48)	(55)	(103)	(160)
Landing fees and other rentals	(372)	(345)	(311)	(265)
Aircraft rentals	(183)	(187)	(192)	(196)
Maintenance materials and repairs	(430)	(390)	(397)	(378)
Other operating expenses	(983)	(1,017)	(976)	(860)
Consumption from third parties	(2,846)	(2,756)	(2,750)	(2,664)
Value added	3,091	2,766	2,805	2,986
Salaries, wages, and benefits	(2,224)	(1,992)	(1,856)	(1,684)
Gross operating income	867	774	949	1,302
Depreciation	(384)	(356)	(318)	(281)
Operating income	483	418	631	1,021
Interest expense	(91)	(106)	(70)	(70)
Capitalized interest	33	17	21	28
Interest income	24	37	43	40
Operating net income before taxes	449	366	625	1,019
Other (gains) losses, net	259	27	203	(2)
Unusual income	259	27	203	(2)
Provision for income taxes	266	152	317	392
Cumulative effect of changes in accounting principles, net of income tax	0	0	0	(22)
Preferred stock dividends	0	0	0	0
Net income (loss) available to common shareowners	442	241	511	603

Table A.6. Southwest Airlines Statement of Intermediate Balances (in Percentage Terms).

For the Years Ended December 31	2003	2002	2001	2000
Passenger	96.7	96.7	96.8	96.8
Freight	1.6	1.5	1.6	2.0
Other	1.7	1.7	1.5	1.3
Total production for the period	100.0	100.0	100.0	100.0
Change in production	7.5	(0.6)	(1.7)	19.3
Change in passenger revenues	7.5	(0.7)	(1.6)	19.8
Change in cargo revenues	11.9	(7.7)	(18.0)	7.8
Fuel and oil	(14.0)	(13.8)	(13.9)	(14.2)
Agency commissions	(0.8)	(1.0)	(1.9)	(2.8)
Landing fees and other rentals	(6.3)	(6.2)	(5.6)	(4.7)
Aircraft rentals	(3.1)	(3.4)	(3.5)	(3.5)
Maintenance materials and repairs	(7.2)	(7.1)	(7.1)	(6.7)
Other operating expenses	(16.6)	(18.4)	(17.6)	(15.2)
Consumption from third parties	(47.9)	(49.9)	(49.5)	(47.2)
Value added	52.1	50.1	50.5	52.8
Salaries, wages, and benefits	(37.5)	(36.1)	(33.4)	(29.8)
Gross operating income	14.6	14.0	17.1	23.0
Depreciation	(6.5)	(6.4)	(5.7)	(5.0)
Operating income	8.1	7.6	11.4	18.1
Interest expense	(1.5)	(1.9)	(1.3)	(1.2)
Capitalized interest	0.6	0.3	0.4	0.5
Interest income	0.4	0.7	0.8	0.7
Operating net income before taxes	7.6	6.6	11.3	18.0
Other (gains) losses, net	4.4	0.5	3.7	(0.0)
Unusual income	4.4	0.5	3.7	(0.0)
Provision for income taxes	4.5	2.8	5.7	6.9
Cumulative effect of changes in accounting principles, Net of income tax	0.0	0.0	0.0	(0.4)
Preferred stock dividends	0.0	0.0	0.0	0.0
Net income (loss) available to common shareowners	7.4	4.4	9.2	10.7

Table A.7. Air France Statement of Intermediate Balances
(in € Millions).

For the Years Ended March 31	2003–2004	2002–2003	2001–2002	2000–2001
Passenger	10,260	10,527	10,378	10,022
Cargo	1,412	1,479	1,448	1,491
Maintenance	508	540	548	566
Other	157	141	154	201
Total production for the period	12,337	12,687	12,528	12,280
Aircraft fuel	(1,302)	(1,369)	(1,443)	(1,625)
Chartering costs	(414)	(415)	(639)	(741)
Aircraft operating lease costs	(458)	(522)	(489)	(410)
Landing fees and en route charges	(913)	(934)	(882)	(814)
Catering	(296)	(319)	(329)	(323)
Handling charges and other operating costs	(756)	(768)	(747)	(697)
Aircraft maintenance costs	(381)	(477)	(652)	(598)
Commercial and distribution costs	(1,051)	(1,157)	(1,133)	(1,199)
Other external expenses	(1,183)	(1,213)	(1,152)	(1,083)
Consumption from third parties	(6,754)	(7,174)	(7,466)	(7,490)
Value added	5,583	5,513	5,062	4,790
Salaries and related costs	(4,079)	(3,856)	(3,738)	(3,436)
Taxes other than income tax	(186)	(187)	(163)	(154)
Gross operating income	1,318	1,470	1,161	1,200
Charge to depreciation/amortization, net	(1,184)	(1,195)	(972)	(915)
Charge to operating provisions, net	(46)	(115)	(39)	62
Other operating income and charges, net	44	2	7	8
Operating income	132	162	157	355
Net financial charges	(60)	(85)	(112)	(137)
Share in net income of equity affiliates	53	29	31	45
Operating net income before taxes	125	106	76	263
Gain on disposal of flight equipment, net	7	30	78	88
Restructuring costs	(22)	(13)	(11)	(5)
Gains on disposals of subsidiaries and affiliates, net	5	4	24	96
Unusual income	(10)	21	91	179
Amortization of goodwill	(15)	(16)	(16)	(62)
Income tax	(2)	13	5	45
Minority interests	(5)	(4)	(3)	(4)
Net income (loss)	93	120	153	421

Table A.8.   Air France Statement of Intermediate Balances
(in Percentage Terms).

For the Years Ended March 31	2003–2004	2002–2003	2001–2002	2000–2001
Passenger	83.2	83.0	82.8	81.6
Cargo	11.4	11.7	11.6	12.1
Maintenance	4.1	4.3	4.4	4.6
Other	1.3	1.1	1.2	1.6
Total production for the period	100.0	100.0	100.0	100.0
Change in production	(2.8)	1.3	2.0	18.9
Change in passenger revenues	(2.5)	1.4	3.6	19.6
Change in cargo revenues	(4.5)	2.1	(2.9)	20.2
Aircraft fuel	(10.6)	(10.8)	(11.5)	(13.2)
Chartering costs	(3.4)	(3.3)	(5.1)	(6.0)
Aircraft operating lease costs	(3.7)	(4.1)	(3.9)	(3.3)
Landing fees and en route charges	(7.4)	(7.4)	(7.0)	(6.6)
Catering	(2.4)	(2.5)	(2.6)	(2.6)
Handling charges and other operating costs	(6.1)	(6.1)	(6.0)	(5.7)
Aircraft maintenance costs	(3.1)	(3.8)	(5.2)	(4.9)
Commercial and distribution costs	(8.5)	(9.1)	(9.0)	(9.8)
Other external expenses	(9.6)	(9.6)	(9.2)	(8.8)
Consumption from third parties	(54.7)	(56.5)	(59.6)	(61.0)
Value added	45.3	43.5	40.4	39.0
Salaries and related costs	(33.1)	(30.4)	(29.8)	(28.0)
Taxes other than income tax	(1.5)	(1.5)	(1.3)	(1.3)
Gross operating income	10.7	11.6	9.3	9.8
Charge to depreciation/amortization, net	(9.6)	(9.4)	(7.8)	(7.5)
Charge to operating provisions, net	(0.4)	(0.9)	(0.3)	0.5
Other operating income and charges, net	0.4	0.0	0.1	0.1
Operating income	1.1	1.3	1.3	2.9
Net financial charges	(0.5)	(0.7)	(0.9)	(1.1)
Share in net income of equity affiliates	0.4	0.2	0.2	0.4
Operating net income before taxes	1.0	0.8	0.6	2.1
Gain on disposal of flight equipment, net	0.1	0.2	0.6	0.7
Restructuring costs	(0.2)	(0.1)	(0.1)	(0.0)
Gains on disposals of subsidiaries and affiliates, net	0.0	0.0	0.2	0.8
Unusual income	(0.1)	0.2	0.7	1.5
Amortization of goodwill	(0.1)	(0.1)	(0.1)	(0.5)
Income tax	(0.0)	0.1	0.0	0.4
Minority interests	(0.0)	(0.0)	(0.0)	(0.0)
Net income (loss)	0.8	0.9	1.2	3.4

Table A.9. China Eastern Statement of Intermediate Balances (in RMB Millions).

For the Years Ended December 31	2003	2002	2001	2000
Passenger	10,261	1,0038	9,587	8,644
Cargo and mail	3,187	2,445	2,092	2,124
Other operating revenues	829	596	474	452
Total production for the period	14,277	13,079	12,153	11,220
Take off and landing charges	(2,254)	(1,988)	(1,703)	(1,572)
Aircraft fuel	(3,045)	(2,564)	(2,613)	(2,327)
Food and beverages	(542)	(606)	(567)	(499)
Aircraft maintenance	(1,329)	(1,078)	(967)	(820)
Commissions	(465)	(380)	(487)	(645)
Other	(570)	(520)	(563)	(568)
Operating lease rentals (aircraft)	(1,048)	(1,026)	(925)	(769)
Operating lease rentals (land and buildings)	(46)	(99)	(90)	(83)
Office and administration	(1,058)	(1,044)	(849)	(724)
Consumption from third parties	(10,357)	(9,305)	(8,764)	(8,007)
Value added	3,920	3,774	3,389	3,213
Wages, salaries, and benefits	(1,449)	(1,036)	(773)	(798)
Gross operating income	2,471	2,738	2,616	2,415
Rental income from operating subleases of aircraft	31	110	126	111
Aircraft depreciation	(1,803)	(1,429)	(1,479)	(1,399)
Other depreciation	(449)	(301)	(268)	(238)
Operating income	250	1,118	995	889
Finance costs, net	(712)	(731)	(814)	(814)
Exchange (loss)/gain, net	(70)	(38)	126	120
Share of results of associates before tax	(29)	(32)	5	(2)
Operating net income before taxes	(561)	317	312	193
Gain on disposal of aircraft and engines	(29)	116	2	112
Revaluation deficit of fixed assets	0	(171)	0	0
Unusual income	(29)	(55)	2	112
Taxation	(247)	(54)	261	(100)
Minority interests	(112)	(122)	(33)	(29)
Profit attributable to shareholders	(949)	86	542	176

Table A.10.   China Eastern Statement of Intermediate Balances
(in Percentage Terms).

For the Years Ended December 31	2003	2002	2001	2000
Passenger	71.9	76.7	78.9	77.0
Cargo and mail	22.3	18.7	17.2	18.9
Other operating revenues	5.8	4.6	3.9	4.0
Total production for the period	100.0	100.0	100.0	100.0
Change in production	9.2	7.6	8.3	10.4
Change in passenger revenues	2.2	4.7	10.9	7.6
Change in cargo revenues	30.3	16.9	(1.5)	22.8
Take off and landing charges	(15.8)	(15.2)	(14.0)	(14.0)
Aircraft fuel	(21.3)	(19.6)	(21.5)	(20.7)
Food and beverages	(3.8)	(4.6)	(4.7)	(4.4)
Aircraft maintenance	(9.3)	(8.2)	(8.0)	(7.3)
Commissions	(3.3)	(2.9)	(4.0)	(5.7)
Other	(4.0)	(4.0)	(4.6)	(5.1)
Operating lease rentals (aircraft)	(7.3)	(7.8)	(7.6)	(6.9)
Operating lease rentals (land and buildings)	(0.3)	(0.8)	(0.7)	(0.7)
Office and administration	(7.4)	(8.0)	(7.0)	(6.5)
Consumption from third parties	(72.5)	(71.1)	(72.1)	(71.4)
Value added	27.5	28.9	27.9	28.6
Wages, salaries, and benefits	(10.1)	(7.9)	(6.4)	(7.1)
Gross operating income	17.3	20.9	21.5	21.5
Rental income from operating subleases of aircraft	0.2	0.8	1.0	1.0
Aircraft depreciation	(12.6)	(10.9)	(12.2)	(12.5)
Other depreciation	(3.1)	(2.3)	(2.2)	(2.1)
Operating income	1.8	8.5	8.2	7.9
Finance costs, net	(5.0)	(5.6)	(6.7)	(7.3)
Exchange (loss)/gain, net	(0.5)	(0.3)	1.0	1.1
Share of results of associates before tax	(0.2)	(0.2)	0.0	(0.0)
Operating net income before taxes	(3.9)	2.4	2.6	1.7
Gain on disposal of aircraft and engines	(0.2)	0.9	0.0	1.0
Revaluation deficit of fixed assets	0.0	(1.3)	0.0	0.0
Unusual income	(0.2)	(0.4)	0.0	1.0
Taxation	(1.7)	(0.4)	2.1	(0.9)
Minority interests	(0.8)	(0.9)	(0.3)	(0.3)
Profit attributable to shareholders	(6.6)	0.7	4.5	1.6

TRANSFER PRICING PRACTICES AND REGULATORY ACTIONS IN THE U.S. AND U.K.: A CROSS-COUNTRY COMPARISON AND ANALYSIS

Rasoul H. Tondkar, Wendy W. Achilles and Joyce van der Laan Smith

ABSTRACT

With the continued globalization of world markets, transfer pricing has become one of the dominant sources of controversy in international taxation. Cross-country differences in transfer pricing practices and regulations present challenges to taxing authorities and multinational enterprises (MEs). In the last two decades, tax authorities in the United States (U.S.) and other countries have brought major court cases against MEs accused of underpayment of taxes through transfer pricing practices. This paper discusses transfer pricing practices, regulatory agencies, penalties related to violations, and proper documentation required in the U.S. and one of its major trading partners, the United Kingdom (U.K.). The paper also examines the acceptable valuation methods allowed as a surrogate for arm's-length transactions as

Advances in International Accounting

Advances in International Accounting, Volume 18, 199–217

Copyright © 2005 by Elsevier Ltd.

All rights of reproduction in any form reserved

ISSN: 0897-3660/doi:10.1016/S0897-3660(05)18010-6

*established by the country's regulatory agency. Finally, the paper dis-
cusses the similarities and differences between the major court cases related to transfer pricing in the two countries.*

INTRODUCTION

Transfer pricing has emerged as one of the dominant sources of controversy
in international taxation. Transfer pricing is the process by which a multinational enterprise (ME) calculates a price for goods and services that are
transferred to affiliated entities. These transfer prices impact the taxable
income reported in each country in which the ME operates. MEs wish to
minimize their tax burden and tax authorities wish to ensure that the tax
base of a ME is divided fairly. Thus, both tax authorities and MEs are
interested in the way in which a transfer price is determined.

Tax authorities view transfer pricing violations as a significant source of
lost revenue. The Internal Revenue Service (IRS) of the U.S. reported that in
1995, as a result of court cases involving transfer pricing violations, it re-
couped $1.64 billion. Similar actions netted $1.2 billion for the IRS in 1994.
In addition, for the 1996–1998 period "the 'gross income gap' in the United
States attributable to transfer pricing was in excess of U.S. $2.8 billion per
year" (Borkowski, 2001, p. 350). The U.S. is not the only country trying to
ensure that it receives its "fair share" of taxes paid by MEs (DeSouza, 1997).
Countries around the world are regulating transfer pricing activities and as a
result, several landmark court cases have emerged in this area.

MEs view transfer pricing as problematic given the potential effect of
differences in tax rates and transfer pricing policies on their reported profits.
Transfer pricing documentation requirements are also costly and time con-
suming for MEs because of differences in each country's regulatory requirements.

Transfer pricing issues are also costly and difficult for regulators because
of the lack of qualified personnel and resources. Oftentimes, the regulators
do not have the staff with the knowledge base necessary to audit large MEs'
transfer pricing practices. Additionally, the regulators may not have the
needed resources to contend in courts with the MEs accused of transfer
pricing violations. In many instances, the regulators are "outgunned" in
court cases because the MEs have more resources to spend on legal teams.

This paper examines the transfer pricing practices, regulatory policies,
and certain court cases involving transfer pricing violations in the U.S. and
the United Kingdom (U.K.). The U.K. is a major trading partner with the

U.S., representing over $33 billion in exports and over $40 billion in imports in 2002 (U.S. Census Bureau). In addition, it is anticipated that the new U.K./U.S. income tax treaty, effective March 3, 2003, will increase cross border trade and investment, increasing the level of transfer pricing issues within each country. The tax authorities within both countries use an arm's-length transaction as the standard for establishing transfer prices. However, within the U.S., the regulations are more detailed providing specific rules for determining the transfer price whereas in the U.K., the burden is on the company to use a transfer price which meets the principle of an arm's-length transaction.

The court cases were selected based on their relevance to the transfer pricing controversy within each country. The discussion of these cases in the two countries address different issues on transfer pricing. Some of the cases discussed provide background information that has led to the development of current transfer pricing regulations, while others are more recent and provide insight into the controversies between the taxpayer and the regulatory agency. This study should be of interest to companies engaged in transfer pricing in the U.S. and the U.K., regulators in these countries, and researchers interested in further examination of transfer pricing issues in the above countries.

TRANSFER PRICING REGULATIONS AND METHODS USED IN THE U.S.

Regulations

The IRS is the regulatory agency that sets transfer pricing rules in the U.S. The guidelines are detailed in Section 482 of the Internal Revenue Code (IRC). It states that intercompany transfer prices must be set at an arm's-length standard. The Treasury Regulations define "arm's-length" as the results of a transaction between controlled entities being similar to the results of uncontrolled corporations. To determine if its pricing strategy meets the arm's-length standard, the company must compare the prices charged to affiliates with those charged to third parties. If the comparable prices are not available, companies must compare their profits to profits earned by comparable third parties (DeSouza, 1997).

The transfer pricing regulations allow for flexibility in the utilization of the transfer pricing methods. Section 482 of the regulations permits the taxpayer to use any other reasonable pricing method, however, documentation supporting the use of the alternative method is imperative.

As part of the transfer pricing regulations, Section 6662 was created to encourage taxpayers, by threat of penalties, to provide the IRS with enough information to determine if the taxpayer is meeting the Section 482 specifications. According to Section 6662, a penalty equal to 20% of the underpayment in tax is levied if there is a substantial miscalculation in the arm's-length price of a transaction. If the company is grossly negligent, the penalty is increased to 40% of the underpayment of tax. Treasury Regulation Section 1.6662-6 details the transfer pricing penalty and documentation requirements.

Section 6662 and Treasury Regulation Section 1.6662 specify the information that needs to be made available for the IRS and identifies documents the company should prepare to detail its transfer pricing policy. The following documentation is required for the U.S. companies:

- Business Overview
- Organization Structure
- Method Selected
- Alternative Methods Rejected
- Analyze Controlled Transaction
- Identify Comparable Methods
- Economic Analysis
- Relevant Data Obtained after Year-End
- Index (Deloitte & Touche, 2002)

Transfer Pricing Methods

The transfer pricing methods used in the U.S. for tangible properties are: (1) comparable uncontrolled price (CUP), (2) resale price (RPM), (3) cost-plus (CPLM), (4) comparable profits (CPM), (5) profit-split, and (6) other reasonable methods. Under the transfer pricing regulations, no method is preferred above other methods. The "best method" is the method "which is the most reliable, with consideration given to the completeness and accuracy of the data, the reality of the assumptions used, and the sensitivity of the results to deficiencies in the data and assumptions employed" (Sherman & McBride, 1995, p. 29).

The CUP method determines an arm's-length price by comparing the transfer price to prices charged to unrelated parties in similar transactions. The CUP method can only be used if the transfer price is adjusted for the differences between the intercompany transaction and the unrelated transaction with which it is being compared. The IRS deems the more differences that exist between the two transactions, the more unreliable the CUP method becomes.

The RPM is most often used when there are no third party transactions to compare the intercompany transaction. With RPM, "a transfer price is computed by subtracting an appropriate gross profit from the resale price charged by the controlled reseller to an unrelated third party" (Sherman & McBride, 1995, p. 30). RPM focuses more on the functions performed by the controlled and uncontrolled resellers than on the transaction itself.

The CPLM calculates the transfer price "by adding the profit (expressed as a percentage of cost) that would be earned on the sale to an uncontrolled party to the cost of producing the property" (Sherman & McBride, 1995, p. 30). Parent and subsidiary groups use this method most often when a subsidiary manufactures a product and sells it to the parent or another affiliated company.

The CPM sets a transfer price by employing "profit measures (such as the return on assets or operating income to sales) to determine a return that would equal that realized by a comparable independent enterprise" (Borkowski, 2003, p. 30). The transfer pricing regulations state that CPM is a "method of last resort" and cannot be used by the IRS to challenge other methods.

The profit-split method includes two methods – the comparable profit-split, and the residual profit-split. With the comparable profit-split, "a profit-split is achieved based on the relative profits of uncontrolled taxpayers engaged in transactions and functions similar to those of the controlled taxpayer" (Kim, Swinnerton, & Ulferts, 1997, p. 20). The residual profit-split requires a two-step process. In the first step, the ME evaluates the functions of the parties involved in the controlled transaction and assigns a fair value to each function based on the value that could be assigned in an arm's-length transaction. The second step requires allocating profit to the company based on the value of each company's input.

The methods prescribed by the IRS for pricing intangible transactions are similar to the methods prescribed for tangible transactions. These methods are: (1) comparable uncontrolled transaction (CUT), (2) CPM, (3) the profit-split, and (4) any other reasonable method. The CUT method for intangibles is basically the same as the CUP method for tangible property. The other intangible methods, CPM and profit-split, are identical to the valuation methods for tangible property (Sherman & McBride, 1995). The U.S. regulations, Section 482-4(a), also contain the commensurate-with-income requirement, which require the value of the transferred intangible property to be based on the income derived from that property. This requirement uses the arm's-length return concept versus arm's-length price (Borkowski, 2001).

Advance pricing agreements (APAs) can be entered into between the taxpayer and the IRS. The APA allows the taxpayer and the IRS to agree upon a transfer pricing method. The APA alleviates the possibility of an IRS challenge to the company's transfer pricing method. The primary disadvantages of an APA are the $5,000 filing fee, the required documentation, and the uncertainty if the APA will be accepted in the other countries in which the taxpayer operates. If there is a tax treaty between the U.S. and the foreign countries, the ME can request the IRS to include the foreign countries' transfer pricing rules as part of the agreement. The U.S./U.K. tax treaty applies an arm's-length standard that is consistent with the Organization of Economic Cooperation and Development guidelines (discussed later).

TRANSFER PRICING REGULATIONS AND METHODS USED IN THE U.K.

The main authority for transfer pricing regulation in the U.K. is the Inland Revenue. The primary legislation that guides the Inland Revenue for taxation is Section 770 (replaced Section 485), Schedule 28AA, and the Income and Corporation Taxes Act of 1988 (Schon, 1997), and the Finance Act of 1998. The Inland Revenue issued the Inland Revenue Tax Bulletin 25, 38, 4, and 46 to cover transfer pricing and the documentation requirements for taxpayers. The U.K. transfer pricing regulations follow many of the regulations identified in the Organization for Economic Co-operation and Development (OECD) Guidelines.

The OECD consists of 30 member countries and is a "unique forum to discuss, develop and refine economic and social policies. They compare experiences, seek answers to common problems and work to co-ordinate domestic and international policies to help members and non-members deal with an increasingly globalized world" (OECD, 2003). The OECD also develops international policies and recommendations on issues, such as transfer pricing, where multilateral agreements are conducive to globalization.

The U.K. applies the arm's-length standard outlined in the OECD Guidelines. The OECD defines arm's-length as the following:

> conditions [that] are made or imposed between the two enterprises in their commercial or financial relations which differ from those which would be made between independent

enterprises, then any profits which would, but for those conditions, have accrued to one of the enterprises, but, by reasons of those conditions, have not so accrued, may be included in the profits of that enterprise and taxed accordingly (OECD, 2001, p. G-1).

Penalties are imposed for failure to comply with the transfer pricing rules and the documentation requirements set forth by the Inland Revenue. Taxpayers are expected to conduct a self-assessment (apply the arm's-length standard to transactions between related parties that appear in their annual tax return) and if the filed tax return is fraudulent or negligent, the tax penalty can be 100% of the unpaid tax. The absence of documentation will constitute negligence; however, there is no penalty if the taxpayer has made an "honest and reasonable" attempt to comply with the law and has evidence to show that it has done so (Schwarz, 1999b).

As part of the self-assessment, documentation requirements exist to ensure a complete and accurate tax return. In practice, burden shifts to the taxpayer to demonstrate reasonable pricing methods. This requirement is effective for tax years beginning after July 1, 1998. The following is a list of documentation requirements for the U.K. companies:

- Business Overview
- Organization Structure
- Method Selected
- Analyze Control Transactions
- Identify Comparable Methods
- Conduct an Economic Analysis (Deloitte & Touche, 2002).

Transfer Pricing Methods

The methods outlined in the OECD Guidelines that are used by the U.K. are: (1) the comparable uncontrolled price, (2) resale method, (3) cost-plus, or (4) any other reasonable method. Since these methods are similar to the U.S. methods, they are not discussed here. The U.K. applies the same transfer pricing methods to both tangibles and intangibles, however, it does not allow the commensurate-with-income approach. The Inland Revenue, like the IRS, has not established an order of most to least preferable method of transfer pricing. Many taxpayers believe the method preferred by the Inland Revenue is the method that produces the best result for the U.K. regulatory agency (Levey, Fox, Penney, Fairley & Palmer, 1994).

The Inland Revenue executes APAs for the U.K. and follows the OECD Guidelines. The OECD Guidelines define an APA as:

> an arrangement that determines, in advance of controlled transactions, an appropriate set of criteria for the determination of the transfer pricing for those transactions over a fixed period of time. An advance pricing agreement may be unilateral involving one tax administration and a taxpayer or multilateral involving the agreement of two or more tax administrations (OECD, 2001, p. G-1).

CASES

The following are discussions of cases involving civil action against a company for transfer pricing violations. A summary of the important aspects of these cases is provided in the Appendix. The litigation in all of the cases arose from disagreements between the company and the tax authority over the calculation of an appropriate arm's-length price. The cases were selected based on their relevance to the transfer pricing controversy within the home country of the company.

U.S. CASES

Section 482

The purpose of Section 482 is to allocate income to the appropriate taxpayer in transactions between affiliated entities and to prevent tax avoidance. In addition, this Section places controlled entities on a level playing field with uncontrolled entities by attempting to compute true taxable income. Under Section 482, the taxpayer chooses the valuation method that best approximates an arm's-length price. The following cases use Section 482 as the basis for the calculation of an arm's-length price for tangible and intangible property.

Section 482: Tangible Property
Microsoft Corp. v. Commissioner. Microsoft Corporation (Microsoft), a Washington-based company, owned Microsoft Puerto Rico (MS-Puerto Rico), a Delaware-based corporation. MS-Puerto Rico manufactured software diskettes and sold them to Microsoft to be packaged with other components. MS-Puerto Rico elected to be treated as a U.S. possession and reported its taxable income under the profit-split method. The IRS wanted

to recalculate Microsoft's combined taxable income for taxable years ending June 30, 1990 and 1991 using 936(h) of the IRC; however, Microsoft argued that the IRS was barred by the statute of limitations from doing so. The IRS contended that diskette duplication activities were not considered a manufacturing activity under 936 and therefore, did not qualify for the profit-split provisions. The IRS recalculated the price of the diskettes sold to Microsoft under the transfer pricing rules of IRC Section 482.

In January 1996, Microsoft and the IRS agreed to extend the statute of limitations related to the calculation of an arm's-length price for the diskettes for taxable years 1990 and 1991 until December 31, 1996. No mention was made of the recalculation of combined taxable income, only the fact that MS-Puerto Rico did not qualify for the profit-split provisions and a new arm's-length price would be calculated. This new price would have substantially increased Microsoft's taxable income as a result of the application of Section 482. The IRS issued Microsoft a deficiency notice related to the recalculation of combined taxable income. A deficiency notice is issued when a difference exists between the tax liability reported on the taxpayer's tax return and the tax liability calculated by the tax authorities.

Microsoft argued the recalculation was not mentioned in the agreement to extend the statute of limitations and thus time had expired. The United States Tax Court agreed with Microsoft and ruled in their favor. This ruling was a major victory for taxpayers because the Court limited the liability of the taxpayer only to what is contained in the plain-language notice from the IRS stating that any agreement between the taxpayer and the IRS must be clearly explained in the notice.

National Semiconductor Corp. v. Commissioner. National Semiconductor Corporation (NSC) manufactured semiconductors and allied products and sold many of these products to its Asian subsidiary. The issue before the Court was whether or not these sales were conducted as an arm's-length transaction under Section 482 of the transfer pricing rules. NSC used the CUP method to calculate the price for the sales. The IRS claimed the calculations did not represent an arm's-length transaction and issued a deficiency notice to that effect. The Court decided neither NSC nor the IRS presented evidence of a true arm's-length price and relied on the expert testimony of several IRS witnesses, with modifications where it was shown the witnesses had erred, to determine an adequate price. The Court determined the amount of income to be reallocated to NSC and entered the amount as the judgment against NSC. This case showed the burden of proof is on the taxpayer but also revealed the arm's-length prices calculated by the

IRS had to be reasonable to be accepted by the Court. If the calculated price of the IRS is not reasonable, the taxpayer only has to prove its transfer pricing was arm's-length. NSC did not prove this in this case.

Compaq Computer Corp. v. Commissioner. Compaq Computer Corporation (Compaq), a Delaware corporation, has its primary business location in Houston, Texas. Compaq is in the business of designing, manufacturing, and selling personal computers. Compaq purchased circuit boards from its Singapore subsidiary to be used in its personal computers. The IRS contended that prices paid by Compaq to its Singapore subsidiary were not arm's-length and the price should be recomputed under the transfer pricing rules of Section 482. Compaq claimed no other subcontractors were capable of producing the circuit boards due to lack of capital-intensive equipment, engineers, processes, and experience.

The IRS audited the tax returns of Compaq for fiscal year ended (FYE) November 30, 1991 and 1992, and issued deficiency notices in the following amount: FYE November 30, 1991: $42,422,470; FYE November 31, 1992: $33,533,968 and Section 6662(a) penalty: $547,619. The Court decided that the amount paid by Compaq for the printed circuit assemblies from the Singapore subsidiary was arm's-length under Section 482. Compaq used the cost-plus method to compute the transfer price charged to the subsidiary and the Court held "the subsidiary's prices were closely related to the prices paid to the unrelated contractors and could be adjusted to account for physical differences, production times, payment terms, freight and duty costs, setup and cancellation charges, inventory costs, and intangible costs." The Tax Court described the IRS' calculations as "arbitrary, capricious and unreasonable based on unrealistic materials, labor and overhead markups."

The IRS lost the case because it failed to prove an alternative method resulted in a more accurate calculation and the Court awarded Compaq a favorable transfer pricing adjustment in the amount of $21 million. This case was unusual in that it was a complete victory for the taxpayer. Generally, the Court does not grant a complete victory to the IRS, or the taxpayer but rules somewhere in the middle.

Section 482: Intangible Property
BMC Software v. Commissioner. BMC Software, located in Houston, Texas, designed and manufactured computer software products. BMC formed a foreign subsidiary in Holland to distribute its products in Europe. BMC and the subsidiary entered into a licensing agreement. The IRS alleged that BMC did not recognize sufficient income in its FYE March 31, 1993 tax

return related to the licensing agreement due to BMC's intercompany transfer pricing policy. The IRS recalculated BMC's tax liability and increased it by $24,124,945. The main issue in this case was the intercompany valuation of intangible transactions of BMC and the subsidiary. The core concept in this case was IRC Sec. 482 and Treas. Reg 1.481-1(b).

A central issue in the dispute was that the IRS wanted access to BMC's computer source code "alleging that it would help refine the calculation of the maintenance fees that petitioner contended should be included in respondent's royalty base." BMC responded that release of the source code contained substantial business risk and the information was irrelevant to the IRS' case. The United States District Court agreed with BMC and the motion to enforce the IRS summons was denied. The ruling in favor of BMC enforced the concept that only relevant information needs to be disclosed to the IRS in relation to transfer pricing documentation.

The decision on the additional tax liability calculated by the IRS to BMC is still outstanding. A decision is expected in the near future.

Seagate Technology v. Commissioner. Seagate Technology Inc. (Seagate), a publicly traded company that manufactures hard disk drives for personal computers, formed a 100%-owned subsidiary in Singapore to manufacture parts for the disk drives. In 1984, the Singapore subsidiary began manufacturing completed hard disk drives. Seagate purchased component parts and completed hard disk drives from the subsidiary for resale to third parties. Seagate generally paid the subsidiary cost plus a markup of 25% for the manufactured parts and completed disk drives. The subsidiary paid Seagate a 1% royalty commission on "certain sales into the United States." Seagate and the subsidiary also had the following agreements: "the subsidiary agreed to pay Seagate a commission of 5% on all of the subsidiary's third party sales, the subsidiary agreed to pay Seagate for certain costs in assisting the subsidiary's operations, the subsidiary agreed to pay for one-half of the research and development cost Seagate incurred and identified as covered under the cost-sharing agreement, and the subsidiary agreed to reimburse Seagate for certain warranty costs incurred by Seagate's repair centers."

Upon audit, the IRS reallocated income from the subsidiary to Seagate using the transfer pricing rules of Section 482 because the IRS did not believe the calculated price was arm's-length. The Court decided that the reallocation amount was unreasonable but did rule in favor of the IRS. The Court also decided that the royalty rate of 1%, the 50% of research and development cost, and the transfer price used by Seagate was not arm's-length. Additionally, the Court ruled that the definition of "sales into the

United States" was not reasonable, and Seagate was not permitted to offset warranty payments. The original deficiency notice issued by the IRS in the amount of $112.3 million was reduced to approximately $45 million. This case is a prime example of the Court rendering a decision where neither party obtains a complete victory.

The cases discussed above portray the transfer pricing controversy in the United States. The primary issues in these cases were calculation of the transfer prices (specifically the methods used to calculate the transfer price), information that should be disclosed to the IRS, and the reliability of agreements between the IRS and ME's. Although this is not a comprehensive list of U.S. cases, the cases are representative of the main transfer pricing controversies facing entities doing business in the United States with operations abroad.

U.K. CASES

The transfer pricing regulations have evolved over many years in the U.K. and several landmark court cases have resulted from disputes in the transfer pricing guidelines. Section 770 (and its predecessor Section 485) addressed transfer pricing issues but did not define certain terms as "arm's-length standard" nor did it provide acceptable transfer pricing valuation methods; however, these Sections did provide the groundwork for the current transfer pricing regulations. Cases discussed in this section relate to the provisions of Sections 485, and subsequently 770.

Section 485

Section 485 was issued under the Income and Corporations Tax Act of 1970. This Section states that if entities are members of a controlled group, the transaction price must be computed as if the entities are not affiliated in any way. This Section is comparable to Section 482 of the U.S. IRC. Although Section 485 was replaced by Section 770 of the Income and Corporation Taxes Act of 1988 (TA 1988), most provisions of this Section are incorporated into Section 770. The cases under Section 485 took place before it was incorporated into Section 770.

Beecham Group plc v. Inland Revenue Commissioners
The Inland Revenue issued Beecham Group plc (Beecham), a well-known pharmaceutical company, an assessment notice for tax years 1977–1985 for

underpayment of taxes related to transfer pricing violations under Section 485 of the Income and Corporations Tax Act of 1970. In the assessment notice, the Inland Revenue requested from Beecham information related to the accounts of its Singapore subsidiary, Beecham Pharmaceuticals (Pte) Ltd from March 31, 1977 until March 31, 1985. The Inland Revenue contended that transactions occurred between Beecham and the Singapore subsidiary during these periods that were not arm's-length. The Inland Revenue requested the information because it wanted to alter the original assessment issued under Section 485 for the years 1977–1985.

Beecham filed a summons before the Court and argued that the original assessment could not be altered. Beecham maintained that if a new assessment was issued, it might contain some contested tax returns that were not mentioned in the original assessment. According to Beecham, this should not be allowed because the statute of limitations had expired for these tax filings.

The Inland Revenue, however, wanted to discard the original summons and further maintained that the question of whether or not the Inland Revenue could invoke Section 485 was an issue that should be heard before the Special Commissioner and not the Court. The Court decided to hear the matter and decided in favor of Beecham. Basically, this implies Beecham did not have to gather extensive information that could be unnecessary and the original deficiency issued by the Inland Revenue is still in effect.[1]

Section 770

Section 770 was issued under the TA 1988. It replaced Section 485 of the Income and Corporations Tax Act of 1970 and contains many of the same provisions as Section 482 of the U.S. IRC. One problem with Section 770 is the missing definition of "arm's-length transaction," which leaves interpretation in the hands of the taxpayer.

Waterloo plc and Others v. Inland Revenue Commissioners

Waterloo, the parent company for a multi-national group, is located in the U.K. and the shares of the company are traded on the London Stock Exchange. Waterloo established a plan so that the trustees could obtain interest-free loans to purchase stock, and stock options for the benefit of the employees of Waterloo's subsidiaries. The Inland Revenue stated that Waterloo had "given business facilities to its subsidiary within Section 773 (4) of the TA 1988 and that Section 770 (1), which provided, that where business facilities were given at an undervalue then in computations for tax purposes the like consequences would ensue as would have ensued if the transaction had been at an arm's-length price."[2] Inland Revenue interpreted the "business facilities" language of Section 770 to include interest-free loans. Waterloo contended they could not compute an arm's-length price but the Court held that business facilities had been transferred and an arm's-length price could be calculated. Thus, the Court rendered a decision in favor of the Inland Revenue. The decision confirms a broad interpretation of the term "business facilities" and expanded the scope of the U.K. transfer pricing rules under Section 770 to include transactions that are conducted through an independent third party.

Newidgets Manufacturing Ltd v. Jones (Inspector of Taxes)
Newidgets Manufacturing Ltd (NW) is a wholly owned subsidiary of Foreign Parent 1 (FP1 – name specified in the court case). NW paid FP1 a royalty (calculated as a percentage of the selling price of widgets sold by NW to third parties) based on a manufacturing licensing agreement between the two parties. The agreement stated that NW had "the exclusive right to manufacture widgets in the British Isles, under technical information provided by FP1, and the non-exclusive right to use the technical information in the manufacturing of spare parts." A copy of the licensing agreement was sent to Inland Revenue for approval under Section 54 of the Taxes Management Act of 1970.

The Inland Revenue approved the agreement for FYE 1991 and 1992; however, no decision was made for FYE 1993. Since NW did not hear from the Inland Revenue concerning FYE 1993, the company assumed the royalty calculations were acceptable and proceeded in that manner. The Inland Revenue decided that the licensing agreement was not an arm's-length transaction under Section 770 and denied the calculation for FYE 1993. The Inland Revenue then assessed an additional tax liability against NW that NW appealed. The Special Commissioner stated that the purpose of Section 54 was to protect the taxpayer with an agreement that had been accepted by both parties. The Court stated that NW had not presented misleading information to Inland Revenue and Inland Revenue had agreed with the royalty calculation. Therefore, the agreement between NW and Inland Revenue was upheld and the appeal by NW was allowed. This decision will give comfort to taxpayers in that they have some protection from additional assessments when an agreement has been reached based on factual information.

Rochester (U.K.) Ltd and another v. Pickin (Inspector of Taxes)
Rochester (U.K.) Ltd (Rochester), a wholly owned subsidiary of a Canadian company, bought seeds from a Dutch supplier, an unrelated third party, for

the purpose of extracting oil. Several years passed and the Dutch supplier sold the seeds to a Swiss company, which was affiliated with Rochester. The Swiss company made arrangements for the extraction of the oil and then supplied oil to Rochester and the Canadian parent.

Upon review of Rochester's tax returns, the Inland Revenue stated that the Swiss company entered into the transactions so that Rochester would pay the Swiss company more than an arm's-length price for the oil and avoid paying U.K. taxes. The Inland Revenue also argued that the U.K. company made payments to the Swiss company for medical research when actually the Swiss Company rendered no services. An assessment notice was issued to Rochester by the Inland Revenue under Section 770 for excess amounts paid to the Swiss company for the oil "and for the payments relating to medical [research] expense on the basis that they were not incurred wholly and exclusively for the purpose of the U.K. company's trade within TA 1988, S74 (1)(a). They were therefore not deductible and remained profits of the U.K. company."

The Special Commissioner ruled in favor of Rochester stating that the Inland Revenue had failed to prove negligence by Rochester and the payments made by Rochester to the Swiss Company were part of a commercial arrangement. This case focused on the documentation and the facts of the transactions. Since, Rochester had documented all transactions and calculated transfer prices within Section 770, the Inland Revenue could not prove the company's calculations were not arm's-length.

The above mentioned cases highlight the main transfer pricing issues facing companies in the U.K. The primary issues in these cases were the calculation of the transfer prices and the reliability of agreements between the taxpayer and the Inland Revenue. As with the U.S. cases, the list is not all-inclusive but does emphasize the most prominent cases that have helped shape U.K. transfer pricing legislation.

DISCUSSION AND CONCLUSION

With the continued globalization of world markets, transfer pricing has become one of the dominant sources of controversy in international taxation. Cross-country differences in transfer pricing practices and regulations present challenges to taxing authorities and MEs. In the last two decades, tax authorities in the U.S. and other countries have brought major court cases against MEs accused of underpayment of taxes through transfer pricing practices.

This paper discusses transfer pricing practices, regulatory agencies, penalties related to violations, and proper documentation required in the U.S. and the U.K. The paper also presents the acceptable valuation methods allowed for arm's-length transactions, as established by the country's regulatory agency. Finally, the paper discusses major court cases related to transfer pricing in the two countries; highlighting the similarities and differences between the court cases in these countries.

The transfer pricing regulations in the countries have evolved in different ways. Transfer pricing regulations in the U.S. are much more detailed and rule based, as compared to the U.K., attempting to answer every foreseeable issue. The current regulations were established much earlier than that of their U.K. counterparts. The final U.S. regulations on transfer pricing were issued in 1994; however, the IRS issued the arm's-length standard that is applied by the U.S. tax authorities in 1968. The IRS applies this arm's-length standard to all inbound and outbound business transaction. These stringent tax laws issued by the IRS put extensive pressure on the tax authorities in other countries to adopt similar transfer pricing regulations to ensure MEs pay an appropriate amount of tax in their country.

Compared to the U.S., the transfer pricing rules took longer to evolve in the U.K. In addition, the U.K. guidelines, unlike the U.S. regulations, do not require any specific method to be used to calculate the transfer price. The Inland Revenue encourages MEs to use the best method for the circumstances of the transaction. However, the Inland Revenue prefers the traditional methods as applied by OECD guidelines. The U.K. in its Treasury explanatory notes of the Finance Act of 1998 adopted the definition of the "arm's-length standard" developed by the OECD in 1979, which is consistent with the U.S. definition.

The transfer pricing documentation requirements within both countries require a company to include the method selected, an analysis of the controlled transactions, and to identify comparable methods. The U.S., as opposed to the U.K., also requires the documentation to include why alternative methods were rejected.

There are also differences in the court cases from the two countries. In the U.S., more cases reach the court system whereas, historically, in the U.K. more cases are settled before reaching this stage. Also, in the U.S. court cases the predominant issue was the transfer pricing method the company used versus the method the IRS thought they should use. This difference in the treatment of the court cases may be a result of the detailed regulations in the U.S. versus the less detailed guidelines provided in the U.K.

As mentioned above, the U.S. regulations on transfer pricing methods are much more detailed than the U.K. regulations. This finding is consistent with the work of Bloom and Naciri (1989) who found that the U.K. tends to place more emphasis on professional judgment and tradition as opposed to the rulebook guidelines not uncommon in the U.S. They also found that in the U.K. as compared to the U.S., more emphasis is placed on substance over form.

This study should be of interest to companies engaged in transfer pricing in the U.S. and the U.K., regulators in these countries, and researchers interested in further examination of transfer pricing issues in the above countries. We also believe that given the current debate occurring in the U.S. on the issue of principles versus rules based accounting standards, further research into the development of the transfer pricing regulations may help us gain a better understanding of the major factors contributing to a principles versus rules based approach to regulation.

NOTES

1. A deficiency notice is the amount by which the actual tax (as it should have been computed) exceeds the amount shown on the return, if any, plus any amounts previously assessed as a deficiency and minus any rebates.
2. Business facilities are transactions that occur in the normal course of business.

REFERENCES

Beecham Group plc v. Inland Revenue Commissioners, Chancery Division (1992). STC 935, 65 Tax Case 219, 6 November 1992.

Bloom, R., & Naciri, M. A. (1989). Accounting standard setting and culture: A comparative analysis of the United States, Canada, England, West Germany, Australia, New Zealand, Sweden, Japan, and Switzerland. *The International Journal of Accounting, 24,* 70–97.

BMC Software v. Commissioner (1999). Docket No. 12731-98, United States Tax Court, 1999 U.S. Tax Ct. Lexis 1647, September 8, 1999, Filed.

Borkowski, S. (2001). Transfer pricing of intangible property: Harmony and discord across five countries. *The International Journal of Accounting, 36,* 349–374.

Borkowski, S. (2003). Transfer pricing documentation and penalties: How much is enough? *International Tax Journal, 29*(Spring), 1–32.

Compaq Computer Corp. v. Commissioner (1999). Docket No. 24238-96, United States Tax Court, 113 T.C. 363; 1999 U.S. Tax Ct. Lexis 52; 113 T.C. No. 25, November 18, 1999, Filed.

Deloitte & Touche. (2002). TransferPricing. www.corptax.com/www/TransferPricing.nsf/Documents/TransferPricing.

DeSouza, G. (1997). Functional analysis. *Journal of International Taxation*, 8(May), 223–228.

Levey, M., Fox, J., Penney, M., Fairley, J., & Palmer, S. (1994). Transfer pricing methods may not be accepted in both the U.S. and the U.K.. *Journal of International Taxation*, 5(April), 153–159.

Kim, S., Swinnerton, E., & Ulferts, G. (1997). 1994 final transfer pricing regulations of the United States. *Multinational Business Review*, 5(Spring), 17–25.

Microsoft Corp. v. Commissioner (2000). Docket No. 16878-96, United States Tax Court, 115 T.C. 228; 2000 U.S. Tax Ct. Lexis 63; 115 T.C. No. 17, September 15, 2000, Filed.

National Semiconductor Corp. v. Commissioner (1994). Docket Nos. 4754-89, 8031-90, United States Tax Court, T.C. Memo 1994-195; 1994 Tax Ct. Memo Lexis 199; 67 T.C.M. (CCH) 2849, May 2, 1994, As Corrected May 2, 1994.

Newidgets Manufacturing Ltd v. Jones (Inspector of Taxes) (1999). Special Commissioner's Decision, STC (SCD) 19S, 17 May 1999.

Organization for Economic Co-operation and Development (2001). Transfer pricing guidelines for multinational enterprises and tax administrations.

Organization for Economic Co-operation and Development (2003). http://www.oecd.org/EN/document/

Rochester (U.K.) Ltd and another v. Pickin (Inspector of Taxes) (1998). Special Commissioner's Decision, STC (SCD) 138, 7 May 1998.

Schon, R. (1997). U.K. transfer pricing: CFC rules will follow self-assessment framework. *Journal of International Taxation*, 8(January), 46–47.

Schwarz, J. (1999b). Transfer litigation in the United Kingdom. *TaxLine Annual Review* (1999/2000): Institute of chartered accountants for England & Wales.

Seagate Technology v. Commissioner (1994). Docket No. 11660-90, United States Tax Court, 102 T.C. 149; 1994 U.S. Tax Ct. Lexis 10; 102 T.C. No. 9, February 8, 1994, Filed.

Sherman, W., & McBride, J. (1995). International transfer pricing: Application and analysis. *The Ohio CPA Journal*, 54(4), 29–35.

U.S. Census Bureau (2003). Foreign Trade Division, Data Dissemination Branch, Washington, D.C. 20233.

Waterloo plc and Others v. Inland Revenue Commissioners (2002). Special Commissioner's Decision, STC (SCD) 95, 24 October 2001.

APPENDIX. SUMMARY OF CASES

Case	Country	Applicable Code Section	Issues in the Case	Outcome of the Case
Beecham Group	U.K.	485	Underpayment of taxes based on transfer price calculations	Finding in favor of Beecham
BMC Software	U.S.	482 Intangible	Calculation of transfer price for licensing agreement Information that needs to be disclosed to IRS	Ruling not issued for deficiency notice Finding in Favor of BMC Software
Compaq Computer	U.S.	482 Tangible	Valuation method used to calculate transfer price	Finding in favor of Compaq Computer
Microsoft Corp.	U.S.	482 Tangible	Calculations of transfer price Language of agreement between IRS and taxpayer	Finding in favor of IRS but for a reduced amount Finding in favor of Microsoft
National Semiconductor	U.S.	482 Tangible	Valuation method used to calculate transfer price	Finding in favor of IRS but for a reduced amount
Newidgets Mfg. Ltd	U.K.	770	Language of agreement between Inland Revenue and taxpayer	Finding in favor of Newidgets on appeal
Rochester Ltd (U.K.)	U.K.	770	Calculations of transfer price	Finding in favor of Rochester
Seagate Technology	U.S.	482 Intangible	Calculations of transfer price	Finding in favor of IRS but for a reduced amount
Waterloo plc	U.K.	770	Expansion of definition of Business Facility Expansion of transfer pricing regulations to transactions with third-party intermediaries	Finding in favor of Inland Revenue

THE IMPACT OF SOCIAL AND ECONOMIC DEVELOPMENT ON CORPORATE SOCIAL AND ENVIRONMENTAL DISCLOSURE IN HONG KONG AND THE U.K.

Jason Zezheng Xiao, Simon S. Gao, Saeed Heravi and Yuk C. Q. Cheung

ABSTRACT

This study compares corporate social and environmental disclosure (CSED) in Hong Kong (HK) and the U.K. through a content analysis of 334 annual reports prepared by 69 listed companies over the period of 1993–1997. We find that U.K. and HK companies differed in the amount, theme and location of CSED, and that there was an upward trend in the amount of CSED in both U.K. and HK firms during the five-year period, although U.K. firms increased more than HK firms. We argue that HK and U.K.'s different stages of social and economic development, by creating differential pressures and demand for CSED and exposing companies to differential political costs and legitimacy threats, contributed towards these differences in CSED.

Advances in International Accounting
Advances in International Accounting, Volume 18, 219–243
Copyright © 2005 by Elsevier Ltd.
All rights of reproduction in any form reserved
ISSN: 0897-3660/doi:10.1016/S0897-3660(05)18011-8

INTRODUCTION

This chapter argues that the stage of a nation's social and economic development is an important factor that affects corporate social and environmental disclosure (CSED). Accounting reflects the information needs of society and different social and economic environments create different information requirements (Burchell, Clubb, Hopwood, & Hughes, 1980). Countries at different stages of social and economic development have different concerns and priorities (Mueller, 1968). Social and environmental issues are of a greater concern to developed countries than to less developed countries (LDCs) and the public and institutions in developed countries generally have higher levels of awareness of such issues than their counterparts in LDCs. Reflecting this difference, companies in developed countries face greater pressures from stakeholders for CSED than firms in LDCs. Furthermore, countries in developed countries are more likely to introduce mandatory CSED requirements than LDCs. Therefore, social and environmental issues expose companies in developed countries, compared with those in LDCs, to greater political costs, according to positive accounting theory (Milne, 2002), and greater legitimacy threats by implication of legitimacy theory (Deegan, 2002). Consequently, CSED in industrialized world would be more extensive than that in LDCs.

We investigate the impact of the stage of social and economic development on CSED by comparing CSED in corporate annual reports published by HK and U.K. companies. These two countries are chosen for two reasons. First, HK is a typical newly industrialized economy whereas the U.K. a typical highly developed country. As a newly industrialized society, many aspects of the HK economy remain developing, with such problems as increasing income disparities and environmental degradation (Tang, 1998, 1999). Table 1 shows that, in terms of GNP (GDP) per capita, HK lagged behind the U.K. until 1993. Even though HK matched the U.K. in economic terms in 1993, it was still less developed than the U.K. as indicated by the social and economic development indicators listed in Table 1. We stress that although HK currently matches and even surpasses the U.K. in certain economic terms, the U.K. became a developed country earlier than HK and the overall social and economic development in the U.K. was more advanced than that in HK before and during the period under examination in this study (1993–1997). In other words, we consider not just current, but also *historical*, stages of *social* and economic development. To the extent that the stages of social and economic development affect CSED, we expect a higher level of CSED in the U.K. than in HK.

Table 1. Social and Economic Performance in HK and the U.K.

Social and Economic Indicators	Year	U.K.	HK
GNP per capita (US$)[a]	1970	2,240	900
	1975	3,900	2,180
	1980	7,960	5,210
	1985	8,470	6,080
	1989	14,570	10,320
GDP per capita (US$)[b]	1990	16,948	13,110
	1993	16,245	19,404
	1995	18,991	22,372
	1996	19,758	24,235
	1997	21,921	26,567
Secondary school enrolment	1970	73	49
(% of children in the age group)[a]	1975	83	49
	1980	83	64
	1985	84	72
	1986	83	72
Enrolment in secondary education – ranking of 125 countries[d]	1995	4	47
Literacy rate – ranking of 98 countries[d]	1995	6	29
Public spending on education	1975	6.6	2.7
as % of GNP[b]	1980	5.6	2.5
	1990	4.9	2.8
	1993	5.4	2.8
TV (radio) receivers	1970	193 (623)	109 (170)
(per 1,000 inhabitants)[b]	1975	359 (694)	190 (500)
	1980	401 (941)	221 (506)
	1985	433 (1,007)	234 (596)
	1990	433 (1,390)	267 (666)
	1995	446 (1,427)	307 (675)
	1996	513 (1,438)	319 (676)
	1997	521 (1,443)	321 (684)
Persons per hospital bed[c]	1970–1975	105	200
	1980–1985	107	204
	1988–1993	160	234
Persons per physician[c]	1970–1975	809	1,500
	1980–1985	613	1,211
	1988–1993	N/A	N/A
Persons per nurse[c]	1970–1975	242	566
	1980–1985	120	795
	1988–1993	N/A	N/A

Sources: [a]World Bank (1991). [b]United Nations (2000). [c]World Bank (1988, 1991, 1995). [d]World Bank (http://wbln0018.worldbank.org/psd/).

Second, because HK had been under British colonial governance for 150 years before it was handed back to China as a "Special Administration Region" on 1 July 1997, a comparison of HK and the U.K. allows us to investigate the impact of different social and economic development stages on CSED in the two countries while taking into consideration the influence of colonization. One implication of colonization is that HK's social and economic systems tend to follow those of the U.K., thus suggesting that CSED is similar between the U.K. and HK (Nobes, 1998).

Under the U.K. rule, HK's legal, economic, education and accounting systems generally followed those of the U.K. (Wallace & Naser, 1995). HK companies ordinance tended to follow British company laws (Chan, 1988, p. 199). The HK Stock Exchange was largely based on the system and practice of its U.K. counterpart. Similarly, HK accounting and auditing standards normally followed those of the U.K. The Hong Kong Society of Accountants (HKSA) and the Association of Chartered Certified Accountants (ACCA) of the U.K. organized joint examinations in HK (Chan, 1988, p. 199). These provide evidence of administrative and accounting knowledge transfer from the U.K. to HK.

Despite this effect of colonization, however, the two countries have attached different importance to CSED. While U.K. companies faced increased pressures for CSED from the 1970s to the 1990s, external pressures for HK firms were minimal during that period. In addition, the U.K. has made some CSED mandatory since 1968 (Gray, Kouhy, & Lavers, 1995a), whereas CSED was voluntary for HK firms before and during the period under investigation in this study (Jaggi & Zhao, 1996; Ng, 2000).

This study contributes to the literature in two ways. First, it proposes and empirically tests a social and economic development perspective on CSED. As discussed later, several perspectives have been adopted in the CSED literature to explain cross-country differences in CSED. However, these perspectives do not formally recognize the impact of the stage of social and economic development on CSED. Our results suggest that this appears to be an important factor that should not be neglected. In addition, the adoption of this perspective opens an avenue for the application of positive accounting theory, legitimacy theory, stakeholder theory, and political economy in international comparative studies of CSED.

Our study also contributes to the literature by comparing CSED between a developed country and a newly industrialized region. Prior research has examined industrialized nations and newly developed countries separately with a focus on the former. With rare exceptions such as Williams and Pei (1999), little comparison of CSED practices between developed countries and newly industrialized country/region (such as HK) can be found in the literature.

PRIOR STUDIES OF CSED

Many cross-country studies of CSED in Western countries have been undertaken. For example, Adams, Hill, & Roberts (1998) analyze 150 annual reports from France, Germany, The Netherlands, Sweden, Switzerland, and the U.K. They find that company size, industrial grouping and country of domicile influence corporate social reporting patterns and that the amount and nature of information disclosed vary significantly across Europe. Guthrie and Parker (1990), by assessing 147 company annual reports, find significant differences between the U.K., the U.S. and Australia with respect to the level, the theme, the method, and the location of the disclosure. However, such cross-country comparisons are predominately based on industrialized nations. In particular, prior research has made little effort to compare CSED between industrialized nations and newly industrialized ones. A rare exception is Williams and Pei (1999) who compare CSED on the Internet by companies in Australian, HK, Singapore, and Malaysia.

Although no study has compared CSED in HK and the U.K., CSED in both countries has been subject to separate academic research. The average amount of the disclosure in the U.K. has increased from about one full page during 1978–1987 to nearly five pages of which 1.53 pages accounted for voluntary disclosures during 1988–1995 (Gray, Kouhy, & Lavers, 1995b; Gray, Javad, Power, & Sinclair, 2001). By contrast, prior studies have found a low level of CSED made by HK companies. Jaggi and Zhao (1996) report that only 13 of 100 HK companies had been consistently disclosing environmental information over the period of 1992–1994. Williams and Pei (1999) find that a sample of HK listed company had, on average, only 10.53 lines of CSED in the 1995 annual reports. A recent study by Ng (2000) discovers that only 9% of 200 HK listed companies reported environmental information in the published accounts. As a newly developed economy, there is a low level of environmental regulation and awareness in HK (Lynn, 1992; Ho, Ng, & Ng, 1994; Ng, 2000). Many HK business managers do not support the view that stakeholders should have rights for environmental information; some do not perceive disclosure of environmental information to be their responsibility (Jaggi & Zhao, 1996). While these studies are somewhat informative on the amount of, and trends in, CSED in each country, they do not enable a direct comparison of these and other aspects of CSED such as the location and themes of disclosure between the two countries. These defects necessitate the current study.

The literature offers several perspectives on cross-country differences in CSED. First, the cultural perspectives emphasize the influences of a country's culture on CSED (e.g., Perera & Mathews, 1990; Williams, 1998). Second, political perspectives attempt to explain the difference in CSED between countries in the context of the social and political structure of the countries and the agenda of political course within a particular society (e.g., Freedman & Stagliano, 1992; Adams et al., 1998; Williams, 1998). In addition, other arguments based on the development of the accounting system and financial markets have also been suggested (Fekrat, Inclan, & Petroni, 1996). However, these perspectives do not formally recognize the influence on CSED of different social and economic development stages.

Several theoretical frameworks have been adopted in the literature to interpret CSED, including positive accounting theory (e.g., Watts & Zimmerman, 1986; Milne, 2002), stakeholder theory (Ullmann, 1985; Roberts, 1992), legitimacy theory (Patten, 1992; Neu, Warsame, & Pedwell, 1998), and political economy (Arnold, 1990; Tinker, Neimark, & Lehman, 1991). While all these approaches focus on the organizational–environmental nexus, only political economy theory considers the impact of social and economic development on CSED. Political economy theory suggests that the economic domain cannot be studied in isolation from the political, social, and institutional framework within which economic development takes place and that social and political as well as economic factors affect CSED (Gray et al., 1995b). Thus, companies produce information that serves corporate political and ideological goals (Guthrie & Parker, 1990; Freedman & Stagliano, 1992). However, these goals are shaped and constrained by the social and economic development of a country where the company is based or operates (Cooper & Sherer, 1984). Therefore, political economy theory can be considered to provide a particular theoretical argument for our social and economic development perspective. We show later in the chapter that the above-mentioned other theories provide additional theoretical arguments.

There is no single motivation for making CSED. Given the complexity of CSED, it is extremely difficult (if it is not impossible) to explain the cross-country variation in CSED from a single theoretical perspective (Gray et al., 1995b). Thus, alternative perspectives might shed additional light on our understanding of CSED. We argue that the difference in CSED between countries can at least partially be attributed to their varied stages of social and economic development.

The financial reporting literature suggests that a country's stage of development is one of many environmental factors that affect corporate financial disclosure (e.g., AAA, 1977; Mueller, 1968; Nobes, 1998; Salter, 1998). Development economists have strongly argued that the social and institutional infrastructure (including the accounting system) in a country is dependent upon economic development and industrialization (Adelman, 1995; Cypher & James, 1997). Cooke and Wallace (1990) list the stage of economic development as part of the internal environment affecting a country's financial disclosure regulation. Moreover, Wallace (1993) suggests that the need for financial reporting increases as an economy becomes more developed.

THEORETICAL DEVELOPMENT AND HYPOTHESES

We argue that the stage of social and economic development is also an important factor affecting CSED, as different stages of social and economic development prompt different national concerns over social and environmental issues and different types and levels of demand for social and environmental information. In developed countries, economies are well developed. These countries have been through the stages of increasing the standard of living by exhausting social and natural resources. People are less concerned about their basic material needs, but more concerned about their social and cultural needs and quality of life. They are more concerned about equity, justice, and issues arising from polluted air, water, land, etc. People are more aware of, and sensitive to, these social and environmental issues, compared with citizens in developing or less developed countries.

By contrast, developing countries are still struggling to meet the basic material needs of their people (Cypher & James, 1997). They have to destroy natural resources to produce enough food and other materials to feed their people. Their pressing priority is current productivity rather than long-term social and economic consequences (Todaro, 1997). They also lack the resources and regulations to protect natural resources from being destroyed or lack the know-how to efficiently utilize resources. Many people in developing countries have to live with social injustice and a poor social welfare system. In general, people lack awareness of the social and environmental issues that are talked about in developed countries. As noted by Gray and Kouhy (1993), a large majority of the populations of developing countries live below a level of basic sustenance commensurate with human dignity. As a result, accounting and reporting issues from the perspective of developing countries themselves might seem relatively trivial compared to more pressing matters. This argument can equally apply to the development of CSED. In reality, a majority of enterprises in developing countries do not have adequate (financial) accounting systems and there is usually no guidance on how such systems can be developed and maintained (Wallace, 1993). Under these circumstances, it would be unrealistic to expect developing countries to have the same level of CSED as developed countries.

These different national concerns and priorities are reflected in public and institutional pressures for corporate social and environmental accountability. Organizations such as Greenpeace and Friends of the Earth have emerged and been actively watching corporate social and environmental activities in developed countries whereas similar organizations, if any, are likely to be imported from developed countries and are less active in developing countries. Moreover, corporate social and environmental issues attract much more press coverage in developed countries than in developing countries.

Finally, social and environmental activities and disclosures are more likely to be subject to governmental regulation in developed countries than in developing countries. According to Gray et al. (1995b), between 1979 and 1991, the total U.K. corporate social reporting rose by over four times, employee-related disclosure fell from approximately 90% to about 78%, and community and environmental reporting rose from about 10% to 32% of total disclosure. In short, adopting the notions from positive accounting theory, legitimacy theory and stakeholder theory, social and environmental issues potentially impose higher "political costs" and a more stringent "social contract," and create more demanding stakeholders for companies in developed countries than for those in developing countries (Milne, 2002; Deegan, 2002). As a result, companies in advanced societies would have to make more CSED to alleviate political costs, maintain the status of legitimacy and satisfy powerful stakeholders.

Between the two poles (developed and developing countries), there are newly industrialized countries such as HK and Singapore. Although, they may not be very different from those traditionally advanced countries in economic terms, they have only begun to consider social and environment issues. There is no legislation in these countries enforcing companies to mandate CSED (Lynn, 1992; Tsang, 1998; Ng, 2000). The level of CSED in these countries is thus generally low. However, as they move closer to traditionally developed countries, their concerns over these issues are increasing. As a result, these countries (e.g., Singapore) have been experiencing a trend of increased CSED over recent years (Tsang, 1998).

The U.K. and HK are illustrative of the above social and economic development perspective on CSED. The U.K. is a traditionally developed country while HK is a newly industrialized economy. The two economies have had quite different experiences in CSED. Since the late 1970s, U.K. firms have been facing growing pressures from the public, European Union, pressure groups, and professional bodies for social and environmental performance and reporting (Gray et al., 1995b). Many efforts have been made to encourage social and environmental reporting, for example, the ACCA's Environmental Reporting Award, the establishment of various social and environment research/promotion bodies (e.g., the Institute of Social and Ethical Accountability; the U.K. Social Investment Forum; the Green Alliance; and the Centre for Social and Environmental Accounting Research, now based at the University of Glasgow). Influenced by European Union social and environmental legislation, the U.K. has stipulated many acts (such as the Environmental Protection Act 1990, the Environment Act 1995, and the Pollution Prevention and Control Act 1999). The U.K. legislation has also made it mandatory for companies to disclose many aspects of corporate social and environmental activities. These include political and charitable donations, information to trade unions, employment of disabled persons, involvement of employees, health and safety at work, and air and water pollution (Gray et al., 1995a).

By contrast, although Friends of the Earth established its offices in HK in 1983, it has made little fundamental difference on the way HK businesses operate. Pollution, safety and many other social problems have accompanied remarkable economic achievements in HK. The government only recently realized the problems and introduced some environmental and social related regulations such as waste disposal and employment related ordinances. However, weak enforcement of environmental legislation has permitted the existence of serious social and environmental problems. For example, it is estimated that only half of HK's daily sewage gets any treatment before it flows into the sea, seriously polluting typhoon shelters and Victoria Harbor (Wong & Tanner, 1997). In addition, unlike the U.K., HK had no mandatory regulatory requirements of CSED before and during the study period (1993–1997) (Jaggi & Zhao, 1996; Ng, 2000). Taking into consideration these and the additional rationale listed below, we expect that differences in CSED will exist between the two countries in terms of the trend, amount, theme, and location of CSED.

Trends in CSED

According to Wallace (1993, p. 131), the international accounting literature suggests that corporate reporting and its regulation in a country is "a response to both technological, economic and social change" and that "in the process of a country's growth, the characteristics and functions of reporting enterprises – and particularly of the needs of the different users, preparers, auditors and regulators of corporate reports – are transformed." Likewise, a country's move towards a higher social and economic stage leads to an increasing demand of stakeholders for corporate social and environmental performance and reporting. This applies to both the U.K., which has been progressing towards a more advanced stage, and HK, which is a newly industrialized economy. Consequently, it is expected that both countries have experienced a trend of increased CSED over the period under study. Furthermore, during the period under study, as HK and the U.K. were at different levels of social and economic development and were under different pressures for CSED, it is expected that the U.K. would experience a greater increase in CSED than HK.

Indirect evidence seems to support such an expectation. Gray et al. (1995b) find that the total CSED contained in annual reports increased by four times in the U.K. between 1979 and 1991 (from just over one page to nearly four and a half pages). By contrast, the available evidence shows that the percentage of listed companies that disclosed information on *corporate environmental issues* in annual reports increased from 1% in 1989 (Lynn, 1992) to 9% in 1998 (Ng, 2000). Although informative, these prior studies do not facilitate a direct comparison of the trends in CSED in the two countries (Fig. 1 shows the trend in CSED in both the U.K. and HK during the period of 1993–1997).

Thus, we formulate and test the following hypothesis:

H1. U.K. companies increase CSED more than HK companies.

Amount of CSED

Compared with their U.K. counterparts, HK companies, regulators and the public are less aware of and less concerned about social and environmental issues (Lynn, 1992). Unlike the U.K., HK had no regulation that mandated CSED before and during the period under our study (Jaggi & Zhao, 1996; Ng, 2000). Anecdotal evidence as cited in the literature review section seems to suggest that the level of CSED in the U.K. is higher than that in HK (see, Gray et al., 2001; Williams & Pei, 1999; Ng, 2000). However, such anecdotal evidence does not enable a direct comparison of the level of CSED in the two countries as these prior studies are based on inconsistent samples, for different time periods and without controlling for confounding factors (such

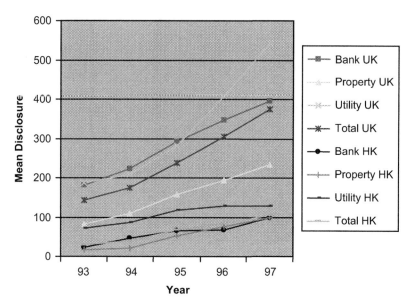

Fig. 1. CSED Trends in Hong Kong and the U.K.

as different company sizes between the two countries). This allows us to frame and test our second hypothesis:

H2. The amount of CSED made by U.K. companies is greater than that by HK companies.

Content Themes of CSED

An industry such as property whose activities modify or affect the environment may make more environmental disclosures than companies in other industries as a result of greater public concern and legislation (Deegan & Gordon, 1996; Hackston & Milne, 1996). By contrast, in the financial and banking industry, as human resources are regarded as one of the most important assets, companies tend to voluntarily disclose employee-related issues to boost a good public image. In short, industries disclose different information related to their different social and environmental responsibilities and corporate strategies. Moreover, compared with those in newly industrialized countries, the public and regulators in an advanced society like the U.K. are interested in a broader spectrum of corporate social and environmental issues and thus expect the companies to disclose a wider range of social and environmental information. In addition, companies in countries at different stages of social and economic development may focus on different issues. On the basis of this reasoning, we formulate the following hypothesis:

H3. There is a significant difference in the categories of disclosure made by companies between the U.K. and HK.

Location of CSED

Prior studies find that investors see some sections of the annual report as more important than other sections. For example, Lee and Tweedie (1976) and Bartlett and Chandler (1997) find that the Chairman's Statement was perceived by British shareholders as the most important section in the annual report, followed by Financial Statements, the Directors' Report, Notes to the Accounts, and the Auditor Report. Roberts (1990) argues that the location of information may reflect the company's attitudes towards environmental and social issues as well as the reader's perceptions of the importance that the company attaches to these issues. Therefore, it is expected that different companies place CSED in different parts of the annual reports. As U.K. companies and the public are more sensitive to social and environmental issues than HK companies, U.K. and HK companies may select the location for CSED differently. Thus we test the following hypothesis:

H4. There is a significant difference in the location of disclosure made by companies between HK and the U.K.

RESEARCH METHODOLOGY

Research Design

To test H1, the CSED trends between U.K. and HK companies were compared by testing the significance of the coefficient of the interaction between year and country using the following regression model:

$$\text{CSED} = \beta_0 + \beta_2\text{Country} + \beta_2\text{Year} + \beta_3(\text{Year} \times \text{Country}) \qquad (1)$$

where: CSED proxies for overall disclosures, disclosures by banking firms, disclosures by property firms, disclosures by utility firms, disclosures on environment, disclosures on energy, disclosures on health and safety, disclosures on human resources, disclosures on community, or disclosures on fairness.

Country is a dummy variable that was set at 1 for HK and 0 for the U.K.

Year is a proxy for the years under study with values ranging from 1 to 5 (representing 1993–1997).

Regression models were estimated for overall disclosures, disclosures by individual industries and disclosures by individual themes respectively.

To test H2, H3, and H4, this study employs content analysis – the most commonly used research method to assess an organization's social and environmental disclosures (Milne & Adler, 1999). Weber (1990, p. 9) describes content analysis as "a research method that uses a set of procedures to make valid inferences from text." It is an objective, systematic and quantitative description of a text assuming that there is a relation between the frequency of the linguistic units and the interest of the text producer (Holsti, 1969). Despite its limitations as discussed in Milne and Adler (1999) and Unerman (2000), it is particularly appropriate for our purposes because of its unobtrusive nature in analyzing narratives and its ability to measure the implicit importance attributed to an information category by the text (e.g., the annual report) producer.

Content Themes

The identification and definition of CSED themes have always been arbitrary. As noted by Gray et al. (1995a), there is no easy separation of these themes as categories and subcategories vary from time to time. This study considers six content themes, namely, environment, energy, health and safety, human resources, community involvement, and fair business practices. Table 2 provides the details of these categories and subcategories. While these categories and subcategories have been broadly used in prior studies, "Sport and Recreation," and "Quality/ISO" are two new subcategories which were not previously examined in the literature. Companies start to consider their employees' health as the direct cost arising from employees' sick leave and medical insurance is huge. Sport and recreation activities organized by employers have become part of corporate culture. Quality/ISO has also become a label for companies with quality service and product. The International Organization for Standardization (ISO) has introduced the ISO14001 series related to environmental management standards.

Table 2.   CSED Content Themes.

Content Themes	Sub-Themes
1. Environment	Pollution control (air, water, land, noise, and visual) Prevention of environmental damage Waste recycling Conservation of natural resources Research and development Environmental audit Environmental policy Other environmental disclosure
2. Energy	Conservation and energy saving Development/exploration of new sources Use of new sources Other energy-related disclosure
3. Health and safety	Health and safety at work Customer safety Product safety Accidents rate Compensation Other health-related disclosure
4. Human resources	Employee development/training programmes Pay and benefits (profit-sharing scheme) Pension scheme Loan to employee Employee share ownership scheme Sport and recreation Other employee related disclosure
5. Community involvement	Charitable donation and service Political donation and service Social activity sponsorship Other community activity disclosure
6. Fair business practices	Employment of women (sexual equality) Employment of minority (racial equality) Employment of disabled people Customer complaints Legal proceedings, litigation and liabilities Quality/ISO Other fair business practice disclosure

Measurement

Some previous studies measured CSED on a dichotomous basis of disclosure or non-disclosure (e.g., Wiseman, 1982; Lynn, 1992). This measurement fails to indicate the extent of the reporting entity's involvement in CSED. Alternative units of analysis in written communication tend to be counts of words, sentences, lines, and pages. In addition, counts of sentences, lines, and pages are also the most simple and convenient way, which has been used, in previous studies. However, these three types of counts have some limitations. For example, it is difficult to make a comparison between two annual reports if fonts, page margins, and components (pictures and graphs) differ. Also, one sentence, line or page may contain more than one category of information and the researcher may have difficulty in deciding which category the sentence/line/page belongs to. Word count is used in this study because words have the advantage of lending themselves to more exclusive analysis. In addition to the number of words, the location of a disclosure was extracted from the annual report to test H4.

Reliability

Two researchers in the U.K. and HK read the collected annual reports. To check whether the two researchers could apply the rules and procedures consistently, three other researchers reanalyzed a selection of 25 U.K. and 10 HK annual reports. The reliability test revealed the average variance was 0.98% for the U.K. annual reports and 0.68% for HK. As the location of an annual report was easily identifiable, there was no mistake made. Only two mistakes were made in classifying disclosures.

SAMPLE

The sample consisted of 33 HK firms from the top 100 listed companies in the HK and 36 U.K. firms from the Financial Times 300 listed companies. This study focussed on three sectors: property, banking, and utility. As property companies account for a significant percentage of total market capitalization in HK, they have a considerable impact on HK's society and environment. Banking is a service industry and its competitive advantage depends on the quality of their employees, and thus, banks may be willing to invest more in staff and disclose more on their human resource information. Utilities were chosen because their activities are sensitive to the

Table 3.   The Sample.

Sectors	U.K. Companies		HK Companies		Total	
	No.	Reports	No.	Reports	No.	Reports
Banking	12	60	10	47	22	107
Property	14	70	17	78	31	148
Utility	10	50	6	29	16	79
Total	36	180	33	154	69	334

environment. The initial sample consisted of all 38 companies in property, banking, and utility in HK's top 100 listed companies and all 46 U.K. listed companies in these same industries from Financial Times top 300 companies. These companies were further screened according to four criteria. First, companies with a merger, major acquisition or takeover during 1993–1997 that resulted in management restructuring were excluded because the new management team might introduce a different policy in issuing their annual reports. Second, companies that changed their accounting dates were excluded because two annual reports might be available for 1 year. Third, companies with less than three annual reports were not included as the time period was too short for a comparison. Finally, companies registered outside the U.K. and HK were not considered. This selection process provided a final list of 33 HK companies with 154 annual reports and 36 U.K. companies with 180 annual reports. Given the limited resources and availability of HK annual reports, the annual reports for 5 years (1993–1997) were sought for each company. The year 1997 was selected as the ending year of the study period with a view to avoiding any external influences from Mainland China on HK's CSED after China took over the sovereignty of HK in later 1997. All 180 U.K. annual reports were collected, whereas only 154 out of 165 HK annual reports were available (see Table 3). If a company prepared a separate social and environmental report, the report was also collected as part of the annual report.

FINDINGS AND DISCUSSIONS

Recent studies have found a positive relationship between company size and the overall level of disclosure in a number of countries (e.g., Hackston & Milne, 1996; Adams et al., 1998; Gray et al., 2001). This is because larger companies are usually exposed to greater public scrutiny and under more pressure to communicate their social and environmental information. It is also argued that management will not disclose social and environmental information when the expected cost exceeds the benefit. A larger company usually has more resources available to cover the costs. In this study we found a strong association, significant at 0.01, between size and the amount of disclosure in both the U.K. and HK with the Pearson correlation co-efficients being 0.532 for the U.K. and 0.548 for HK. This size effect was controlled for in testing Hypotheses 2, 3, and 4 using one-way analysis of variance (ANOVA). That is, company size was used as a covariate in the analysis. Company size was measured by turnover for utility and property, and interest received and receivable for banks for all purposes of the paper unless otherwise stated. Alternatively, we also measured company size by total assets.

Table 4 indicates the trends in CSED in the U.K. and HK for the period 1993–1997. In this table, positive numbers for "Year × Country" indicate greater CSED in HK than in the U.K. and negative numbers indicate greater CSED in the U.K. than in HK. As Table 4 indicates, the increase in overall CSED was significantly greater in the U.K., which supports H1. U.K. companies also had a significantly larger trend of disclosure of information on utility, environment, and human resources. These results are consistent with

Table 4. Disclosure Trends in the U.K. and HK (Based on Word Count).

	Year × Country	F-Ratio	Adj. R^2
Total	−41.95**	51.02**	0.09
Industry			
Bank	−43.96	14.76**	0.08
Property	−17.72	18.57**	0.07
Utility	−77.72	13.99**	0.10
Themes			
Environment	−36.26**	7.31**	0.07
Energy	−8.22	3.71**	0.03
Health	−2.55	12.53**	0.12
Humanity	−218.92**	172.98**	0.67
Community	−25.40	9.08**	0.09
Fairness	39.66**	25.39**	0.23

Notes: Positive numbers for "Year × Country" indicate greater CSED in HK than in the U.K. and negative numbers indicate greater CSED in the U.K. than in HK. These results are produced after controlling for company size that is measured by turnover for utility and property firms and interest received and receivable for banks. Using total assets as a proxy for company size does not significantly alter these results. **Significant at the 0.01 level.

the predictions of the social and economic development perspective. However, HK companies increased more significantly in the disclosure of fairness than U.K. companies. This is because the focus of CSED in the U.K. shifted from fairness disclosure at the end of the 1970s and 1980s towards mainly on community and environmental disclosure in the early 1990s (Gray et al., 1995b, p. 62). This shift reflected U.K.'s advance to a higher level of social and economic development. In the 1970s and early 1980s, the social focus of the economy was mainly in the area of employment (including related issues such as equal opportunity, pension rights, and trade union). In the 1990s, the social concerns ranged from environmental problems to social inclusion, citizens charters, community supports and sponsorship, and staff training. By contrast, in the early 1990s, HK just began to develop CSED and its central social and economic issues related to employment, consumerism and social democratic transition (specifically the preparation of the handover to China). As a result, the public were mainly interested in issues relating to fairness such as equal opportunity in employment, customers rights, and quality of products and services. By contrast, HK was relatively late in addressing environmental issues compared with the U.K. and other Western economies (Jaggi & Zhao, 1996).

Table 5 shows that the total CSED by U.K. companies was greater than that by HK companies. This was also the case for the banking and property industries. Moreover, when total assets were controlled for as an alternative proxy for company size, then there was also a difference in the utility sector with the F-value being 11.00 significant at 0.01. Thus, there is strong evidence to support H2. As company size was controlled for in the statistical test, this difference should not be regarded as being caused by the differences in size between HK and U.K. companies. Instead, the difference supports our argument that different stages of social and economic development result in different amounts of CSED in the two countries. For example, the difference was partly caused by the mandatory nature of some CSED in the U.K. Gray et al. (2001) report that 1.10 out of the 4.89 pages of CSED made by U.K. companies during 1988 and 1995 fell into the category of mandatory disclosures. Taking the regulation of CSED as a characteristic of social and economic development, this chapter does not formally distinguish between mandatory and voluntary CSED.

As shown in Table 6, U.K. companies disclosed more than HK companies in the categories of health and safety and human resources. However, no difference was found in the amount of disclosures concerning environment, energy, community, and fairness between the two countries. However, when total assets were controlled for as an alternative proxy for company size,

Table 5.   The Amount of Disclosure in the U.K. and HK
(Based on Word Count).

Industry	U.K.		HK		F-value
	Mean	S.D.	Mean	S.D.	
Total	7,415	3,978	2,080	1,492	30.08**
Bank	8,644	3,241	1,819	935	16.01**
Property	4,672	2,994	1,725	1,573	15.44**
Utility	9,779	3,977	3,349	1,580	4.20

Note: These results are produced after controlling for company size that is measured by turnover for utility and property firms and interest received and receivable for banks. **Significant at the 0.01 level.

Table 6.   Theme-Based Disclosure in the U.K. and HK
(Based on Word Count).

Theme	U.K.		HK		F-value
	Mean	S.D.	Mean	S.D.	
Environment	603	1,097	153	351	3.78
Energy	80	235	0	0	2.86
Health	204	283	17	64	9.50**
Human resources	5,581	2,712	1,298	828	53.5**
Community	595	768	228	388	1.07
Fairness	353	318	383	319	2.22

Note: These results are produced after controlling for company size that is measured by turnover for utility and property firms and interest received and receivable for banks. **Significant at the 0.01 level.

then there was also a significant difference in the theme of environment with the *F*-value being 5.38 significant at 0.05. The results partially confirmed H3 that, due to different stages of social and economic development, U.K. and HK companies focussed on different social and environmental issues. In particular, over the period under study, HK showed great interest in fairness while the U.K. moved on to deal with other pressing issues such as environmental problems, social inclusion, and human resources. This probably contributed towards narrowing the gap in the disclosure of information on fairness issues while enlarging the gulf in the disclosure of information on issues relating to the environment and human resources.

From Table 7, it can be seen that no or little CSED was included in the Mission Statement, the Auditors' Report, and Financial Statements by either U.K. or HK companies. This might be because, technically, these sections of the annual report are probably less suitable for disclosing CSED; the Mission Statement is normally fairly short whereas the Financial Statements and the Auditors' Report are driven by accounting standards and auditing standards that focus on the financial results and conditions of the company, rather than on social and environmental issues.

In the other sections of the annual report where CSED was found, however, U.K. and HK companies placed an emphasis on different locations. The amount of CSED by U.K. companies declined in the following order: Notes to the Accounts, Separate Section or Report, Directors' Report, Operations Review, and Chairman's Statement. By contrast, the amount of CSED by HK companies followed a different pattern (in order of declined importance): Operations Review, Notes to the Accounts, Directors' Report, and then Chairman's Statement. Table 7 shows that U.K. companies disclosed more social and environmental information in a Separate Section or Report, the Directors' Report, and Notes to the Accounts than HK firms. These differences were statistically significant. These results can be interpreted as U.K. companies in general attaching more importance to CSED than HK companies, especially if a separate section in the annual report or a

Table 7. The Location of Disclosure in the U.K. and HK (Based on Word Count).

Location	U.K.		HK		*F*-value
	Mean	S.D.	Mean	S.D.	
Mission statement	2	13	29	105	1.84
Chairman's statement	165	223	241	214	1.00
Separate section/report	2,228	2,314	27	87	19.6**
Operations review	922	1,636	679	1,128	0.07
Directors' report	1,515	1,124	303	300	25.8**
Audit report	0	0	0	0	–
Financial statements	0	0	2	13	0.86
Notes to the accounts	2,583	1,283	536	471	59.3**

Note: These results are produced after controlling for company size that is measured by turnover for utility and property firms and interest received and receivable for banks. **Significant at the 0.01 level.

separate social and environmental report signifies more perceived importance of CSED. Thus, there is evidence to support H4.

CONCLUSIONS

This study compared CSED in HK and the U.K. by analyzing 334 annual reports from 69 companies over the period of 1993–1997. It found that, despite the colonial impact, U.K. firms made significantly more CSED than their HK counterparts. The difference existed for all three industries (banking, property, and utility) and for the themes of health and safety, human resources, and environment, but not for the themes of energy, community and fairness. During the five-year period studied, there was an upward trend in the amount of CSED in both the U.K. and HK, although U.K. firms increased more than HK firms did. Moreover, U.K. companies made more CSED in a separate section of the annual report or a separate social and environmental report, the Directors' Report and Notes to the Accounts than HK firms. These results were obtained after controlling for company size because there appeared to be a strong association between company size and the amount of disclosure in both countries. This size effect is consistent with the findings of prior studies (e.g., Adams et al., 1998; Gray et al., 2001).

These findings reflect a higher level of public awareness of social and environmental issues and greater public, institutional and regulatory pressures and demand for CSED in the U.K. than in HK. They also suggest that social and environmental issues represent greater political costs and legitimacy threats for U.K. companies than for HK firms. Moreover, the results indicate that CSED was perceived as more important by U.K. firms than by HK firms. Our findings generally support the argument that social and economic development is an important cause for the difference in CSED between the two countries. They are also consistent with the key notions of positive accounting theory, stakeholder theory, and legitimacy theory, suggesting that these theories can be adopted in comparative studies of social and environmental reporting under the social and economic development perspective.

Although making two important contributions as noted in the introduction, the limitations of this study should be noted. The results would have been more inclusive if a longer time period and more industries had been examined. In addition, this study has only considered annual reports. We did not consider other media because the annual report is the most important and statutory document for corporate communications (Gray et al., 1995a). This focus is in line with the vast bulk of the CSED literature. We did not expand the scope to CSED on the Internet for two reasons. First, the findings would be contaminated by the uneven usage of the Internet between HK and the U.K. during the period of study since the percentage of the largest 30 companies without a website in the mid-1999 was 37% and 3% in HK and the U.K. respectively (Lymer, Debreceny, Gray, & Rahman, 1999). Second, Internet-based corporate disclosures are largely a copy of hardcopy disclosure (Lymer et al., 1999).

Moreover, other factors may also contribute towards the difference in the CSED between the U.K. and HK. Potential factors include the role of government and culture. Future research would benefit from using samples involving more sectors and covering more companies, distinguishing mandatory from voluntary disclosures, considering additional determinants of CSED and other media used by companies to disclose social and environmental information.

ACKNOWLEDGEMENT

The authors thank the editor, Sonja Gallhofer, Wan-Ying Hill, Zhijun Lin, and the participants of Napier University Accounting Research Seminar Series on 25 October 1999 and the 12th Asian Pacific Conference on International Accounting Issues for comments on earlier drafts. Jason Xiao acknowledges financial support provided by the Chinese Accounting, Finance and Business Research Unit at Cardiff University. The authors thank He Yang's research assistance.

REFERENCES

AAA (American Accounting Association). (1977). Report of the committee on international accounting operations and education, 1975–1976. *The Accounting Review, 52*(Suppl.), 65–132.

Adams, C. A., Hill, W. Y., & Roberts, C. B. (1998). Corporate social reporting practices in Western Europe: Legitimating corporate behaviour? *British Accounting Review, 30,* 1–21.

Adelman, I. (1995). *Institutions and development strategies.* VT: Edward Elgar Publishing Company.

Arnold, P. J. (1990). The state and political theory in corporate social disclosure research: A response to Guthrie and Parker. *Advances in Public Interest Accounting, 4,* 144–181.

Bartlett, S. A., & Chandler, R. A. (1997). The corporate report and the private shareholder: Lee and Tweedie twenty years on. *British Accounting Review, 29,* 245–261.

Burchell, S., Clubb, C., Hopwood, A., & Hughes, J. (1980). The roles of accounting in organizations and society. *Accounting, Organizations and Society, 5*, 5–27.

Chan, A. M. Y. (1988). The speculative accounting systems in Hong Kong: Understanding Hong Kong's accounting reality. In: V. K. Zimmerman (Ed.), *Recent accounting and economic developments in the far east* (pp. 197–218). Champaign, IL: Centre for International Education and Research in Accounting, University of Illinois.

Cooke, T. E., & Wallace, R. S. O. (1990). Financial disclosure regulation and its environment: A review and further analysis. *Journal of Accounting and Public Policy, 9*, 79–110.

Cooper, D., & Sherer, M. (1984). The value of corporate accounting reports: Arguments for a political economy of accounting. *Accounting, Organizations and Society, 9*, 207–232.

Cypher, J. M., & James, L. D. (1997). *The process of economic development.* New York: Routledge.

Deegan, C. (2002). The legitimising effect of social and environmental disclosures – a theoretical foundation. *Accounting, Auditing, and Accountability Journal, 15*(3), 282–311.

Deegan, C., & Gordon, B. (1996). A study of environmental disclosure practices of Australian corporations. *Accounting and Business Research, 26*, 187–199.

Fekrat, M. A., Inclan, C., & Petroni, D. (1996). Corporate environmental disclosures: Competitive disclosure hypothesis using 1991 annual report data. *The International Journal of Accounting, 31*, 175–195.

Freedman, M., & Stagliano, A. J. (1992). European unification, accounting harmonization, and social disclosures. *The International Journal of Accounting, 27*, 112–122.

Gray, R., & Kouhy, R. (1993). Accounting for the environment and sustainability in lesser-developed countries: An exploratory note. *Research in Third World Accounting, 2*, 387–399.

Gray, R. H., Javad, M., Power, D. M., & Sinclair, C. D. (2001). Social and environmental disclosure and corporate characteristics: A research note and extension. *Journal of Business Finance and Accounting, 28*, 327–356.

Gray, R. H., Kouhy, R., & Lavers, S. (1995a). Methodological themes: Constructing a research database for social and environmental reporting by UK companies. *Accounting, Auditing and Accountability Journal, 8*, 78–101.

Gray, R. H., Kouhy, R., & Lavers, S. (1995b). Corporate social and environmental reporting: A review of the literature and a longitudinal study of UK disclosure. *Accounting, Auditing and Accountability Journal, 8*, 47–77.

Guthrie, J., & Parker, L. D. (1990). Corporate social disclosure practice: A comparative international analysis. *Advances in Public Interest Accounting, 3*, 159–176.

Hackston, D., & Milne, M. (1996). Some determinants of social and environmental disclosures in New Zealand. *Accounting, Auditing and Accountability Journal, 9*, 77–108.

Ho, S., Ng, P., & Ng, A. (1994). A study of environmental reporting in Hong Kong. *Hong Kong Accountant, 5*, 62–65.

Holsti, O. R. (1969). *Content analysis for the social sciences and humanities.* New York: Addison-Wesley.

Jaggi, B., & Zhao, R. (1996). Environmental performance and reporting: Perceptions of managers and accounting professionals in Hong Kong. *The International Journal of Accounting, 31*, 333–346.

Lee, T. A., & Tweedie, D. P. (1976). The private shareholder: His sources of financial information and his understanding of reporting practices. *Accounting and Business Research, 6*(Autumn), 304–314.

Lymer, A., Debreceny, R., Gray, G. L., & Rahman, A. (1999). *Business reporting on the internet*. London: IASC.

Lynn, M. (1992). A note on corporate social disclosure in Hong Kong. *British Accounting Review, 24*, 105–110.

Milne, M. J. (2002). Positive accounting theory, political costs and social disclosure analysis: A critical look. *Critical Perspectives on Accounting, 13*, 369–395.

Milne, M. J., & Adler, R. W. (1999). Exploring the reliability of social and environmental disclosures content analysis. *Accounting, Auditing and Accountability Journal, 12*, 237–256.

Mueller, G. (1968). Accounting practices generally accepted in the United States versus those generally accepted elsewhere. *The International Journal of Accounting, 3*(2), 91–103.

Neu, D., Warsame, H., & Pedwell, K. (1998). Managing public impressions: Environmental disclosures in annual reports. *Accounting, Organizations and Society, 23*, 265–282.

Ng, A. Y. (2000). Going green: More cause than concern. *Australian CPA, 70*, 64–69.

Nobes, C. (1998). Towards a general model of the reasons for international differences in financial reporting. *Abacus, 34*, 162–187.

Patten, D. M. (1992). Intra industry environmental disclosures in response to the Alaskan oil spill: A note on legitimacy theory. *Accounting, Organizations and Society, 17*, 471–475.

Perera, M. H. B., & Mathews, M. R. (1990). The cultural relativity of accounting and international patterns of social accounting. *Advances in International Accounting, 3*, 215–251.

Roberts, C. B. (1990). Environmental disclosures in corporate annual reports in Western Europe. In: D. L. Owen (Ed.), *Green reporting: Accountancy and the challenge of the nineties* (pp. 139–165). London: Chapman & Hall.

Roberts, R. W. (1992). Determinants of corporate social responsibility disclosure: An application of stakeholder theory. *Accounting, Organizations and Society, 17*, 595–612.

Salter, S. B. (1998). Corporate financial disclosure in emerging markets: Does economic development matter? *The International Journal of Accounting, 33*, 211–234.

Tang, K.-L. (1998). East Asian newly industrializing countries: Economic growth and quality of life. *Social Indicators Research, 43*, 69–96.

Tang, K.-L. (1999). Planning for the unknown: Social policy-making in Hong Kong 1990–1997. *International Journal of Sociology and Social Policy, 19*, 27–56.

Tinker, A. M., Neimark, M., & Lehman, C. (1991). Falling down the hole in the middle of the road: Political quietism in corporate social reporting. *Accounting, Auditing and Accountability Journal, 4*, 28–54.

Todaro, M. (1997). *Economic development*. MA: Addison-Wesley.

Tsang, E. W. K. (1998). A longitudinal study of corporate social reporting in Singapore: The case of the banking, food and beverages and hotel industries. *Accounting, Auditing and Accountability Journal, 11*, 624–635.

Ullmann, A. A. (1985). Data in search of a theory: A critical examination of the relationships among social performance, social disclosure, and economic performance of US firms. *Academy of Management Review, 10*, 540–557.

Unerman, J. (2000). Methodological issues: Reflections on quantification in corporate social reporting content analysis. *Accounting, Auditing and Accountability Journal, 13*, 667–681.

United Nations. (2000). *Statistical year book*. New York: UN.

Wallace, R. S. O. (1993). Development of accounting standards for developing and newly industrialized countries. *Research in Third World Accounting, 2*, 121–165.

Wallace, R. S. O., & Naser, K. (1995). Firm specific determinants of the comprehensives of mandatory disclosure in the corporate annual reports of firms listed on the stock exchange of Hong Kong. *Journal of Accounting and Public Policy, 14*, 311–368.

Watts, R. L., & Zimmerman, J. L. (1986). *Positive accounting theory.* London: Prentice-Hall.

Weber, R. D. (1990). *Basic content analysis.* Beverly Hills, CA: Sage.

Williams, S. L. M. (1998). *Voluntary environmental and social accounting disclosure practices in the Asia–Pacific region.* Unpublished doctoral thesis, Murdoch University, Australia.

Williams, S. L. M., & Pei, C. A. H. W. (1999). Corporate social disclosures by listed companies on their web sites: An international comparison. *The International Journal of Accounting, 34*, 389–419.

Wiseman, J. (1982). An evaluation of environmental disclosures made in corporate annual reports. *Accounting, Organizations and Society, 7*, 53–63.

Wong, A. Y-S., & Tanner, P. A. (1997). Monitoring environmental pollution in Hong Kong: Trends and prospects. *Trends in Analytical Chemistry, 16*, 180–190.

World Bank. (1988, 1991, 1995). *Social indicators of development.* London: Johns Hopkins University Press.

World Bank. (1991). *World tables 1991, a World Bank publications.* London: Johns Hopkins University Press.

COMPLIANCE WITH MANDATORY DISCLOSURE REQUIREMENTS BY NEW ZEALAND LISTED COMPANIES

Joanna Yeoh

ABSTRACT

Annual reports are a primary medium in which listed companies communicate with the public. In New Zealand, legislation, along with other reinforcing features, regulates the information disclosures found in companies' annual report. However, the existence of a regulatory framework does not guarantee its compliance. This paper reports a descriptive study of the compliance behaviour of New Zealand registered companies listed on the New Zealand Stock Exchange (NZX) with regard to required disclosures in their annual reports over a 3-year period, 1996–1998. Compliance with reporting requirement is measured by using a researcher-created disclosure index consisting of 495 mandated information items. The sample consists of 49 companies spanning the 1996–1998 period. The overall results show a high degree of corporate compliance with the financial reporting requirements. However, the compliance rate is higher with respect to the Statements of Standard Accounting Practices (SSAPs) than to both the Financial Reporting Standards (FRSs), and

Advances in International Accounting
Advances in International Accounting, Volume 18, 245–262
ISSN: 0897-3660/doi:10.1016/S0897-3660(05)18012-X

*listing rules of the stock market. This is a cause for concern, as the
SSAPs will eventually be replaced by FRSs.*

INTRODUCTION

This paper reports the results of an empirical study assessing the degree of
compliance with annual report mandatory disclosure requirements by New
Zealand (NZ)-registered companies listed on the New Zealand Stock
Exchange (NZX) over a 3-year period (1996–1998). The results indicate a
high degree of compliance with mandatory disclosure requirements. The
results are consistent with prior literature (see Adhikari & Tondkar, 1992;
Riahi-Belkaoui, 1995) that listed companies in developed markets tend to
comply more with mandatory disclosure requirements than their listed
counterparts in developing markets.

Although prior studies (McNally, Eng, & Hasseldine, 1982; Hossian,
Perera, & Rahman, 1995) have reported instances where accounting information have voluntarily been disclosed in annual reports of NZ companies,
several other studies have documented noncompliance with certain individual
accounting standards (see Ryan, 1994). For example, Tower, Gnosh, Rahman, Tan, and Cuthberston (1990) found that the non-compliance rate with
accounting standard on depreciation (SSAP-3) was between 32% and 48%.
While the degree of compliance with individual financial accounting standards
in NZ has previously been examined for pre-Financial Reporting Act (FRA)
periods, no study has focused on the degree of compliance with FRSs after the
enactment of the FRA. Also, no study, in the context of NZ, has focused on
the accounting information required to be disclosed in corporate annual reports in its entirety. This study, therefore, fills the void in the literature by
assessing the degree of compliance with statutory and regulatory financial
reporting requirements by companies listed on the NZX for post-FRA period
(1996–1998). Studies of this genre provide useful and timely information for
standard setters to isolate those standards with low compliance.[1]

FINANCIAL REPORTING FRAMEWORK

NZ lies in the southern Pacific Ocean about 1,600 km east of Australia. It
consists of two large islands (the North and South islands), and a number of
smaller islands. Its total land area is 268,021 sq. km, comparable to the size

of the United Kingdom. However, it is considerably less populated. As of early 2002, its total population was approximately 3.8 million. Eighty percent of the population consists of people of European origin, and 15% of the Maori race. The country also has many other minorities, including those of Polynesian and Chinese descent. It was formerly a British colony, but is now a self-governing democratic nation within the British Commonwealth. It is rich in natural resources, and is economically dependent on exports of agricultural commodities such as dairy produce, meat, forestry products, and fish. Its major export trading partners are Australia, Japan, and the United States (U.S.).

The financial reporting practices of companies in NZ are regulated by both the Companies Act 1993 and the FRA. However, whereas the Companies Act prescribes the administrative (and certain content) requirements, the FRA establishes the overall regulatory framework for financial reporting in the country. Further, while the Companies Act applies to all companies, the FRA applies to all companies and all issuers.[2] The Companies Act requires directors of companies to maintain accurate accounting records, which can be adequately explained. It also requires all companies to prepare an annual report, which must include all contents prescribed under section 211 of the Act. The prescribed contents include financial statements, an audit report, and additional information regarding accounting policies, directors, employees, and donations. The prescribed additional information can be excluded with shareholders' consent. Financial statements consist of balance sheet, profit and loss statement, statement of cash flows, and accompanying notes as defined by section 8 of the FRA.

The requirements for an audit are set out in both the Companies Act and the FRA. The Companies Act requires all companies to appoint an external auditor except for non-issuer companies with unanimous shareholder approval to waive this requirement. The FRA requires the financial statements of all issuers to be audited. Implicitly, non-issuer entities are subject to statutory audit requirements.

Evolving from the British tradition of self-regulation, the accountancy profession in NZ, the Institute of Chartered Accountants of New Zealand (ICANZ), is influential in the financial reporting practices of companies in the country. Although the ICANZ has no exclusive right to develop FRSs in the country, it has been the sole developer of Accounting Standards Review Board (ASRB) approved standards. The ASRB-approved FRSs have legal endorsement under the FRA. Apart from developing FRSs, it monitors their compliance through its members serving in the capacity either as reporting accountants, auditors, or directors.

The FRA requires financial statements of all reporting entities to show a "true and fair view" in addition to meeting generally accepted accounting practice (GAAP). Compliance with GAAP would usually be sufficient to enable financial statements to show a "true and fair view". However, when this is not the case, section 11 of the FRA requires additional information to be provided to achieve a "true and fair view". Section 3 of the FRA defines GAAP as compliance with any applicable FRSs, and where no applicable FRS exists, appropriate accounting policies having authoritative support.[3]

Under the FRA, a failure to comply with an applicable FRS is punishable by a maximum fine of NZ$100,000 per director. However, the FRA does not prescribe any penalty for failing to comply with appropriate accounting policies having authoritative support. Westwood (2000) points out that, in practice, the Registrar of Companies may invoke an alternative penalty for failure to comply with authoritative support by using the FRA section 18 filing requirement in conjunction with section 16(2). The section 16(2) requires external auditors to report any breach of GAAP to the Registrar of Companies, who in turn, must report the breach to the ASRB and the Securities Commission. During 1995/96, for example, the Securities Commission enquired into aspects of financial statements of 29 listed companies, and reviewed 138 financial statements referred to it by the Registrar of Companies because their audit reports were qualified (Securities Commission, 1996).

In addition to the reporting requirements of the Companies Act and the FRA, listed companies are obliged to conform with the NZX's continuous periodic reporting requirements. The NZX has a market surveillance panel responsible for the creation and enforcement of its rules, with power to censure and suspend a company's shares from trading in the market.

RESEARCH DESIGN AND METHODOLOGY

Sample Selection

The sample consists of NZ-registered non-financial companies that were listed on the NZX during 1996–1998. Only NZ-registered companies were chosen because foreign-registered companies do not have to comply with NZ GAAP. The companies selected were from those NZ-registered companies listed on the NZX, and whose annual reports were available for each of the 3 years. The final sample consists of 49 companies per year. The yearly sample represents approximately 39 percent of the NZ-registered companies listed on the NZX as at the end of each year examined.

Therefore, the results of this paper can be generalised to the population of NZ-registered non-financial companies listed on the NZX.

Measuring Disclosure Compliance Level

A disclosure-measuring template was developed and used to capture the mandatory disclosure compliance level (DCL) for each company in the sample. The disclosure template is similar to the one used by Owusu-Ansah and Yeoh (2002). The disclosure-measuring template consists of all information items required to be disclosed in an annual report of a NZX-listed company. The information items are compiled from the Companies Act 1993, promulgations of the professional accounting body (FRSs and SSAPs), and the NZX listing rules.

An applicable mandated information item is scored one when disclosed in an annual report of a sample company, and zero otherwise. A problem with scoring disclosures in annual reports is whether or not an undisclosed information item is applicable to a sample company. Several measures employed in prior literature to minimise the impact of this problem were adopted here. First, following Cooke (1989), the annual reports were thoroughly read before they were scored so as to ascertain if undisclosed information items were indeed inapplicable to the companies. Second, applicability of any information item was confirmed by reviewing preceding and succeeding years' annual reports as NZ companies are required to disclose comparative figures for each financial statement item. This procedure is consistent with Owusu-Ansah (2000). Third, the applicability of some items was determined by logical reasoning (Owusu-Ansah, 2000). For example, it is logical to expect a company to disclose its accounting policy for inventory valuation, if it owns some kind of inventory.

Another problem with the disclosure index methodology is that some of the information items in the index may not be applicable to all sample companies. Following prior studies, a relative score was computed for each company. The relative score is the ratio of what a company disclosed in its annual report to what it is expected to disclose under the regulatory regime in each year investigated. Because the constituents of the disclosure index are mandated information items, the relative score obtained by a company is interpreted as its DCL, derived by using the following formula:

$$\text{DCL}_{ijt} = \frac{\sum_{i=1}^{m_{jt}} d_{ijt}}{\sum_{i=1}^{n_{jt}} d_{ijt}} \tag{1}$$

where

d_{ijt} = disclosure value of information item i applicable to j sample company in year t, taking a value of one, if company j discloses it, or zero, if it does not, m_{jt} = number of mandated information items applicable to the sample company j that it actually disclosed in year t, n_{jt} = the number of mandated information items applicable to sample company j, which are expected to be disclosed by company j in year t.

To ensure that the DCL for each company reflects its true disclosure compliance behaviour, the reliability of the disclosure-measuring template was evaluated. To do this, annual reports of 20 sample companies were randomly selected and given to an independent person to re-score. A correlation analysis was done on the scores obtained by this person, and those by the present investigator. The results of this analysis indicate that there was no significant bias introduced by the scorers, and that the DCL for each company is reliable.

RESULTS AND DISCUSSION

As panel A of Table 1 indicates, there was a high degree of compliance with mandatory disclosure requirements by the companies in the sample in each of the years investigated. The DCLs cluster together in the upper end of the fourth quartile. They range from a minimum compliance level of 84.1% to a maximum level of 99.5% (see panel B of Table 1). A closer inspection of panel A of Table 1 reveals that the number of companies disclosing less than 90% of the applicable mandated information items declined over time.

The number of companies whose compliance rate was between 90% and 100% of statutory and regulatory disclosure requirements consistently increased over time from 84% in 1996 to 98% in 1998. This upward trend in the degree of compliance with disclosure requirements could be due to the regulatory agency having proved that it is not a big lion without teeth. The upward trend in compliance level could also be due to increasing economies of scale. Thus, the marginal cost of complying with more disclosure requirements by the sample companies declines over time.

While Table 1 summarizes the overall compliance level with mandatory disclosure requirements in the country, a more detailed item-by-item comparison between actual compliance level and corresponding disclosure requirements would be insightful. Hence, such a comparative analysis was done, and is reported in Tables 2–4.

Table 1. Yearly Descriptive Statistics of Disclosure Compliance Behaviour of Companies.

Panel A: *Mandatory Disclosure Compliance Level*

Disclosure Compliance Level (%)	Companies					
	1996		1997		1998	
	No.	%	No.	%	No.	%
Between 95 and 100	25	51.02	20	40.82	23	46.94
Between 90 and 94	18	36.73	24	48.98	25	51.02
Between 85 and 89	6	12.24	5	10.20	1	2.04
Between 80 and 84	0	0.00	0	0.00	0	0.00
Between 75 and 79	0	0.00	0	0.00	0	0.00
Less than 75	0	0.00	0	0.00	0	0.00
Total	49	100.00	49	100.00	49	100.00

Panel B: *Summary Statistics*

	1996	1997	1998
Mean (%)	93.9	94.3	94.5
Minimum (%)	85.1	85.3	88.6
Maximum (%)	99.4	99.3	99.4

Table 2 is a detailed item-by-item comparison of the actual compliance level and corresponding disclosure requirements of FRSs, Table 3 is a detailed item-by-item comparison of the actual compliance level and corresponding disclosure requirements of SSAPs, and Table 4 is a detailed item-by-item comparison of the actual compliance level and corresponding disclosure requirements of the NZX.

The figures in the column headed "Applicable (Not Applicable)" represent the number of sample companies, on the basis of their annual reports, that are (are not) to disclose the information items under the regulatory regime that prevailed in each year. Because disclosure requirements can be complied with at varying levels, sample companies obliged to comply with a particular requirement (column 1) have been categorised into two: (i) those fully complying with all sub-items (figures in columns 2c, 3c and 4c), and (ii) those not complying with at least one of the sub-items (figures in parentheses in columns 2c, 3c and 4c).

Table 2. Item-by-Item Comparison of Actual Disclosure Against Disclosure Requirements: Financial Reporting Standards.

(1) Sources of mandatory disclosure requirements/ mandated disclosure items (sub-items not shown)	Applicability of Disclosure Items														
	1996 (n = 49)					1997 (n = 49)					1998 (n = 49)				
	(2a) Applicable (not applicable)		(2b) Complying (not complying)			(3a) Applicable (not applicable)		(3b) Complying (not complying)			(4a) Applicable (not applicable)		(4b) Complying (not complying)		
Financial Reporting Standards	No.	%	No.	%	Rank	No.	%	No.	%	Rank	No.	%	No.	%	Rank
FRS-01 Accounting policies	49 (0)	100	47 (2)	96	3	49 (0)	98	48 (1)	98	1*	48 (0)	100	45 (3)	94	4
FRS-02 Presentation	49 (0)	100	45 (4)	92	6	49 (0)	98	45 (4)	92	3	48 (0)	100	44 (4)	92	6
FRS-04 Inventories	47 (2)	96	45 (2)	96	3	44 (5)	88	38 (6)	87	6	38 (10)	79	36 (2)	95	3
FRS-05 Events occurring after balance date	29 (20)	59	22 (7)	76	12	35 (14)	70	29 (6)	83	8	5 (43)	10	2 (3)	40	16
FRS-07 Extraordinary items & fundamental errors	20 (29)	41	20 (0)	100	1*	22 (27)	44	19 (3)	86	7	1 (47)	2	0 (1)	0	20**
FRS-09 Disclosure of information	30 (19)	61	11 (19)	37	21	20 (29)	40	6 (14)	33	26	48 (0)	100	15 (33)	31	17
FRS-10 Cash flows	48 (1)	98	32 (16)	67	15	46 (3)	92	28 (18)	60	20	47 (1)	98	36 (11)	77	11
FRS-13 Research and development	25 (24)	51	18 (7)	72	13	34 (15)	68	26 (8)	76	13	18 (30)	38	12 (6)	67	14

FRS-14 Construction contracts	23 (26)	47	19 (4)	83	9	30 (19)	60	26 (4)	87	6	0 (48)	0	0 (0)	100	.
FRS-19 Goods and services tax	9 (40)	18	6 (3)	67	15	10 (39)	20	6 (4)	64	16	2 (46)	4	2 (0)	100	1*
FRS-20 Dividend election plans	23 (26)	47	14 (9)	58	18	23 (26)	46	18 (5)	79	11	1 (47)	2	1 (0)	100	1*
FRS-26 Debt defeasance	24 (25)	49	15 (9)	63	17	28 (21)	56	20 (8)	72	14	2 (46)	4	2 (0)	100	1*
FRS-27 Right of set-off	10 (39)	20	3 (7)	30	22	11 (38)	22	2 (9)	25	27	0 (48)	0	0 (0)		.
FRS-29 Prospective financial information	3 (46)	6	3 (0)	100	1*	2 (47)	4	1 (1)	67	15	1 (47)	2	1 (0)	100	1*
FRS-30 Share ownership arrangements	30 (19)	61	16 (14)	53	19	34 (15)	68	21 (13)	63	17	10 (38)	21	3 (7)	30	18
FRS-31 Financial instruments	28 (21)	57	7 (21)	25	23	20 (29)	40	7 (13)	33	26	45 (3)	94	7 (38)	16	19
FRS-32 Superannuation schemes	13 (36)	27	3 (10)	23	24	8 (41)	16	0 (8)	11	28**	6 (42)	13	3 (3)	50	15
Mean compliance level				67					66					66	
Overall compliance level				80					70					77	

*Denotes full compliance with requirements.

**Denotes total failure to comply with requirements.

Table 3. Item-by-Item Comparison of Actual Disclosure Against Disclosure Requirements: Statements of Standard Accounting Practices.

(1) Sources of mandatory disclosure requirements/ mandated disclosure items (sub-items not shown)	Applicability of Disclosure Items														
	1996 ($n=49$)					1997 ($n=49$)					1998 ($n=49$)				
	(2a) Applicable (not applicable)		(2b) Complying (not complying)			(3a) Applicable (not applicable)		(3b) Complying (not complying)			(4a) Applicable (not applicable)		(4b) Complying (not complying)		
Statements of Standard Accounting Practice	No.	%	No.	%	Rank	No.	%	No.	%	Rank	No.	%	No.	%	Rank
SSAP-03 Depreciation	48 (1)	98	46 (2)	94	4	49 (0)	98	48 (1)	98	1*	47 (1)	98	47 (0)	100	1*
SSAP-08 Group accounting	32 (17)	65	20 (12)	63	17	28 (21)	56	13 (15)	48	25	42 (6)	88	34 (8)	81	10
SSAP-12 Income tax	48 (1)	98	30 (18)	63	17	48 (1)	96	23 (25)	49	23	47 (1)	98	39 (8)	83	9
SSAP-15 Contingencies	29 (20)	59	27 (2)	93	5	23 (26)	46	21 (2)	91	4	44 (4)	92	44 (0)	100	1*
SSAP-17 Investment properties	13 (36)	27	11 (2)	85	8	8 (41)	16	5 (3)	63	17	14 (34)	29	13 (1)	93	5
SSAP-18 Leases and hire purchases	44 (5)	90	34 (10)	77	11	38 (11)	76	35 (3)	92	3	39 (9)	81	37 (2)	95	3

SSAP-21 Foreign currency	21 (28)	43	21 (0)	100	1*	16 (33)	32	14 (2)	88	5	39 (9)	81	36 (3)	92	6
SSAP-22 Related parties	26 (23)	53	24 (2)	92	6	22 (27)	44	13 (9)	61	19	41 (7)	85	36 (5)	88	8
SSAP-23 Segments	45 (4)	92	37 (8)	82	10	38 (11)	76	29 (9)	77	12	47 (1)	98	36 (1)	77	11
SSAP-25 Joint ventures and partnerships	27 (22)	55	17 (10)	63	17	32 (17)	64	17 (15)	55	21	10 (38)	21	0 (10)	0	20
SSAP-28 Fixed assets	31 (18)	63	22 (9)	71	14	21 (28)	42	13 (8)	64	16	47 (1)	98	35 (12)	74	13
Mean compliance level				80					71					80	
Overall compliance level				76					70					77	

*Denotes full compliance with requirements.

Table 4. Item-by-Item Comparison of Actual Disclosure Against Disclosure Requirements: NZX Listing Requirements.

(1) Sources of mandatory disclosure requirements/ mandated disclosure items (sub-items not shown)	Applicability of Disclosure Items																				
	1996 (n = 49)						1997 (n = 49)						1998 (n = 49)								
	(2a) Applicable (not applicable)		(2b) Complying (not complying)			(3a) Applicable (not applicable)		(3b) Complying (not complying)			(4a) Applicable (not applicable)		(4b) Complying (not complying)								
NZX listing requirements	No.	%	No.	%	Rank	No.	%	No.	%	Rank	No.	%	No.	%	Rank						
Sec 10 Signing financial statements	49 (0)	100	48 (1)	98	2	49 (0)	98	47 (2)	96	2	48 (0)	100	48 (0)	100	1*						
Sec 26 Substantial security holders	46 (3)	94	31 (15)	66	16	47 (2)	94	24 (23)	52	22	46 (2)	96	45 (1)	98	2						
Sec 8.4.2 Sec 8.4.2 Principal security and directors	48 (1)	98	47 (1)	98	2	48 (1)	96	39 (9)	82	9	47 (1)	98	42 (5)	89	7						
Sec 8.5.3 Reporting period changes	23 (26)	47	20 (3)	87	7	29 (20)	58	22 (7)	77	12	2 (46)	4	2 (0)	100	1*						

Sec 3.3.4 Alternate directors	6 (43)	12	3 (3)	50	20	5 (44)	10	3 (2)	67	15	8 (40)	17	7 (1)	88	8
Sec 10.5.4 Appointed directors	3 (46)	6	3 (0)	100	1*	4 (45)	8	3 (1)	80	10	2 (46)	4	1 (1)	50	15
Sec 8.3.2 & 8.4.3 Audit committee existence	49 (0)	100	29 (20)	58	18	49 (0)	98	30 (19)	62	18	48 (0)	100	36 (12)	75	12
Mean compliance level				80					74					86	
Overall mean compliance level				76					70					77	

*Denotes full compliance with requirements.

Several inferences can be drawn from Tables 2–4. First, the sample companies fully complied with certain mandated disclosure requirements at least once during the 3-year period studied. These requirements are: SSAP-3 (*Accounting for Depreciation*), SSAP-15 (*Contingencies*), SSAP-21 (*Foreign Currency Translations*), FRS-1 (*Disclosure of Accounting Policies*), FRS-19 (*Goods and Services Tax*), FRS-20 (*Dividend Election Plans*), FRS-26 (*Debt Defeasance*), FRS-27 (*Extraordinary Items and Fundamental Errors*), FRS-29 (*Prospective Financial Information*), SEC 8.5.3 (*Reporting Period Changes*), SEC 10 (*Signing Financial Statements*), and SEC 10.5.4 (*Appointed Directors*).[4]

The full compliance with these disclosure requirements, ranked first in Table 2, might be due to three factors. First, the compliance with these requirements may not give away proprietary information to competitors, which can be detrimental to the compliant companies. Second, certain disclosure requirements such as FRS-27 (*Extraordinary Items and Fundamental Errors*) attract regulatory scrutiny as they are generally abused by the management. Hence, full compliance minimizes potential political cost. Finally, the relatively low cost of producing and disseminating certain disclosure requirements such as SEC 10 (*Signing Financial Statements*), SEC 10.5.4 (*Appointed Directors*), SEC 8.5.3 (*Reporting Period Changes*), FRS-19 (*Good and Services Tax*), and FRS-20 (*Dividend Election Plans*).

The high compliance rate for FRS-29 (*Prospective Financial Information*) is surprising because disclosure of such information can invite possible legal suits. Perhaps, what might have motivated such high compliance with this requirement is that NZ's environment is relatively less litigious than the U.S.

A second inference that can be drawn from Table 2 is that certain disclosure requirements were moderately complied with (between 60% and 99%) by the sample companies. These requirements constitute about 59% of all those disclosure items, from the three regulatory sources in each of the years investigated, that the companies were required to comply with. The requirements that were moderately complied with by the companies include FRS-13 (*Research and Development*), SSAP-17 (*Investment Properties and Properties Intended for Sale*), SSAP-18 (*Accounting for Leases and Hire Purchase Contracts*), SSAP-23 (*Accounting for Segments*), and a NZX Listing rule (*Section 8.4.2: Principal Security Holders and Directors' Shareholding*).[5]

The third inference is that about a quarter of all the disclosure requirements were poorly complied with by the companies. Those that were lowly complied with at least two out of the 3 years investigated include SSAP-8 (*Group Accounting*), FRS-9 (*Information to be Disclosed in Financial*

Statements), FRS-31 (*Disclosure of Information About Financial Instruments*), and FRS-32 (*Financial Reporting by Superannuation Schemes*). Plausible reasons for the low compliance are cost and complexity of some of these requirements. For example, FRS-31 (*Disclosure of Information about Financial Instruments*) addresses controversial issues, which though referred as a FRS, is yet to be approved by the ASRB (which has authoritative support of the accounting profession).

Fourth, it can be discerned from Table 2 that the listing requirements of the NZX has the highest mean compliance rate, followed by the SSAPs and then by the FRSs.[6] There are two plausible reasons accounting for this phenomena. First, the NZX's market surveillance panel monitors compliance with its requirements more rigorously than the Securities Commission, the Registrar of Companies, and the ICANZ. Second, cost of complying with the NZX listing rules is relatively lower than the cost of complying with SSAPs and FRSs.

Also, Table 2 indicates that the companies consistently complied more with SSAPs than FRSs over the period investigated. The mean compliance rate for SSAPs ranges from 53% (in 1996) to 80% (in 1998). In contrast, the mean compliance rate for FRSs ranges from 40% (in 1996) to 66% (in 1998). The differences in the compliance rates between SSAPs and FRSs may be due to three factors. First, because the SSAPs have relatively been in existence for years, the companies have acquired experience in their applications. Thus, this is a learning curve effect. Second, the FRSs are more costly to comply with than the SSAPs. Third, some of the FRSs cover recent and controversial issues, thus non-compliance may indicate the preparers disagreement with the views of ASRB.

CONCLUSION

This study investigates the mandatory disclosure compliance levels by NZ-registered companies listed on the NZX over a 3-year period. The results show a high rate of compliance with mandatory disclosure requirements by these companies over the period investigated. However, the mean compliance rate with NZX listing rules was higher, followed by that for SSAPs, and then, the FRSs.

Like all studies, the present study has several weaknesses, which should be taken into consideration in interpreting the results. First, information items in the disclosure index were treated equally in terms of their information content for methodological convenience. Second, the study examined information required to be disclosed in corporate annual reports – one of the media by which companies communicate with the public. Third, the assumption that increases in the quantity of disclosure improves the quality of information is questionable. Research shows that more information does not necessarily mean quality information (Hirshleifer, 1971; Baiman, 1975).

Despite the weaknesses above, the study suggests several lines of future inquiries. First, a research that would survey preparers of corporate annual report in NZ to elicit their reasons for not complying with certain mandatory disclosure requirements is needed. Second, for public policy purposes, a further study would be needed to identify those companies that failed to comply with mandatory disclosure requirements. Finally, future studies could attach weights to the disclosure items to portray their relative importance.

NOTES

1. Westwood (2000) attributes low compliance with accounting standards to their low quality, which in turn, is a consequence of standard setting process being reactive rather than proactive. He states that low-quality accounting standards may be caused by lack of precision in prescribed accounting treatments due to the existence of optional treatments, inconsistencies between required treatments, and/or lack of coverage (due to limitations in the scope of a standard's subject matter or because a standard does not exist in respect of a particular subject).

2. Section 4 of the FRA defines an issuer as: (i) an entity which has allocated securities to the public by way of a registered prospectus; (ii) an entity which has securities quoted on the NZX; (iii) a life insurance company that has issued any life insurance policy according to an offer of securities to the public; (iv) a unit trust in which securities have been allocated according to an offer of securities to the public; and (v) a registered bank that has allocated securities to the public. Essentially, an issuer is any party that has made a public issue of debt or equity securities (Westwood, 2000). Issuers include companies, building societies, industrial and provident societies, friendly societies, credit unions, and incorporated societies, as well as unincorporated bodies, trusts or organizations and individuals (Deegan & Samkin, 2001).

3. According to Westwood (2000), appropriate accounting policies having authoritative support essentially refer to sources of accounting guidance which are appropriate to the circumstances of the entity reporting and that have authority within the accounting profession in NZ.

4. The high compliance rate for SSAP-3 is consistent with the results reported by Ritchie (1994).

5. There is a major improvement in the compliance rate for SSAP-18 as compared to Davy's (1994) results.

6. Also, a one-way ANOVA test suggests that there is a significant difference between the overall mean compliance rate between the NZX listing rules, SSAPs, and FRSs at the 0.01 level.

ACKNOWLEDGEMENTS

I appreciate the research grant provided by the University of Canterbury, New Zealand. I thank Selena Robb, James Arbuthnott, and Dylan Fitzgerald for their assistance in data collection, and Grace Ooi and Warwick Anderson for their editorial comments. I also thank the staff at Macmillan Brown library of the University of Canterbury for tracing the annual reports of the sample companies in the library's special collection on New Zealand and the Pacific Islands. I am grateful to Stephen Owusu-Ansah for his insightful comments on earlier drafts of this paper. The views expressed in this article (chapter) are those of the author and do not necessarily reflect the views of the Institute of Chartered Accountants of New Zealand.

REFERENCES

Adhikari, A., & Tondkar, R. (1992). Environmental factors influencing accounting disclosure requirements of global stock exchanges. *Journal of International Financial Management and Accounting, 4*(2), 76–105.

Baiman, S. (1975). The evaluation and choice of internal information systems within a multiperson world. *Journal of Accounting Research, 13*(1), 1–15.

Cooke, T. E. (1989). Disclosure in the corporate annual reports of Swedish companies. *Accounting and Business Research, 19*(74), 113–124.

Davy, A. (1994). SSAP-18: Accounting for leases and hire purchase contracts. In: J. B. Ryan (Ed.), *New Zealand company financial reporting 1994*. Auckland, New Zealand: Premier Print Series.

Deegan, C., & Samkin, G. (2001). *New Zealand financial accounting*. Auckland, New Zealand: McGraw-Hill Book Company.

Hirshleifer, J. (1971). The private and social value of information and the reward of incentive activity. *The American Economic Review, 61*(4), 561–574.

Hossian, M., Perera, M. H. B., & Rahman, A. R. (1995). Voluntary disclosure in the annual reports of New Zealand companies. *Journal of International Financial Management and Accounting, 6*(1), 69–85.

McNally, G. M., Eng, L. H., & Hasseldine, C. R. (1982). Corporate financial reporting in New Zealand: An analysis of user preferences, corporate characteristics and disclosure practices for discretionary information. *Accounting and Business Research, 13*(49), 11–20.

Owusu-Ansah, S. (2000). Noncompliance with corporate annual report disclosure requirements in Zimbabwe. In: R. S. O. Wallace, J. M. Samuels, R. J. Briston & S. M. Saudagaran (Eds), *Research in accounting in emerging economies 4* (pp. 289–305). London, England and Greenwich, CT: JAI Press.

Owusu-Ansah, S., & Yeoh, J. (2002). The impact of Financial Reporting Act on corporate disclosure practices in New Zealand. In: *Proceedings of the 14th Asian-Pacific conference on international accounting issues (Nov 23–26)*, Los Angeles.

Riahi-Belkaoui, A. (1995). Accounting information adequacy and macroeconomic determinants of economic growth. *Advances in International Accounting, 8*, 67–77.

Ritchie, K. A. (1994). SSAP-3: Accounting for depreciation. In: J. B. Ryan (Ed.), *New Zealand company financial reporting 1994*. Auckland, New Zealand: Premier Print Series.

Ryan, J. B. (1994). *New Zealand company financial reporting 1994*. Auckland, New Zealand: Premier Print Services.

Securities Commission [New Zealand]. (1996). Securities Commission's 1996 Annual Report.

Tower, G. D., Gnosh, M., Rahman, A. R., Tan, L. M., & Cuthberston, J. (1990). SSAP-3: Depreciation of fixed assets and measurement of fixed assets. In: J. B. Ryan (Ed.), *New Zealand company financial reporting 1989*. Levin, New Zealand: Kerslake, Billens and Humphrey.

Westwood, M. (2000). *Financial accounting in New Zealand* (4th ed.). Auckland, New Zealand: Pearson Education.

Printed and bound by CPI Group (UK) Ltd, Croydon, CR0 4YY

08/05/2025

01864950-0001